PENGUIN
TARGET 3 BILLION

A.P.J. Abdul Kalam is one of India's most distinguished scientists. He was responsible for the development of India's first satellite launch vehicle, the SLV-3, and the development and operationalization of strategic missiles. As chairman of the Technology Information, Forecasting and Assessment Council, he pioneered India Vision 2020, a roadmap for transforming India into an economically developed nation by 2020, focusing on PURA as a development system for countrywide implementation.

Kalam held various positions in the Indian Space Research Organisation and the Defence Research and Development Organisation and became principal scientific adviser to the Government of India, holding the rank of a cabinet minister.

The President of India between 2002 and 2007, Kalam has been awarded honorary doctorates from thirty-eight universities and the country's three highest civilian honours—Padma Bhushan (1981), Padma Vibhushan (1990) and Bharat Ratna (1997).

Kalam has authored fifteen books on a variety of topics that have been translated into many languages across the world. His most significant works are *Wings of Fire, India 2020: A Vision for the New Millennium* and *Ignited Minds*. He now conducts lectures on societal development in many international institutes and is involved in research on different societal missions.

Srijan Pal Singh studied at the Indian Institute of Management, Ahmedabad, where he won a gold medal for the best all-rounder student and was the student council head. He worked in a Naxalism-affected region in Orissa on a project to establish a transparent public distribution system using IT interventions.

Srijan has actively travelled across rural India and participated in various international initiatives to study and evolve sustainable development systems. Many of his articles on sustainability and development have been published in reputed journals. Srijan is currently working with Dr Kalam to promote PURA as a sustainable development system.

TARGET 3 BILLION

PURA: Innovative Solutions towards Sustainable Development

A.P.J. ABDUL KALAM

&

SRIJAN PAL SINGH

With regards on 60th wedding anniversary

From: Mukesh - Deepika

PENGUIN BOOKS

PENGUIN BOOKS
Published by the Penguin Group
Penguin Books India Pvt. Ltd, 11 Community Centre, Panchsheel Park,
New Delhi 110 017, India
Penguin Group (USA) Inc., 375 Hudson Street, New York, New York 10014, USA
Penguin Group (Canada), 90 Eglinton Avenue East, Suite 700, Toronto, Ontario,
M4P 2Y3, Canada (a division of Pearson Penguin Canada Inc.)
Penguin Books Ltd, 80 Strand, London WC2R 0RL, England
Penguin Ireland, 25 St Stephen's Green, Dublin 2, Ireland (a division of Penguin
Books Ltd)
Penguin Group (Australia), 250 Camberwell Road, Camberwell, Victoria 3124,
Australia (a division of Pearson Australia Group Pty Ltd)
Penguin Group (NZ), 67 Apollo Drive, Rosedale, Auckland 0632,
New Zealand (a division of Pearson New Zealand Ltd)
Penguin Group (South Africa) (Pty) Ltd, 24 Sturdee Avenue, Rosebank,
Johannesburg 2196, South Africa

Penguin Books Ltd, Registered Offices: 80 Strand, London WC2R 0RL, England

First published by Penguin Books India 2011

Copyright © A.P.J. Abdul Kalam and Srijan Pal Singh 2011

10 9 8 7 6 5 4 3 2

The views and opinions expressed in this book are the authors' own and the facts are
as reported by them which have been verified to the extent possible, and the publishers
are not in any way liable for the same.

ISBN 9780143417309

Typeset in Adobe Garamond Pro by Eleven Arts, Delhi
Printed at Thomson Press India Ltd, New Delhi

CONTENTS

PREFACE
EMPOWERING 3 BILLION

The fundamental ingredient in the evolution of happy, peaceful and prosperous nations and societies is laying the foundation for sustainable development. As global society—particularly in developing and emerging nations—stands at its defining moment in history, the needs of our times consist of prosperity with inclusion, development with equity and industrialization with environmental concern. Large-scale divides between the rural and the urban areas of the world—which are manifested in the income levels and the quality of human amenities—are not only a loss of opportunity, but also a matter of concern as regards the sustenance of prosperity and peace.

Overcoming the prejudices of prosperity and fundamental human living standards is a significant national challenge as well as an international responsibility. Today, in the underdeveloped, the developing and some parts of the developed nations of the world, more than 3 billion people live in villages, often in a condition of underutilization of talent and resources, and of deprivation. We shall address here the opportunities that elude this half of the human population. These 3 billion entities of humanity are important from the point of view of global policy-making, national governance and the corporate sector. In an increasingly democratic world, they will hold the key to global government and also present an immense and growing market and a sourcing centre for industries around the world. Moreover, it is now widely believed that the world population will reach 7 billion within the year, and thus the need for ensuring the prosperity and peace of humanity will now be a task that will require sustainable models of growth with added focus on employment generation.

This book is based on the first-hand experience of the authors and bears testimony to the evolution and implementation of a sustainable development system in various regions that enjoy diversity in input conditions and strategies. This book will integrate the challenges and opportunities of the present human civilization and demonstrate how to meticulously evolve a sustainable development system of PURA (Provision of Urban Amenities in Rural Areas) by harnessing the potential of the rural masses of the world.

We shall use the Indian experience as a showcase and refer to existing examples to show how, in a limited time period, societal transformation has been achieved through the implementation of PURA systems. It is noteworthy that the PURA model for development is now being implemented across India by the Central and the state governments, along with many private and educational sector initiatives. PURA is also spreading to other regions of the world with plans of customized implementation in parts of the United States and Africa.

The book will expatiate on how PURA is an amalgamation of technology, people, traditions, skills and entrepreneurial spirit aimed at achieving sustainable development that is financially viable, socially equitable and eco-friendly. The book closely interlinks and connects a theoretical understanding of rural development with living examples from around the world which are practical implementations of the concept. We shall also discuss how a variety of stakeholders—the government, the private sector and the community—can closely work towards a socio-economic development based on empowerment rather than endowment.

In the later chapters, the book proposes the evolution of a step-wise, enterprise-driven model of PURA in the form of the PURA Corporation—a concept which sees human development as an investment, and which is now gathering momentum with the youth. Finally, the book takes PURA on to the international front and describes how nations around the world can empower their people by using the sustainable development model.

The book is not merely an explanation of the sustainable development system of PURA. It is also an assessment of the challenges and the opportunities presented by the rural sector—especially in India—and a guide for any potential entrepreneur from across the world to venture into the vast and largely untapped domain of villages.

Finally, we believe that the implementation of a sustainable development system will be complete only when prosperity comes with peace. Man discovered fire about 1.6 million years ago, which changed the course of human existence on this planet. A new fire needs to be discovered for achieving the twenty-first-century mission of peace with prosperity. The famous French philosopher, Pierre Teilhard de Chardin said, 'Some day, after mastering the winds, the waves, the tides and gravity, we shall harness for God the energies of love, and then, for a second time in the history of the world, man will have discovered fire.' This is the twenty-first-century fire we need to discover—the fire of love for the other being.

INTRODUCTION
THE ELIXIR OF RURAL EXPERIENCE FROM A NATION OF DIVERSITY

Throughout my professional career of about six decades, working in a spectrum of organizations and in varying capacities, I had an opportunity to traverse throughout the nation, across its length and breadth. Even during the presidential years, from 2002 to 2007, I made it a point to visit, interact with and learn from many rural areas. India's heart resides in its villages, and just like a doctor whose work begins with the diagnosis of the heartbeat, the planning and execution of any policy for the nation of a billion, has to begin with the learning derived from its 600,000 villages.

I recall my visit to the far eastern Indian state of Nagaland in October 2002, amidst the fading eastern end of the mighty Himalayas. The state of Nagaland is small in size but very rich in its biodiversity and culture. Comprising a population of about 2.5 million, largely tribal, the state has many different dialects and cultures unique to each of the tribes present. One of the places I visited there was Tuensang. Tuensang is the largest district of Nagaland and a strategically important area as it forms the border of India with Mynamar. While I was there, I participated in the tribal council meeting of the nearby areas. The tribal leaders of Nagaland are very special people who are not only the political representatives of their people but also the custodians of their unique culture. They came in their traditional colourful and vibrant attire, each well prepared for the meeting with a set of papers with their handwritten agendas. I was told that they generally prefer to sit under the shade of some large tree in the open, but because of my presence, they decided to conduct the meeting in a closed room. They greeted me and then each other and then professionally took their pre-allocated seats around a circle. Then the discussions began with utmost seriousness. The agenda for that day was about how the tribal council initiatives have augmented the productivity of vegetables and fruits in the local areas. Someone raised a point, 'I am happy to announce that the production, for the first time, now exceeds the demand by a large margin!' Everyone applauded. I, too, was happy to know the brilliant performance of the villages. But then a young leader got up and said, 'Respected members! While it is good news that the productivity and quality have both gone up, the question is, now with this asset, how do we build an economically viable model for prosperity?' Someone from a corner was struck by an idea. She said, 'We need to find out which markets we can export to. I have a small team that can study the demand patterns of the nearby villages and urban areas; we should explore these options.' Everyone agreed with her. Then a senior tribal started speaking as others listened with respect and interest. He said, 'Mr President and my fellow council members, we have one major hurdle to this, which is the non-availability of roads between villages and urban areas. We also do not possess vehicles for transporting our goods.' The ensuing discussion went on for an hour. After many ideas being pondered over, they took the decision to form a cooperative society, which would buy the excess vegetables and fruits and take the responsibility for transportation. It would hire a swift and robust truck, which can travel in difficult terrain and take the produce into faraway markets and even beyond the state of Nagaland. Then they further discussed how to improve the tourism industry in the region. They prepared a memorandum to the chief minister of the state for construction of a number of helipads to improve the access to Nagaland for tourists and also to transport excess agricultural produce.

I observed this situation of lack of physical access impeding economic activity in a number of remote and tribal places in India. In January 2005, when I visited the Nicobar Island after the December 2004 tsunami, I also met the tribal leaders of the place. I asked them why they did not use the ocean's wealth for economic growth. I told them, 'There is so much of marine wealth at your disposal. Fishermen from the neighbouring countries are even illegally exploiting our seas. Why don't you use this national resource?' The tribal leaders thought about my questions and then responded. They were of the unanimous view that while they had deep traditional knowledge about fishing, they lacked proper knowledge on how to market the excess fish beyond their village need and were interested in learning about the technology for fish processing. This lack of knowledge was hindering their economic growth.

Another surprising message I got from the Nicobar tribal leaders was when I observed the curious absence of orphanages as a part of the relief effort. When in New Delhi, I had been told that the tsunamis had engulfed many parents and rendered children orphans. So I asked them, 'When I visited Andaman I saw three orphanages constructed after the tsunami. What about Nicobar?' The Nicobar tribal leaders told me, to my great surprise, and like a silver lining in the destruction left behind by the tsunamis, that there were 'no orphans here'. One senior but highly energetic leader told me with deep thought, 'The children who have been left without surviving parents after the tsunami, are indeed children of every home. We don't need orphanages. Our own homes are taking care of these children. After all, we are one big family on this little island.' Such a beautiful custom of transmitting love, of caring and of compassion is indeed inspirational and needs to be preserved and emulated across the nation and the world. When we talk of development, this aspect has to be kept in mind.

Let me take you some 1,200 kilometres to the west to the southern Indian state of Kerala. Kerala is a unique state on the map of India, which has a Neolithic history at least 7,000 years old and in modern times is ranked as the state with the highest literacy rate (about 95 per cent) and the lowest level of corruption in India. I have been associated with the state for very long. I would like to recall one of my recent visits to the town of Wayanad in Kerala, which left a special mark on my memory. On 17 February 2011, I was invited to inaugurate a unique education programme by the district education department and later I was also scheduled to interact with the students from various schools in the district at the Jawahar Navodaya Vidyalaya. We were supposed to leave Delhi at

9.30 a.m. for Bangalore and then board a connecting flight to Calicut, reaching it at about 3.30 p.m. and then drive to Wayanad from there to reach the venue of the function at 5 p.m. Everything was perfectly planned—but then the most meticulously chiselled plans sometimes collapse before unforeseen tragedies. We reached the Delhi airport on time, only to be informed that the flight to Bangalore had been delayed due to 'unavoidable' circumstances. Our first impression was that the delay would be of some minutes, until one hour passed, then another, and then another, while we waited in the airport waiting room, trying to utilize our time by refining the lectures, reading books and discussing with the team. By the time we finally got a boarding call, we had lost five hours and certainly missed our connecting flight to Calicut. Thankfully, we were not subjected to any in-flight delays and reached Bangalore by 5.30 p.m. Of course, our connecting flight had departed long back, and in fact had landed in Calicut by that time.

I was anxious about the children and other people who were waiting for us in Wayanad and called up the organizers to explain the situation. To my surprise they all said, 'Sir! None of us will move from here. We are waiting for you, even if it means waiting here all night. We know you will not disappoint us.' I was moved and was determined to reach Wayanad in whatever possible way. Our team discussed the various possibilities and finally concluded that given our options, the only way to reach Wayanad the same day, was by road, through the forests of Kerala, across hundreds of kilometres, and reach Wayanad in about six hours. It was 6 p.m. then, which meant we would reach Wayanad by about midnight. I decided to take the option and conveyed it to the organizers. So began one of the longest single-stretch road journeys I have ever undertaken.

In less than 100 kilometres, except for the road, all the typical marks of human civilization vanished, giving way to a green lush forest with its own unique sounds and sights. In the moonlit night, we could see the long shadows cast by our own vehicle's lights as the sounds of its engine were occasionally matched by the trumpeting of elephants. The forest wealth was immense, and testimony to the great national asset we possess. After the long non-stop journey through the hills, and after spending more than six and a half hours on the road, we were finally greeted with the signboard 'Welcome to Wayanad'. Mobile signals were connecting again, and man-made lights starting competing with the night stars as we entered the town. We headed straight for the venue of the first function, the Chandragiri Auditorium. As soon as we reached there was a loud cheer and I was surprised to see more than 2,000 people and young students who had filled up the hall to greet me. I was touched by the gesture and moved by the hardships they had endured while waiting to meet me in the middle of the night. I shared my joy and empathy with them. India is a unique country, and people here are like no other. When we are driven by some purpose or mission, Indians in any part of the nation can perform feats that are unimaginable. What I saw in Wayanad was one example of this.

While at the function, I inaugurated the Arividam Programme for spreading education to a higher level in the district. 'Arividam' means *a place of knowledge and information*. Knowledge makes an individual great, hence the objective of the Arividam project is to evolve great citizens for the state of Kerala. The focus of the Arividam Programme is the delivery of educational information and knowledge to the students, teachers and the public in order to bridge the digital gap in education at the regional level. This includes creation of video-conferencing facilities for principals and headmasters and officials, individual websites for all the schools and creation of a people's network. IT and computers, coupled with innovative planning and execution, can be a wonderful tool in taking knowledge to the masses. Applications like Facebook and Orkut have reached millions of users, so why can we not use the same philosophy to reach a large rural audience with education and knowledge? After this function I swiftly went to the Jawaharlal Nehru School, where thousands of children from Wayanad had gathered, at 2.30 a.m. in the night, full of vibrant energy. After the function, one student asked, 'Sir! How can science and technology help in removing illiteracy?' Of course, a couple of hours ago, I had come across one good example to tell him about—Arividam.

Let me now move to the extreme north of the nation. In 2005, a severe earthquake caused massive destruction of life and property in the Kashmir Valley. After this earthquake, while a large-scale rescue and rehabilitation mission was being undertaken I visited the regions of Uri, Ursa and Tangdhar, all of which mark the border between India and Pakistan. I attended a meeting between the locals of these regions, largely farmers, and the representatives of the government including the Governor, chief minister and senior officers from the armed forces. While at the meeting, I recalled my visit to these places the previous day and particularly noted that they had few means of livelihood. So I asked the locals about their livelihood and why they did not grow fruits in their farms, especially apples, a fruit for which Kashmir is famous. Their answer surprised me and caught some of the officials present with me rather unprepared. They said, 'Sir! We don't have land. Our land is with the army.' I looked at the Governor, the CM and the senior defence officers. There was an uncomfortable silence. I knew I had to respond to this issue. Realizing the difficulty of the locals, I told the officers that it is essential to allot certain cultivable land to the border areas, so that we can bring economic prosperity to the region. I further stressed the need to establish proper linkages to the markets. Security concerns should not be allowed to become an impediment to development. In fact, development is the greatest answer to any form of societal unrest. But I must also mention a great contribution by the Indian armed forces in this region. I saw the army units in the border areas assisting in the reconstruction of houses and providing water and education facilities, thereby playing a vital role in the societal missions of the region.

In the last year of my presidency in 2007, the army chief, General Joginder Jaswant Singh invited me to visit the Chinese border in the north-eastern state of Arunachal Pradesh. The general, popularly known as 'General JJ', is a veteran with a strong overwhelming personality and an evergreen smile. So when JJ insisted that I address our soldiers at the border, I could not refuse. We arrived at a place called Kibutu at the frontier where the Chinese and Indian territories meet. We were in a valley on the Indian side with mountains reaching the skies around us. On the other side I could see the Chinese post, a little higher in altitude than ours, where a few curious Chinese soldiers had gathered, probably attracted by the commotion created by our visit. I looked at our young soldiers and then looked at the Himalayan mountains towering above. I was touched by the hardships the soldiers had to face in difficult weather conditions. No matter what support we create for them, the hard reality of the Himalayan battlefield is that it is often the weather more than the enemy which is a bigger adversary. Then I turned to the local people assembled, largely tribals. Their cheerful faces and smiles were not enough to conceal the most obvious signs of poverty and hardship—overworked hands, frayed clothes and frail bodies. These frontier dwellers of India are living in such tough conditions, often without any special support and undertake a number of supporting and logistical roles for the army. As I walked past them, I heard the usual greeting in these tribal areas—an enthusiastic 'Jai Hind'.

I then addressed the integrated army command, with all the soldiers and officers, and I found in them the enthusiasm for the work in difficult situations and the willingness to face any challenges. When I saw a number of young officers after my address to them, I asked them, 'Friends! Brave officers and men of India! I realize that you are working day and night for the peace and safety of the nation and its people. I am proud of you all. Can the young officers and young men share with me one of your most cherished dreams?' There was a moment of silence and then several hands went up. A young soldier rose, smartly gave a salute and said in a loud voice, 'Sir! Whenever I see the Chinese placed in the Himalayas I am reminded of my visit to Tawang. My strongest ambition is to fight and win any aggression by the Chinese.' Another young officer added, 'Sir, my life's ambition is to recover the 50,000 sq km of land belonging to us back from Chinese possession. I will fight till my last breath for getting back this land.' Hearing him, the locals assembled burst into applause and starting chanting *Jai Hind! Jai Hind!* at the top of their voices. I was amazed at the spirit of the officers, soldiers and the locals and their resolve towards their nation. We need to nurture these regions and such spirit needs widespread propagation.

Let us now move across the length of India to the west. It was 15 May 1998. India had just conducted its five successful nuclear tests, elevating its defence stature. The mood in the nation was that of jubilation. I and my team of scientists were returning from Pokhran, the site for the tests. Pokhran is a place deep in the western Indian deserts of Thar, and little life and civilian movement exists in these remote deserts. Those days of May were particularly hot with temperatures soaring above 50°C in the day as the sun was beating down and was being reflected in the golden sand. On our way back, meandering across the desert roads, we came across a small village, Bhadariya. Seeing the signboard my friend Dr K.N. Rai's eyes immediately lit up. He exclaimed that he knew the place and that he had heard about a certain ashram. On his request, we decided to take a small detour and visit the place. Bhadariya is a small hamlet and we could locate the ashram easily; but what was difficult was to believe what we saw there. It was a large place, filled with greenery in the middle of the desert. Upon seeing us, the head priest of the ashram, Baba Sri Bhadariya Maharaj greeted us and took us to see the unique library he had created. He then took us down the staircase into an underground chamber which led to the library. We were pleasantly surprised to find the room remarkably cool and filled with more than 200,000 books—belonging to different subjects, different languages and different times in history. Some of them were even handwritten on parchment. Baba Sri Bhadariya Maharaj told us that due to the architectural design of the building, even when the outside temperature soars, the library remains naturally air-conditioned. He showed us books that were hundreds of years old and told us that the ashram had conserved traditional knowledge from earlier times.

While we were reading in the library, mesmerized by the cultural wealth, he brought us huge glasses of milk. I asked him, 'Baba, in the middle of this desert, where do you get such delicious fresh milk from?' He smiled and asked us to follow him; he took us behind the ashram where we saw a huge cow shelter with about 1,000 cows. Baba then said, 'Kalam, these are all discarded cows. People drove them away from their homes when they stopped giving milk. For them these cows were useless.' He laughed and added, 'But you see, just like you I am also a technologist. I have a special method of treating the same stray cows and today they all are healthy and happy and produce large quantities of quality milk, which you have in your glass.' I was amazed to hear about such a noble mission. I asked, 'But Baba, where do you find fodder for all these animals?' Baba Sri Bhadariya Maharaj then asked me to sit down on a small charpoy under the shade and started telling me the story of the transformation of Bhadariya. He told me, 'Kalam, years ago, the people of this place were very poor and were addicted to many types of toxicants, including liquor, tobacco and other forms of local weeds. This place was barren and devoid of trees. There was a plethora of problems of poverty, hunger, health care and malnutrition. Water was scarce and yet poorly managed. Look at what we then did, with cooperation and support from the villagers. We started with a de-addiction campaign, right here in the ashram, which now spreads to over seventy villages around Bhadariya. We executed a mission of greening Bhadariya and the surrounding areas with local support and planted lakhs of trees here. We got tube wells dug up and initiated agriculture in this place—with special ways to conserve water.' Baba then passionately continued, 'This ashram is also providing knowledge on naturopathy and herbal medicines to the rural community and on the treatment of cattle. The medicines are made from locally available herbs, using a technology that suits the conditions here.' He finally told me, 'You know Kalam, the villagers were so happy about all this that they provide fodder for these cows. Of course, when the cows started giving milk I began to offer milk and butter free of cost to the needy and to the travellers passing through this place. Like yourself, Kalam!' He laughed once again as he said that and offered me a refill of the glass, which I was happy to accept. 'One final question, Baba: where does all this knowledge about local herbs, cow rehabilitation techniques and the other things you are doing come from?' Baba Bhadariya's eyes shone in the light as he smilingly pointed to the underground library, 'From there!'

I believe real service to religion is to serve the villages on remote hills and in distant deserts. True servants to religion will choose to move away from urban comforts and head to unknown places where people face unimaginable difficulties. That is how religious service can truly enrich the heart. Bhadariya is a small place in the middle of the Thar Desert, but has that great lesson for the world. It is also an example of how the integrated development of communication, dissemination of knowledge, medicare, cattle rearing, fodder management are all taking place together in a desert area, to transform land, resources and human life using local and traditional knowledge coupled with modern science and technology. This is a fundamental aspect which we will discuss in this book, and it is valid not just for a nation or a group of nations, but for the entire international context.

A.P.J. Abdul Kalam

1

THE 'OTHER' HALF OF MANKIND

THE CHANGING WORLD AND ITS CONNECTEDNESS

The world is changing—perhaps more dynamically than ever before in its history. Since the early 1800s, a multidimensional force of science and technology, economics, politics and religion has been continuously and rapidly making, breaking and reshaping all borders, natural and man-made alike. Out of the relatively long history of about 200,000 years through which humanity has survived and thrived, the last two centuries—which roughly constitute not more than one-thousandth of its existence—represent an era that has seen tremendously new alterations being sculpted. This new-age, lightning-speed leap in the pace of transformation has been enabled by a world which is integrally connected by four rapid forms of connectivity. These are environment, people, economy and ideas.

We all know that global warming and climate change are no longer the problems of individual nations, states or cities; they are worldwide problems that affect us all. In the present times, a single product may be made out of components sourced from different continents and may provide services to markets far away from its place of origin. Products have absorbed cultural flavours from different parts of the world and transcended their national identity. Truly, global products are now a household brand across the world. Today, a multinational company like Coca-Cola has more than 3,300 product variants to suit local conditions and reaches almost 200 countries. In fact, there are now only three countries where Coca-Cola still does not reach—Syria, North Korea and Iran.[1] The Industrial Revolution and mass production have reformed the scale equations of manufacturing. A century and a half ago, a metre of cloth took more time to produce than a modern automobile plant takes to manufacture an entire car today.

We have also seen how the economic turbulence that originated in one part of the world shook the whole world and how a volcanic eruption in an island country brought the airline industry to a temporary halt.[2] Advances in modes of transportation have progressively made the movement of people across nations and regions more feasible. First the fossil-fuelled steam engine and then the advent of powerful IC engines,* coupled with the introduction of commercial flights, have all increased the mobility of human beings exponentially, even by about 1,000 times in the developed world, during the past two centuries.[3] This has led to the globalization of skills and talents that can flow seamlessly from one nation to another. On the other hand, this has also resulted in the globalization of human diseases, the most recent instance being the different kinds of flu which have rapidly spread across the globe.

Similarly, ideas and innovations are no longer geographically or politically confined. An invention made today in one place takes almost no time in finding a market thousands of miles away. The expansion of information and communication technology and the convergence of technological tools are structuring a new world knowledge platform, where problems of one part of the world can be solved by various experts based at different points of the globe. The seamless flow of information and people also means that local or regional issues will invariably gain global prominence, and unaddressed problems and unmitigated poverty can mutate rapidly into global terrorism which we are already witnessing. This flow of ideas has also led to increasing importance being given to

---

*The steam engine was first invented by James Watt in the later half of the eighteenth century (which was actually an improvement over the version invented by Thomas Newcomen). It paved the way for the Industrial Revolution. IC engines are internal combustion engines, characterized by the combustion of the fuel occurring in a closed combustion chamber. They are significantly more efficient than external combustion engines and more robust too. Much of the work on the development of combustion engines happened in the late nineteenth century. Modern automobiles are all fitted with IC engines.

global human rights and to the propagation of the idea of democracy and people empowerment.

BRIDGING THE GAP BETWEEN YESTERDAY'S METHODS AND THE PROBLEMS OF THE FUTURE

The combined advances in technology, economics and connectivity act as a double-edged sword in terms of bringing equity in opportunity. Muhammad Yunus, Nobel laureate and microfinance banker-entrepreneur, highlights how the affordable mobile phone has enabled the women entrepreneurs of Bangladesh to have access to markets.[4] Similarly, India's experience with the progress in wireless communication and space-based knowledge applications for societal applications has been positive.

But there is another side to the picture. Augmentation of wealth and resources has been matched with its concentration to a few hands. The Human Development Report of the United Nations Development Programme (UNDP), has revealed that the top fifth of the world's population in the wealthiest nations benefits from 82 per cent of the expanding export trade and 68 per cent of foreign direct investment, while the bottom fifth, in terms of wealth, is left with around 1 per cent

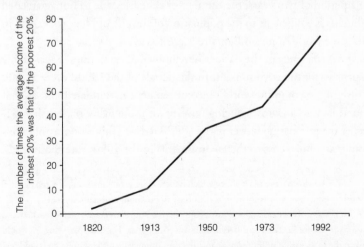

FIGURE 1.1: The income gap between the fifth of the world's people living in the richest countries and the fifth in the poorest nations

of each.[5] This is reflected in the income gap between nations around the world as depicted in Figure 1.1 which shows that, in 1992, the ratio of the 20 per cent of the people living in the richest nations to the 20 per cent in the poorest nations, stood at about seventy-two times.[6] In fact, the top three richest people in the world possess more financial assets than the combined assets of the poorest 10 per cent of the world. It is clear that while, at individual levels, some technologies have brought equities, at the aggregate level, policies have failed to deliver the benefits to the needy.

The methods of the twentieth century do not hold much promise for the challenges of the twenty-first century. What worked yesterday may have difficulty succeeding today and almost certainly would fail tomorrow. A consumption-centric economic will and a theoretical assumption of the 'trickle-down'* effect have brought about the menacing problems of inefficiency and inequity. They cause harm to the environment which, if not addressed immediately, will result in irreparable damages. The vertical growth of economies has already failed to expand horizontally to cover a larger spectrum of people and, despite the beneficial tools that make life easier for some, many exist in the unseen shadows of deprivation. Today, we live in a world where 25,000 people die of starvation every day.[7] Thus, in a period of two years, the number of casualties due to hunger-related ailments is equivalent to the population of the city of New York. And in the same world, a new billionaire is created every alternate day.

Low efficiency of the current developmental economics is also highly expensive for the environment. In the decade of the 1990s, every $1,000 worth of growth in the world's income per person, translated into $6 that found its way towards reducing poverty for those living on less than $1, as per the purchasing power parity (PPP)† a day.[8] This economy of excess comes at a huge cost to the environment. In the 1990s, the Biosphere 2

---

* 'Trickle-down' refers to a policy which believes that providing non-targeted benefits would in sometime indirectly benefit the broad population, especially the needy.

† It is a way of estimating the adjustment needed on the currency exchange rate between nations to accommodate the differences in prices of goods. For example, what $1 would buy in the USA would be quite less than what the currency equivalent of Rs 45 would buy in India. In India, $1 in PPP is about Rs 17 in urban and about Rs 11.5 in rural areas.

experiment* was conducted to determine the amount of resources an average human being requires as per our current consumption patterns. Some startling revelations followed. One was that an average Englishman would require close to 5 hectares—roughly six football fields—to satisfy his needs at the current consumption levels and to absorb the waste subsequently generated. An average North American would require twice that amount of land, about 10 hectares. The earth, although immense, is limited in size. Even if all the cultivable land were allotted to human beings, the average size per person would work to about 1.67 hectares only. If every human being were to start living like a North American, we would need six planet earths to match our consumption. Current models are not only ineffective but also perilously taxing on the environment.[9]

Ironically, an influx of donations, allocations and charities also falls short of achieving the targets of modern inclusive development. Our experience across the world clearly shows that some of the best-funded projects and missions have failed despite the mammoth resources at their disposal, while it is an undisputed fact that significant success can only be achieved by relatively smaller but better directed approaches. For instance, the Indian government has been spending $7–8 billion every year on the Food Subsidy programme.[10] The scheme has come under intense criticism for its inefficient delivery and leakages, as a result of which about half the children in the nation are still undernourished.

Many of the international aid agency efforts during the late twentieth century were directed towards the pressing issues of children and general living conditions. Despite the spending of both the private and the public sectors, the results were far from satisfactory. The United Nations Children's Fund (UNICEF) reports that, out of the 2.2 billion children

*Biosphere 2 was an experiment conducted in 1991. It was a massive airtight container of glass, cement and steel covering 1.25 hectares in the Arizona desert. Four volunteers were placed in the container and provided with an engineered habitat to supply all their needs, replicating Biosphere 1—which is the earth. It was conducted to determine the dependencies of human beings and the planet, and to calculate the resource requirement for average living and its impact on the biosphere. The participants of the experiment were forced to quit after two years as the biosphere within the dome could not support the living conditions of human beings.

in the world, half live in poverty. One-third of them (640 million) lack adequate shelter; about one-fifth of them lack access to safe water; and one-seventh have no access to health-care services.[11] Imagine growing up in a life where food was not only poor in quality but also rationed in quantity, with roofs which would give way to the scantiest rainfall and then getting water that often would be an agent of disease. The odds of life, learning and growth are unevenly stacked when poverty lives on your side and unplanned donations can hardly deliver. Hence, visible and sustainable results in development are more a function of precise actions and directed investments than of superfluous expenditures.

THE DISPARITY IS GLOBAL

With the exception of China, which through its township and village enterprises has achieved remarkable success in addressing the problem of poverty, the global quest for reduction of poverty has at best been stagnant, at times with outright negative results. Figure 1.2 shows that if

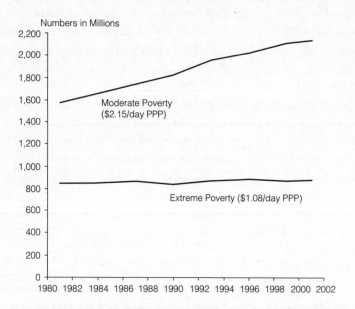

FIGURE **1.2:** Moderate and extreme poverty in absolute numbers cumulatively across the world, excluding China[12]

China is excluded from the equation, then, since 1981, the number of cases of extreme poverty ($1.08 per day per person in PPP) has actually risen from about 848 million to about 873 million in 1999; and the cases of moderate poverty have risen by about 36 per cent in the same period from about 1.57 billion cases to about 2.1 billion cases.[13]

It is estimated that with the current economic models of development, $166 of extra production would be needed to achieve a single dollar of poverty reduction.[14] The conclusion is that production efficiencies would have to conform to an effort of holistic matching between what consumers need and what they get.

To a large extent, economic disparity has followed political boundaries, leading to divisions along the parameters of developed, emerging and underdeveloped worlds—all coexisting and unequally sharing limited resources. But even within these economically divided worlds, there exists another internal division—along the lines of rural and urban—which almost unanimously cuts across sharply, dividing living standards, income classes and amenities into two asymmetric parts.

Even poverty has some patterns. Today, of every ten cases of extreme poverty (less than $1.25/day), seven would live in villages and rural areas all over the world. But that is not the complete picture. Driven by the need for education, health care and better income, rural poverty is migrating to urban areas in the hope of getting a better chance and an equitable share in opportunities, but often ending in despair and destitution. The first- and second-generation migrant urban impoverished face even more challenging realities: they are constrained for the very necessities of life and that too at compromised quality standards and exorbitant rates. Professor C.K. Prahlad, in his works on urban poverty, had pointed out that the urban poor actually end up paying a 'poverty penalty', citing that the needy communities in Mumbai slums pay five to twenty-five times more for basic products like water and medicine than the rich in the posh areas of the same city.[15] Hence, success in overcoming rural poverty and empowering rural households will lead to the reduction of urban poverty levels as well.

In the analysis that follows, we shall focus on how a sustainable development system can be envisioned, implemented and replicated for the neglected half of the world. This will require the evolution of a new and unique model which is investment-oriented and focused on sustainability, and which strives for empowerment in the long run. Empowerment-based models of development have a distinct advantage over approaches that are endowment based or oriented towards consumption augmentation. They are self-sustained and stable—economically, socially and environmentally. They focus on creating empowered productivity and, more artificially through external assistance, creating a virtual realizability. This means that they can be rapidly scaled—which is a very significant aspect when we consider the impact zone of more than 3 billion living in a variety of locations and often in regions lacking in resources.

THE RISE OF THE NEW VILLAGE

A typical household in any of the 600,000 villages in India—or elsewhere in the world—would present the image of a truly versatile and self-sufficient economic unit. It would often grow its own food, construct its own house, build the mud path around the house, manage its livestock, and may even be adept in basic traditional health care. One may also be pleasantly surprised to find households that weave their own cloth.

Roughly half the world population lives in these rural areas, often relying on archaic technology, untapped resources, underdeveloped skills and assistance, even donation-oriented policies for their basic livelihood. The challenges and opportunities for the 3 billion of the world are a matter of urgent concern to the global community at large.

First, while basic skills for a variety of products and services have been passed from one generation to the next, there is a lack of specialization—from the perspective of both technology and capability. In an increasingly knowledge-oriented society, where science governs every area of our life—from the way our automobiles run to the way our plants grow—knowledge is a prerequisite to prosperity. Even in an environment of specialization, the system will run efficiently only if adequate avenues are created for facilitating an exchange of goods and services, both among rural areas and between rural and urban areas. This is manifested in the need for creating markets that are efficient, accessible and well connected. Knowledge and markets would lead to a better income, but the quest for a better life needs to go a step beyond mere economic goals. Economic empowerment has to lead to societal transformation and thus the final focal area has to be the creation of facilities and amenities that are accessible by and affordable for the needy of the world, wherever they may be.

In the following chapters, we will evolve a framework for sustainable and efficient development emanating from various rural regions and based on examples from around the world in the area of development of the impoverished. It can be a vibrant tool for economic development, and the villages can act as action areas of social transformation leading to a happy, peaceful and prosperous global society.

As we continue to expound on the evolution of empowerment-focused sustainable development systems for the 3 billion, we will use India as an example to illustrate the opportunities, initiatives, effects and challenges which the system poses.

INDIA AS A FOCAL EXAMPLE

India has eighteen officially recognized languages; hundreds of dialects; a variety of religions, castes and sub-castes that share complicated relationships with each other varying with time; agro-climatic conditions from the sub-zero Himalayas to the baking desert sands of Thar—and all this held integrally together under a democratic framework of governance. The socio-economic developmental issues and experiences of the villages of India, with their 750 million people, are a perfect projection and assessment of what any global effort would reflect on a worldwide scale.

Mahatma Gandhi was the greatest advocate of non-violence. His belief in the principle of non-violence emanated from a deep understanding of grass-roots level issues. About eight decades ago, he linked the evolution of peaceful societies with the need to develop the rural world. He said: 'You cannot build non-violence on a factory civilization, but it can be built on self-contained villages.'

Today, as mankind once again stands at the crossroads of growth with depleting peace; prosperity with depleting equity; and technology with depleting values, the issue of the 3 billion becomes a fiercely urgent matter for all global leaders, corporate bodies and industry. As we embark upon the journey of evolving such a system, three factors will define and underline our approach—empowerment of the masses, integrated action and sustainability on all fronts.

2

SUSTAINING THE GROWTH TRAJECTORY

A VISION OF INDIA IN 2020

In the mid-1990s, I was given the task of chairing the Technology Information, Forecasting and Assessment Council (TIFAC). I recall that in our very first meeting we decided that TIFAC must evolve a plan for transforming India into an economically developed nation by the year 2020. India in the 1990s was different from the one the world knows today. Through the previous two decades (1970–89) the nation had seen slower growth rates and been subject to numerous fundamental problems such as unemployment, economic instability, conflicts and a food crisis. Given the then prevailing economic and social conditions of the country, when the suggestion was first mooted for an economically developed nation, everyone speculated over India's ability to embark on this long-term mission. But that was the right time: the then prime minister and his government had just announced economic liberalization and growth measures for the Indian economy, and the impact was beginning to get felt.

The council, consisting of many young members, was excited and energized by the idea and for one full day we discussed how we could translate thought into action. At a time when the economy was growing at around 5–6 per cent per annum in GDP, we had to envisage a growth rate of at least 10 per cent per annum, consistently for over ten years, to realize the development vision for 1 billion democratic people with multilingual, multi-religious and multicultural characteristics. This really ignited the minds of all of us in the council. The members of TIFAC at that time included the principal secretary to the prime minister; nine secretaries to the Government of India; the chiefs of the Confederation of Indian Industry (CII), the Associated Chambers of Commerce and Industry of India (ASSOCHAM) and the Federation of Indian Chambers of Commerce and Industry (FICCI); the chairmen of the Industrial Bank of India (IDBI), the Industrial Credit and Investment Corporation of India (ICICI) and the Industrial Finance Corporation of India (IFCI); the chairmen of public sector corporations and the chief executives of a number of private sector institutions; the vice chancellors of different universities; and scientists from the Department of Science and Technology (DST). We debated and formed seventeen task teams with over 500 members who held consultations with more than 5,000 people in various sectors of the economy. Committees worked for over two years, resulting in twenty-five reports which we presented to the then prime minister of India on 2 August 1996.

The idea which we were pursuing was to formulate an action plan for the whole nation to replace the hesitant 'Can we do it?' with the assertion 'We can do it!' The reports included vision on areas such as agro-food processing; advance sensors, civil aviation, electric power, waterways, road transportation; telecommunications; food and agriculture; engineering industries; health care; life science and biotechnology; materials and processing; electronics and communications; the chemical process industry; services and strategic industries. As we formulated India Vision 2020, the group also studied what the possible driving forces could be and the associated impedances and roadblocks which would need to be addressed.

Transforming India into a developed nation implied that every citizen of the country lived well above the poverty line; that education and health were of a high standard; national security was assured; and that core competencies in certain major areas would enable the production of quality goods for home consumption and for exports, competitively; and, above all, that there would be prosperity for all citizens. The additional thrust would be on creation of employment and development of skills. Based on various inputs, the government announced a vision statement that India would become a developed nation by 2020. The issuing of such a statement was unusual since every government is elected only for a period of five years, but the stance taken by the Parliament and the government of committing themselves to a programme over a twenty-year time frame set a new precedent for the nation.

The visualization of India in 2020[1] consists of an integrated development based on the following ten pillars:

A DISTINCTIVE PROFILE OF THE NATION

1. A nation where the rural–urban divide has been reduced to a thin line.
2. A nation where there is equitable distribution and adequate access to energy and water.
3. A nation where agriculture, industry and the service sector work together in symphony.
4. A nation where education with a value system is not denied to any meritorious candidate through societal or economic discrimination.
5. A nation which is the best destination for the most talented scholars and scientists and investors.
6. A nation where the best health care is available to all.
7. A nation where the governance is responsive and transparent.
8. A nation where poverty has been totally eradicated, illiteracy removed, and none in society feels alienated.
9. A nation that is prosperous, healthy, secure, safe from terrorism, peaceful and happy, and continues on a path of sustainable growth.
10. A nation that is one of the best places to live in and is proud of its leadership.

INTEGRATED ACTION FOR A DEVELOPED INDIA

To achieve this distinctive profile for India, we have the mission of transforming it into a developed nation. We have identified five areas where India has a core competency for integrated action:

1. Agriculture and food processing
2. Education and health care
3. Information and communication technology
4. Good quality infrastructure in the form of reliable and quality electric power, surface transport and waterways for all parts of the country
5. Self-reliance in critical technologies

These five areas are closely interrelated, and we have assessed that, harnessed in a coordinated way, they will lead to food sufficiency and economic and national security.

For India to realize this objective, the convergence of technologies and innovation for harnessing the potential of every state, every village and every individual of the nation is required. One of the necessary conditions for achieving this development profile is the economic growth rate (GDP) of 10 per cent per annum, with contribution by all sectors, societal groups and regions of the nation. Such a phenomenal growth rate can come only by continuous economic innovation and a balanced growth of all the three sectors of economy—agriculture, manufacturing and services. It will require dedicated capacity-building missions and the infusion of technology in everyday life. Above all, it will require the knowledge empowerment of the citizens of the nation.

INDIA IN 2011

The 1990s set the tone for the advancement of the nation, and the growth rate achieved during that decade was very encouraging. In 2011, India finds itself less than a decade away from fully realizing the vision of an economically developed nation by 2020. Post-liberalization, the Indian economy has indeed grown at one of the highest rates compared to many other nations.

Such leadership in growth requires out-of-the-box and innovative development missions and policies. In the 1990s, it was the opening up of the economy which spurred international exports and competitive products and services. In the following decade, it was primarily due to the growth in sectors like information technology (IT) and IT-enabled services (ITES); pharmaceuticals and health care; automobile and other services and manufacturing industries. The question that now rises is: What type of socio-economic innovations does the nation require to move forward on a path of sustainable growth in this decade and beyond?

Since Independence, India has witnessed the emergence of global-standard cities in the nation, which contribute to national wealth and trade. The growth of the cities has been rather centralized with a rapid expansion of population and size, due to migration from the rural and the suburban regions. This has also opened up the possibility of the next potential engine for Indian growth—the 600,000 villages. Let us understand the difference between urban and rural growth models and fit it into the Indian context. Such an analysis can be extrapolated to the global context as well.

WHAT IS NEEDED

There has been an asymmetry between the rural and the urban areas. Given the fact that it is the urban areas which are the seat of large companies and politics, the better amenities like education and health care and a good life are seen to be necessarily established first in urban areas. There is a definite evidence of economies of scale present in the urban context. Wealth begets more wealth, and a higher economic and industrial activity begets stronger economies and better employment.

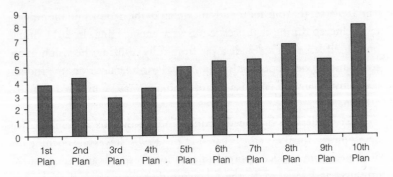

FIGURE 2.1: The GNP growth rate over different plans at 1999–2000 prices

Source: Derived from data available in the India Economic Survey, 2009–10

TABLE **2.1:** India's global ranking in National Product per capita

RANKING BY YEAR	1975	1984	1994	2004
India's relative ranking across all nations	90	89	80	75

In the past four decades—and more specifically post-1990—the Indian economy has definitely posted significant growth rates. The top three growth rates were recorded in the three Five-Year Plans post-1991, which proves that India's new economic policies have worked in positive directions (Figure 2.1).

The per capita National Product—which is a better measure of individual level prosperity—has risen from Rs 5,700 (US$125) per capita (at the 1999–2000 price level) in 1950 to above Rs 18,300 (US$400) in 2003–04, by 3.2 times. But in a relative sense, India has been moving upwards rather slowly in terms of global ranking and, since 1975, has gained fifteen positions over a thirty-year time frame.

The most important reasoning that emerges here is that this economic growth will be unsustainable unless it is inclusive of 70 per cent of the population's habitat—the villages with 750 million people—which also need to be a site for empowerment and entrepreneurship.

While we fly the best aircraft in the world, ferrying more than hundred million passengers every year between Indian cities,[2] there are still many villages which lack access to all-weather roads. While international cities like Mumbai boast of the richest individuals on the planet, the villages in the same state have seen more than 41,000 distressed farmers choosing to end their life due to indebtedness and bankruptcy in the past twelve years from 1998 to 2009.[3] And while we are now a trillion-dollar-plus economy, with 550 million youths, we must deal with the fact that we have more people living in poverty, more children to bring quality nourishment to, more people to provide with clean drinking water and more people who need to be brought under literacy than any other nation. These are our fundamental challenges for the twenty-first century.

Rural development is not at all a loss-making proposition. What is loss-making is poor implementation—but then that holds true for any type of initiative at any place in the world. During the course of this book, we will cite many rural examples where, consistently over the decades, far higher returns have been achieved than on any stock exchange in the world. With more than Rs 1,00,000 crore[4] (US$22 billion) being put into rural development by the government alone, it cannot be claimed that there is a lack of investment in the sector. The only thing which is lacking is, perhaps, an integration of efforts to meet with well-defined and measurable objectives, in a mission-mode striving towards prosperity.

One clear issue here is that of rural to urban migration. Migration from the rural areas is due to inequality in opportunity and outcome between the rural and the urban areas. The underemployed or unemployed population may move to the cities for better living conditions and higher income levels. Moreover, setbacks—such as financial or medical—can force migration. It can also occur as the desire for better amenities and higher education which is felt in a progressive rural population.

Per se, limited migration for better income and living standard is not bad. However, a better alternative would be the creation of facilities and income assets in rural areas in a sustainable manner and beneficial to the population in their model. Then, every village in the nation would have the productivity and the opportunities of an urban setting with the rural ambience and environment preserved.

There are some fundamental issues to be addressed in this context:
- It is difficult to motivate professionals—doctors, engineers and teachers—to live in the rural regions due to the lack of good living conditions and facilities and capacity-building and capacity-utilizing assets.
- The next challenge is to make these models of rural development financially sustainable and eco-friendly.
- For them to succeed, it is necessary to make them available to all—in terms of economy, quality assurance and physical accessibility.

A REVIEW OF 'URBANIZATION'

The asymmetry which has been created due to migration has also taken its toll on cities around the world, as about 37 per cent of their inhabitants live in slum areas.[5] This figure is expected to reach a staggering number of 2 billion urban slum dwellers by 2030.[6] The economy of scale which forms the basis of the urban economic juggernaut is confined by limitations of size.

As the population increases, city planning comes under tremendous pressure for expansion of facilities. With most of the existing space above and below the ground occupied, and the population increasing beyond critical mass, any form of expansion becomes extremely costly; there is pressure on real estate and housing, leading to huge price escalations.

For instance, Mumbai, India's financial capital, has one of the highest real estate rates in the world, as more than 1.8 million people live in a crescent bay. This reflects a population density more than thrice that of the Japanese capital, Tokyo. Such high densities with peak population increase the cost of living and bring down the comfort level of the people. Driven to the urban peripheries by the escalation in costs, many citizens travel several hours every day—by a variety of transport and at high cost—to reach their places of work. The excessively crowded roads and local railways in urban cities also make daily commuting risky. As an example, on an average every day, about ten people lose their lives on Mumbai's local trains[7] and approximately five fatalities occur on Delhi roads.[8] The high cost of transport, commodities and real estate makes entrepreneurship costly and precarious, and creates the 'urban poor' whose living standards are often characterized not only by deprivation but also the poorest ecological conditions. The urban poor are often the most exploited in the economic sense as well. Studies show that the underprivileged and needy, as compared to the economically well-off in the city of Mumbai, end up paying about thirty-seven times more for municipal grade water, more than eight times for certain medications and about seventy-five times more for credit services.[9] We believe these observations go beyond political borders, and every nation is grappling with the pressures of excessive migration.

Is such an intensely concentrated population growth necessary to maintain a staggering growth? Cities and civic amenities can find alternative ways of growth. Let us look at modern industries and the scenario emerging out of them. The mass production of yesterday is confined to only a few areas now. Today, it is possible to have well-networked but decentralized industries which adhere to world-class standards and integrate with each other to emerge as a globally competitive industry. With more than 475,000 villages in India that have access to electricity, most of the nation can now be electrically powered. The vital telecommunications and IT infrastructure enable a global exchange of information—easy, fast, reliable and cheap.

It is possible to connect clusters of villages by annular roads or other transport mechanisms, with well-designed traffic to facilitate movement from one village to the next. This will enable agro-industries, service and even high-tech knowledge industries to relocate in the villages, supported by the movement of some government offices and the provision of necessary incentive structures. Market forces will also take care of further development. Each of the clusters has to be managed in an entrepreneurial and innovative manner involving local panchayats,* professionals, the administration, business concerns and key local human resources. Such clusters can be replicated all over the nation.

Each of these rural clusters will have to ensure the provision of not only better income levels and quality jobs but also cost- and quality-competitive social assets and amenities, where the augmented income levels can be used for better living conditions. The clusters will also have to consider the issue of preserving the cultural heritage, human values and environmental assets present within them. Technology and innovation will play a huge role in achieving this ambition. At present, several technologies exist to make this possible provided we use the multiple connectivity approach as brought out in Technology Vision 2020. The Indian experience clearly demonstrates that the true handicap suffered by the rural areas is poor connectivity, which can be rectified. The conventional tendency of people to move from rural to urban areas, leaving the vast rural potential underutilized, will have to be reversed. A new way of urbanization—where urban jobs, urban income levels and urban amenities reach and expand into the clustered rural areas—needs to be realized.

* Panchayat: It is a unit of local governance which exists in India and other South Asian countries. Article 40 of the Indian Constitution directs the government to set up the panchayat system. Typically, each panchayat has two to three villages within its governance and is represented by an elected body—the gram sabha (village council). Over time, the panchayati raj system has gained prominence as the government has been increasingly using it as a medium for the delivery of many schemes, including the Mahatma Gandhi National Rural Employment Guarantee Act (MGNREGA).

THE PATH AHEAD

India's greatest strength is its 550 million youths who have to be empowered with knowledge and quality value-adding employment across the nation. It is estimated that by 2020 three out of every ten additions to the global workforce will be Indians.[10] India's sense of purpose to achieve a developed and inclusive economy has to be matched with its action for building capacities, harnessing competencies and undertaking an integrated development mission across the nation. The innovative development tool for achieving the vision for an empowered society will essentially require ideas and actions in:

- Harnessing core competencies and customization: In each state, district, city and village of the nation, core competencies need to be identified, nurtured and developed as a sustainable economic entity. This will require customization of solutions to fit local needs and strengths. Decentralization of the last mile solution will be the key.

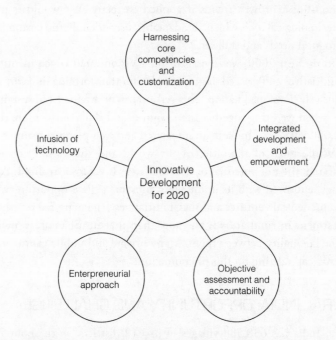

FIGURE **2.2:** The multi-pronged necessary action approach

- Integrated development and empowerment: Development can be sustainable only when it is multi-pronged and when it focuses on the empowerment of the needy rather than merely on alleviation of poverty. Capacity-building is the key ingredient and it will help ensure permanent income generation and skill sets that are universally applicable for employment.
- Objective assessment and accountability: It is important to establish transparent, objective, participative and accountable ways of measuring the effect of a particular development initiative. The impact should be expressible in real gains of outcome rather than on outlay.
- Entrepreneurial approach: During the next decade, the development tool for empowered development should be entrepreneurial in spirit and action. It would mean maximizing yields and returns by using management techniques, opening access to markets and by quality consciousness.
- Infusion of technology: Technology is the tool which can lead to non-linear growth trends if applied correctly. We would require technological tools which are adaptable, user-friendly and customized to local needs and skill sets.

In the year 2000, we envisaged India Vision 2020 which identified key initiatives and devised the growth plan for transforming India into an inclusively developed nation. This version can be attained and sustained only when we bring together the resources and skills of the more than 600,000 villages of India in an integrated and well-planned manner.

While most of the cities of the world and the nation are now saturated, the full potential of the rural areas is yet to be realized. Each village, endowed with its uniqueness, presents a great opportunity for entrepreneurial ventures and social initiatives. The marginal return on investment in rural areas is far more than that in urban areas, owing to the inequality between them. Many private and public ventures are already capitalizing on this phenomenon.

RURAL INDIA: OPPORTUNITY AND CHALLENGE

Rural India has 638,588 villages in its 612 districts. With about 750 million rural Indians, India has the largest rural population in the world.

At present, the net domestic product of the rural economy stands at over Rs 13,70,000 crore (US$304 billion) with a rural GDP of about Rs 15,46,018 crore (US$343 billion). With information and communications technology (ICT) reaching the rural masses (209 million mobile phone users in rural India in 2007, and 643 million rural subscribers to wireless technology in 2008,[11] the villages of India are increasingly achieving equality in terms of access to information, technology and markets. With

THE 600,000+ VILLAGES OF INDIA HAVE:

- 94.8 per cent of land area;
- 70 per cent of population;
- 50 per cent of National Domestic Product (NDP) of India;
- 42 per cent of services and industrial sectors;
- 40 per cent target for rural consumers in the mobile user segment;
- 20 per cent of all the professional colleges in the nation;
- More than 500 million youths below thirty-five years.

the proper skills-building and technology interface for harnessing the potential, this 'electronic connect' can lead to a seamless flow of knowledge and economic returns.

There is a significant thrust at the policy level for strengthening the rural base in terms of financial services which includes priority lending. In fact, under the policy regulation, at least 18 per cent of the net bank credit has to be towards agriculture and 10 per cent for the weaker sections of society.[12]

Owing to improving connectivity, better ambience and economical factor costs, many industries and academic institutions are now based in rural areas. About 40 per cent of colleges and 20 per cent of professional colleges are located in rural areas, a share which is now increasing.[13] All these institutions provide a pool of knowledge volunteers and even potential entrepreneurs who can bring in better technology, greater integration and more efficient management for the conversion of competencies into income and human development.

The government, at the Central and the state levels, has also been aiding rural development and empowerment through many schemes of different kinds. They include income-generating schemes like the Mahatma Gandhi National Rural Employment Guarantee Act (MGNREGA) and the Swarnjayanti Gram Swarozgar Yojana (SGSY); societal schemes like the Indira Awaas Yojana (IAY); the Total Sanitation Campaign; and the Sarva Shiksha Abhiyan (SSA). Thanks to schemes like Bharat Nirman, rural infrastructure has been developed, with efforts in place to connect all villages with a population of over 1,000 by means of all-weather roads.[14] Besides these schemes, there are departmental initiatives in the areas of horticulture, food processing, fisheries, agro-research, handicrafts, livestock and others, all aimed at creating better income, better assets and better human life at the rural levels. A recent trend has been that of the private sector coming up as an agent of development through non-profit initiatives under corporate social responsibility and also profitable initiatives like microfinance.

The rural sector also presents unique challenges which need to be tackled. Out of India's below-the-poverty-line population of about 300 million, 80 per cent live in rural areas.[15] The average rural consumer expenditure is Rs 625 as compared to Rs 1,170 in urban regions.[16] This further translates into the fact that as much as 53 per cent of the total expenditure of every rural household in on food, while only about 10 per cent is capacity-building expenditure like on health care and education.[17] The situation is even worse for the rural poor—below the poverty line (BPL)—where almost 65 per cent of the total consumption is on food alone.[18]

This means that any capacity-building initiative has to begin at the level of income-generation and address the problem of underemployment and unemployment. The new models of sustainable development will have to look at how to customize with reference to the 'present state', and each rural area will have to evolve a unique path to achieve the 'desired future'. The other challenge—especially for a development entrepreneur—is the need to find vertical integration and the convergence of various schemes of the public and the private sectors, and match them to the needs and strengths at local levels.

To achieve such a profile of development, we need to have a framework which is integrated and, at the same time, totally customizable to accommodate a variety of stakeholders, beneficiaries, investors, initiatives and technologies, which can make the Indian rural sector a vibrant

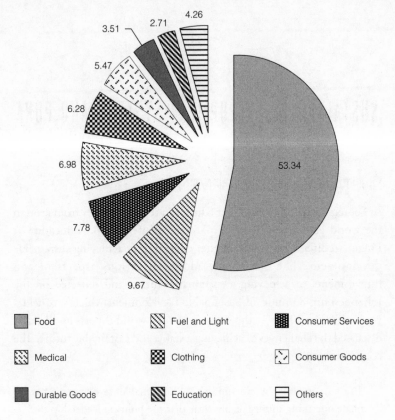

▨ Food	▨ Fuel and Light	▨ Consumer Services
▨ Medical	▨ Clothing	▨ Consumer Goods
■ Durable Goods	▨ Education	▤ Others

FIGURE 2.3: The spending pattern of an average rural family

forerunner for national growth during this decade. We shall formulate it as the Global Sustainable Development System for Providing Urban Amenities in Rural Areas (PURA).

3

SUSTAINABLE DEVELOPMENT SYSTEMS AND PURA

SUSTAINABLE DEVELOPMENT

In September 2003, 130 higher education representatives from around the world gathered at the International Conference on Education at Prague to discuss the role of higher education in achieving sustainable development. The conference addressed various aspects of and impediments to achieving a sustainable future and reflected on the Johannesburg Summit on Sustainable Development which was held a year earlier, in 2002. At the summit various world experts and leaders discussed the challenges of achieving a stable and sustainable future. The conference report says:

> The Johannesburg world summit for sustainable development has made one thing unmistakably clear that the political leadership the world over is incapable of rising to the challenge of sustainability. Yet, most of the hundred or so world leaders who attended have a higher education degree from some of the world's most prestigious universities—the higher education sector is failing society by producing leaders incapable of addressing the most pressing problems. If higher education is the nursery of tomorrow's leaders then the sector bears profound responsibilities to create a sustainable future. This implies that graduates of every discipline need a sound working knowledge about sustainability.[1]

Sustainable development and inclusive growth in all fields will be the major factors in reducing potential conflicts in the country and in a world without borders. That will be our key to achieving a society which is peaceful, prosperous and happy. Let us understand sustainable development in more detail.

SUSTAINABLE DEVELOPMENT AND PEACEFUL SOCIETIES

Sustainable development based on a foundation of inclusion is the cornerstone for building a peaceful and prosperous society across the world. Economic and social empowerment of the people is the solution for attaining productive engagement of every citizen.

Post-Independence, one of the most alarming threats to the security and peace of India has been the surging left-wing extremism, in the form of 'Naxalism' which, in some form or the other, affects 118 districts[2] stretching across one-third of the nation. In the past half a decade, more than 10,000 people have lost their lives to this increasing form of unrest.[3] It is evident from the Annual Report of the home ministry, 2009–10, that extremism thrives in the 'Red Corridor' that largely covers the regions which are economically underdeveloped or socially backward. While the

TABLE 3.1: State-wise left-wing extremism violence, 2008–09

States	2008		2009	
	Incidents	Deaths	Incidents	Deaths
Andhra Pradesh	92	46	66	18
Bihar	164	73	232	72
Chhattisgarh	620	242	529	290
Jharkhand	484	207	742	208
Madhya Pradesh	7	–	1	–
Maharashtra	68	22	154	93
Orissa	103	101	266	67
Uttar Pradesh	4	–	8	2
West Bengal	35	26	255	158
Others	14	4	5	–
Total	1591	721	2258	908

causality between the lack of amenities and the threat to peace may be debatable, the correlation between the two is beyond doubt. Besides the efforts to improve the security coverage, our primary tool for overcoming the problems and for achieving peace and stability across India, would be a fresh approach that aims at sustainable development measures which would also bring about economic prosperity and growth.[4]

This situation is not unique to India. Although post-World War II interstate conflicts have remained more or less constant and generally low intensity, there has been a significant rise in civil conflicts within nations, hinting at a connection between lack of sustainable development and state failures.

In fact, data from around the world (Figure 3.1) show that the majority of conflicts are concentrated in regions of the world where extreme poverty, hunger and disease are most prevalent.[5] This is depicted in Figure 3.2 in a map of the world showing different forms

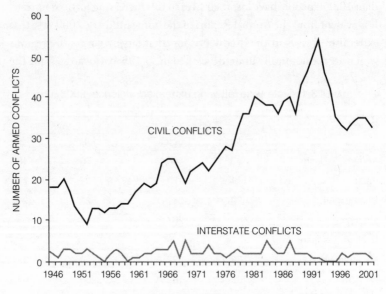

FIGURE 3.1: Annual number of civil and interstate conflicts from 1946 to 2001

Source: Population Action International (2003)

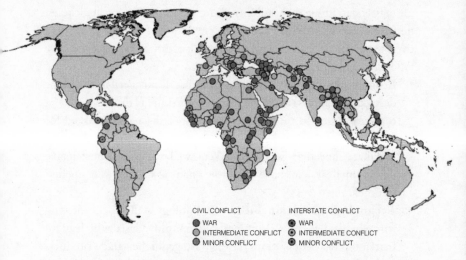

FIGURE 3.2: Zones of armed conflict in the world, 1990–2000

Source: Population Action International (2003)

of conflicts during the decade 1990–2000. The geographical correlation between the poverty-affected zones and the prevalence of conflict is abundantly clear. In an interconnected and mobile world, this aspect extends further—today, tensions in one part of the world can result in a ruthless manifestation thousands of miles away in a completely different region. Economic prosperity and sustainable growth will lead to peaceful societies. Sustainable development systems are thus not only a national or a regional, but a global need.[6]

CONSTITUENTS OF SUSTAINABLE DEVELOPMENT

We have already stressed the need for evolving and executing sustainable development systems, especially for the integrated transformation of rural India. It is important to know the implications of sustainability. The challenges and the opportunities which we, as a nation and the world, face are multi-pronged and unique to our times. The definition of sustainable development has to take into account a network of parameters which will ultimately determine the feasibility of the model for direct beneficiaries, non-beneficiaries, national values, the environment and the stability of the system. Broadly speaking, 'sustainability' can be defined with the following constituents:

- **Economic sustainability**: This implies that the financial model of the development tool is sound and robust. It also implies that development tools are tuned to the core competency of the region marked for implementation; that the products are matched to market demand; and that connectivity with the market is well maintained. Sustainable development systems have to achieve financial stability over a period of time.

- **Technological sustainability**: Technology will be the driving force behind the development tool employed. It will lead to better and faster operations, lower wastage, higher-grade products and services, and will cut down the costs. Modern sustainable development tools have to be technologically sustainable, which means that they should be upgradable and capable of applying competitive technologies.

- **Social sustainability**: Modern institutions, whether government or private, have to accept that one of their primary interfaces comprise people who would not necessarily be their customers. The new requirement of sustainable development systems is to be a partner in the lives of the people, in order to bring about a positive change in human development. This may come about not only as corporate social responsibility and welfare schemes, but also as dedicated enterprises in the area of societal uplift, which would work closely with the local community, building capacities and living standards. Societal sustainability will also lead to peaceful societies, a necessary condition for sustainable growth.

- **Environmental sustainability**: One of the most crucial challenges of the twenty-first century is that of climate change due to global warming caused by man-made greenhouse gases. Today, globally, we release into the atmosphere close to 30 trillion kg, that is, 30,000,000,000,000,000 kg,[7] of carbon dioxide-equivalent greenhouse gases which come from our industries, power plants, vehicles, homes, shops and agricultural fields. Out of this, roughly half is absorbed by natural sinks like oceans, the soil and forests, while the rest is released into the atmosphere, forming a 'blanket' of greenhouse gases which trap the infrared radiation from the earth's surface and prevent it from going out into space. The net effect is that global mean temperatures are rising; the decade of 2000–09 was the warmest ever recorded.[8] India, too, contributes a significant 5 per cent share to the total emissions generated globally, though our per capita emission is lower than that of the world.[9]

> **ELEMENTS OF ENVIRONMENTAL SUSTAINABILITY**
>
> - Reducing emission
> - Reducing water and soil pollution
> - Protecting biodiversity
> - Preserving natural resources—flora and fauna
> - Waste recycling; waste-to-wealth, using technology
> - Awareness of ecology in the community
> - Accountability on environment

The aspect of environment—covering emission control, reducing pollution of water and soil resources, preserving biodiversity—is, indeed, an important consideration in any sustainable development model.

- **Value sustainability**: Development should be accompanied by the creation of a value-based society and lead to the evolution of enlightened citizens, who are powered by knowledge and skills, and guided by moral values. Such a value creation in the societal fabric will help reduce societal conflicts, bring about tolerance and respect for diversity, harmonious interaction and a reduction in crime.

- **Learning and adaptability**: Sustainable development systems require infrastructure, opportunity, incentives for continuous learning from each other and evolution. This will lead to innovations and improvements which would improve the yield, enhance capacity, bring down costs or add value. Development systems also have to be adaptable to conditions of local input and needs. This focus on being dynamic would additionally lend long-term stability to the system which would, in turn, assimilate external alterations and be self-reliant.

THE EVOLUTION OF A SUSTAINABLE DEVELOPMENT SYSTEM IN INDIA

In Indian history, very rarely has the nation come across a situation that involved, simultaneously, an ascending economic trajectory; a continuously rising foreign exchange reserve; a reduced rate of inflation; global recognition of its technological competence; the energy of more than 550 million youths; the umbilical connectivity of 20 million people of Indian origin in various parts of the planet; and the eagerness shown by many developed countries to invest in our engineers and scientists and to set up new research and development centres. The distinction between the public and the private sectors and the illusory primacy of one over the other are vanishing. India, the largest democracy in the world, has a reputation for upholding its democratic principles and for providing leadership to its one billion people with a multicultural, multilingual and multi-religious background. Our technological competency, as also our value systems obtained through our ancient civilization and heritage, is highly respected. Foreign institutions see investing in India as an attractive proposition. Indians, too, are investing and opening new business ventures in other countries. The Indian economy is growing and has an average annual growth rate of about 8 per cent of GDP.

However, there is a pressing need to raise the economic conditions and living standards of over 300 million people living in extreme poverty out of the 1 billion plus population. One of the reasons for this situation is that a large part of the growth comes from the manufacturing and the service sectors. Moreover, the benefits of these two sectors thin down significantly as they reach the rural interior regions of the nation.

While the economy has generally been growing impressively, agriculture has been growing at just 1.2 per cent since the 1990s.[10] If we are to uplift the 300 million people living below the poverty line and provide them with a better life, we have to ensure that the agriculture sector grows at least at 4 per cent per annum. We also need to ensure that fruitful employment is made available to the rural masses and the youths in Indian villages, with avenues for building capacity. The nation and the world need systems which can alter the lifestyle of the 750 million people living in rural India, and give every man and woman the opportunity to build competencies, to be economically active for the family and to have better living standards. During this decade and onward, we require development initiatives which will integrate competencies, skills, employment and market access, and will make available quality education for children and health care for the rural families.

For providing this growth, India and other nations have to extend the development process to the rural sector. Technology needs to reach the doors of the common man, in the most useful form. The skills imparted need to match the competencies and the available resources, and seamless investments need to follow good entrepreneurship, which would, in turn, generate jobs and income. This would lead to an environment of employment generation at the local levels where the skills and opportunities for income generation will be well matched. The villages, individually and collectively, should evolve as economic engines for the nation's development; they should provide better and healthier living conditions to the inhabitants; and become centres of reliable goods and services to the markets with value addition. To achieve such a profile, we need a framework which would enable the movement of goods, services, people, ideas and investments within and outside village complexes.

WHAT IS PURA?

PURA stands for 'Providing Urban Amenities in Rural Areas'. It is a socio-economic system for sustainable growth. As envisioned, it is meant to ensure a better life for millions of Indians who live in deprivation—often a generation behind in basic human facilities—especially in the rural regions. Put into action, PURA stands for a well-planned drive towards achieving an inclusive and integrated development, starting at the village household level.

A common impediment to rural development is the fact that reputable professionals find rural life unattractive. This tendency is manifested in doctors playing hooky from the PHCs (primary health-care centres) and the rural hospitals, and teacher absenteeism from rural schools. Even NGOs (non-government organizations) and the organizations based on rural enterprises and village development mostly have their professional staff and offices based in cities. One factor behind this crippling situation is the total lack of adequate services and amenities in rural areas—a problem which PURA needs to address. Hence, one of its fundamental efforts is to create, in a rural environment, amenities of urban standards. We will study how this can be, and has been, successfully realized in various PURA missions across the nation.

The model of a PURA creation begins at the individual village household level, which is the atomic level of PURA implementation. Here, it has to ensure the participation of all households according to their skills and needs, with an opportunity for capacity-building and gaining access to basic amenities. Typical human-resources-building exercises that are undertaken should again focus on how to attract participation by every household in a rural area. The performance evaluation of PURA implementation should account for the impact created by each household.

The next in the PURA hierarchy is the village, where its implementation requires a careful analysis of the available resources and the prioritization of the needs of the local population. Also, it is in this area that the acceptability of PURA's various initiatives needs to be developed to make it a process of community participation.

The next higher grouping is the PURA Village Cluster, which is a group of villages sharing basic economic and social assets, such as connecting roads, markets, advanced health-care services, higher educational facilities and electronic connectivity. Depending on the terrain and the population, the size of a PURA cluster can vary from ten to even fifty villages. The clusters would be located close to each other, physically as well as culturally and linguistically, and may typically have some common elements in the resources they possess or the skills they have developed. A PURA cluster would be the basic 'element' of the PURA design, each possessing its unique qualities, economic inputs and outputs, and be capable of existing independently. It is at this aggregate level that PURA planning should start.

Each cluster would exist independently as a socio-economic entity. Beyond this level, our focus would move to inter-PURA coordination. PURA clusters may collaborate for mutual benefit, dividing fixed costs, exchanging knowledge and sharing markets, core competencies or products. They may also establish common brands and standards for strengthening their position in the market.

There is no doubt that, in India, development of the rural sector is very important. The government and the private and the public sectors have been undertaking rural development, but in a haphazard manner. For example, during the last few decades, they have set up educational institutions and health-care centres; laid roads, built houses and marketing complexes; given communication links in a particular rural area, but as disconnected activities. It has been our experience that these initiatives start well—just like heavy rain resulting in multiple streams of water. As soon as the rain stops, a few days later, the streams dry up because there are no water bodies to collect and store the surplus water. Now, for the first time, PURA envisages an integrated development plan with employment generation as its focus, driven by providing good habitation, health care and education, and by developing skills; through physical and electronic connectivity, and marketing. This will lead to the generation of stable employment for sustained development.

India—taken as an entire country—needs 7,000 PURAs covering more than 600,000 villages. The theme of PURA—apart from concentrating on reinforcing agriculture—is to emphasize agro-processing, develop local crafts, dairy farming, fishing and silk production, so that the non-farm revenue for this sector is enhanced, based on the core competency of the region. Moreover, its economy will be driven by sources of renewable energy, such as sun, wind, biofuels and the conversion of municipal waste into power. In this approach, the objective is sustainable development, using the core potential of the rural sector.

One such sustainable development system is the mission of PURA. It involves:

PHYSICAL CONNECTIVITY

- Ring Road
- Rail connectivity
- Public infrastructure
- Enables movement of people and goods
- Improves access to schools and health-care centres
- Reduces investments in distribution of power, water and communication networks

PHYSICAL CONNECTIVITY

The villages must be connected with each other and with main towns and cities by good, well-networked roads and, where needed, by railway lines. This connectivity would depend on the local climatic and terrain conditions. For example, in the case of deltaic, island or coastal PURAs, the most efficient way might be to use carefully planned waterways or seaways with a proper traffic management system. There must be other infrastructure, such as schools, colleges, hospitals, irrigation networks and amenities for the local population and visitors. This is Physical Connectivity.

Physical Connectivity goes beyond the mere creation of assets; it has to attain full utilization. So, building connecting roads between villages and cities would be useful only if it were backed by a public transport system which could ferry people between them. Physical Connectivity in the form of a school building would be beneficial only if it were accessible to both teachers and students. Of course, the creation of such a system can be shared between multiple partners and often be market-driven.

It is important to understand that Physical Connectivity would act as an 'enabler': it would facilitate the movement of goods and people, and thereby enable enterprises, assets or societal missions to have a wider access to their inputs, markets or intended beneficiaries. A network of good roads or seaways with proper traffic management would connect enterprises with their suppliers and buyers and bring down the time and cost of transport. Similarly, in the case of services, a school or a hospital building would be a fundamental enabler upon which further societal missions could be based, to benefit a large section of people at one common location with limited human investment.

ICT AS A LEVELLER

The spread of information and communication technology (ICT) tools promises to be the greatest leveller of twenty-first-century societies. ICT tools are facilitators which enable low-cost access to knowledge and the networking of people. This can lead to:

- Access to real-time information on input.
- Low-cost dissemination of information about efficient processes and access to education and training.
- Increase of scale by allowing connection with a large network of thousands of individuals.
- Direct access to remote markets.
- Facility of accessing from home which encourages participation, especially by women.
- Mechanism for transparent feedback and redressal of grievances at low cost and in less time, thereby ensuring accountability.
- Add-on services like education, health care and financial services.
- Standardized processes that allow replication at low cost.

ELECTRONIC CONNECTIVITY

In this era of emerging knowledge, native intelligence has to be preserved and enhanced with the latest tools of technology, training and research. Villagers, wherever they are, must have access to good education from the best teachers, the benefit of good medical treatment and the latest information on their occupations such as agriculture, fishery, horticulture and food processing. This means that they must have Electronic Connectivity.

Like Physical Connectivity, Electronic Connectivity has to be customized so that it can be availed of by the intended user. The 'true' value of Electronic Connectivity would be a function of its relevance and user-friendliness.

Value of Electronic Connectivity = Relevance × Usability

Relevance would be the balancing factor between the technology available and the cost economics. Usability would derive from the number of people who could use the connectivity with little or no training, and

TABLE **3.2:** Customization of Electronic Connectivity

Measure	Explanation
Assistance	Availability of guidance at the electronic interface centres to facilitate usage.
Technological	Adaptation into native language, user-friendly interface and usage. Built-in robustness within the system.
Training	Building-capacity for spreading awareness and knowledge of using Electronic Connectivity for oneself.
Value-adding Services	Using Electronic Connectivity as a tool for delivering value-adding services, such as finance, education, health care, and creation of income via areas like business process outsourcing (BPO).

INDIA'S ELECTRONIC CONNECTIVITY INITIATIVES: NATIONAL E-GOVERNANCE PLAN (NEGP) OF INDIA

NeGP was set up in 2006 with the aim of improving the quality of and access to government services in India with the help of ICT. The components of NeGP are:

1. SWAN (State Wide Area Network): To connect each state and Union Territory (UT) headquarters with the district headquarters and similarly, the district headquarters with block headquarters with 2 Mbps-leased lines.
2. National and state data centres across the nation.
3. Common Service Centres (CSCs): They have been conceived of as the front-end delivery system with a special focus on IT services for the government as well as the private sector for the remotest villages. A network of about 100,000 CSCs to cover each of the panchayats (or a cluster of five to six villages) across 600,000 villages is being currently aimed at. As of July 2008, about 75,000 CSCs were already in place, forming a network between villages.

The CSCs are designed as ICT-enabled kiosks with a PC and basic support equipment like a printer, a scanner, a UPS, with wireless connectivity as the backbone and additional equipment for edutainment, tele-medicine and projection systems.

the support system behind it. User-friendliness and usage-frequency can be enhanced in a variety of ways.

Electronic Connectivity is essentially a facilitator to help create knowledge networks; enhance educational initiatives; connect hospitals with remote locations; bring in better banking services; and open up market access in a faster and more transparent manner.

KNOWLEDGE CONNECTIVITY

Once the Physical and the Electronic Connectivity are enabled, the Knowledge Connectivity has to be set up. This can facilitate an increase in productivity; utilization of spare time to tackle underemployment; and the spread of awareness of health welfare. It can ensure a market for products; increase quality consciousness; interact with partners; help obtain the best equipment; and increase transparency. This, in short, is Knowledge Connectivity.

This connectivity will essentially be a 'value-adder' to either the local strength or the capacity of human resource. Knowledge Connectivity has to map and match the local competencies at the village cluster level. It is an excellent avenue for creating enterprises, especially among women and the young. It would bring the best relevant practices to a ground-level realization. As PURA matures, Knowledge Connectivity itself will enable the creation of knowledge-service enterprises, providing value addition

---

ELECTRONIC CONNECTIVITY

Establishing Electronic Connectivity through Broadband/Fibre/Satellite/Wireless/Leased Line.
Tele-Education
- Satellite Link
- Wireless Connectivity
- Fibre Connectivity
- Public Call Offices (STD/ISD/ISDN)
- Leased Line Connectivity
Tele-Medicine
- Village Internet Kiosks
- e-Government Access
- e-Market Access
- Tele-Training on Farming
- e-Banking
- ATM Centres for Villagers

KNOWLEDGE CONNECTIVITY

- Schools/Hospitals
- Vocational Training
- Knowledge Training
- IRS Imagery for
  - Land and Crop Management
  - Water Management
  - Forest Management
  - Environment
  - Proactive Health Care
  - Cooperatives Product Marketing

to the lives of the local people. Some of the prominent functions which it would have to perform for each village include:

- Waste management
- Soil and fertilizer management
- Agro-processing technologies
- Mapping of land, water and other resources
- Value-adding practices in non-farming activities
- e-Health care and distance education
- Environment and forest management
- Value-based education and inculcating morals
- Entrepreneur training and incubation
- Weather management
- Any special local or seasonal needs

ECONOMIC CONNECTIVITY

Once the Physical, the Electronic and the Knowledge Connectivity have been established, they will facilitate Economic Connectivity in the area.

Economic Connectivity would essentially lead to the creation of employment, entrepreneurship and income augmentation of the rural area through the setting up of agro-based, manufacturing and service industries. Its role in the overall PURA scenario is important since PURA complexes strive to be economically independent and, thereby, contribute to the economic growth of the nation in a positive manner. Moreover, the Economic Connectivity model would have to be customized according to the state of the PURA complex in terms of:

- Agro-climatic conditions of the region
- Quality of human resources
- Specialized skills
- Special competencies
- Connectivity to the markets and cities, and within the villages
- Support industries
- Services most needed at the local level which may be seasonal in demand

KNOWLEDGE CONNECTIVITY THROUGH VILLAGE RESOURCE CENTRES

Village Resource Centres (VRCs) were established by the Indian Space Research Organisation (ISRO) as part of its societal mission of bringing space-based services emanating from Satellite Communication (SatCom) and Earth Observation (EO) to rural society. While SatCom provides the method for an effective delivery of information and services across vast regions, EO provides community-centric information regarding geo-referenced land records; natural resources; the environment; sites for exploiting ground water for potable use and recharging; wasteland and reclamation; watershed profile; and cropping patterns. It can also provide customized local area information. These systems are very useful for predicting disaster, giving early warning and vulnerability-related information.

ISRO has undertaken the mission of assisting the VRC programme with a portfolio of services which are being established in collaboration with forty partner agencies across twenty-two states. A total of 473 VRCs have been set up with plans for rapid expansion in the future. Each VRC essentially has digital connectivity; specialty health-care providers enabled via the Indian National Satellite System (INSAT); spatial information on natural resources; facilities for primary health care and distance education. Thus the VRC service portfolio includes:

- Tele-education: for development of skills and livelihood support. It also includes supplementary teaching for children and non-formal education to adults
- Tele-health-care: both preventive and curative, VRCs have customized health-care software with diagnostic instruments. With the help of local doctors and paramedics, expert consultation is provided to the villagers from specialty hospitals
- Land and water resource management
- Interactive advisory services: VRCs facilitate interaction between the local people and experts at knowledge centres such as agriculture universities and technical institutes.
- e-Governance services
- Weather information and forecasts
- Tele-fishery: information pertaining to potential fishing zones (PFZs) and other data
- Local services as needed by the villages

So far, VKCs have conducted over 6,500 programmes benefiting several hundred thousand people in the rural regions of the nation.

ECONOMIC CONNECTIVITY

- Small-scale Industries
- Agro-industries
- Warehouse
- Micro Power Plants
- Renewable Energies
- Village Markets
- Employment Opportunities
- Value System—Economic Strength
- Women's Empowerment
- Urban Decongestion
- Improved Quality of Life
- Increased Purchasing Power

The Economic Connectivity model has to be based on a holistic prediction of the demand for support services in the future. For example, while setting up an agro-processing unit, the PURA initiator must also acknowledge the additional services in terms of logistics and the capacity-building which would be needed to support it. PURA's Economic Connectivity would be achieved by a mix of institutions of various sizes, stake-holding patterns and activities.

There would be a distinct and direct correlation between the economic activity in terms of the agro sector and creating a demand for the services. As the income of the rural population rises, there would be a corresponding increase in the disposable income level. Some part of

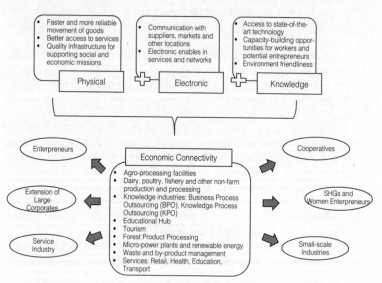

FIGURE 3.3: Block model of Economic Connectivity for PURA

it would initially go towards better and more food, but a larger and increasing share would go into non-food expenditure. If we have a value-driven society where this extra income is not wasted on non-productive activities, much of the income generated would translate into capacity-building and human development services. This would create an opportunity for economic activities based on a demand for local services as well, generating further employment activities.

With the rise in income, the demand for services gradually increases. Initially, it is slower since the rise in income will largely provide for better food and nutrition. But as the income keeps rising, a larger share will go towards creating local demands. This will contribute further to income augmentation with employment in the service industry of the PURA complex, and will also help handle the problem of underemployment. As better services become available, the capabilities of the population will get upgraded. This will help generate a larger yield in terms of employee productivity in the agro or the manufacturing sector, thereby enhancing production, provided the necessary space is available for expansion in terms of Physical and Electronic Connectivity. All this would translate into the income of the household rising further by a combined effect of agro-manufacturing and the service industries.

To achieve this profile of an increased income and better human resources through Economic Connectivity issuing out of the other three—Physical, Electronic and Knowledge—the following conditions are necessary:

1. Vertical integration of the agro-manufacturing processes.
2. Adequate entrepreneurship and planning in the service sector as the demand increases.
3. A value-based society at the domestic level so that the augmented income is used for creating capacity and not frittered away; this would impede the process of increasing productivity.
4. Adequate room for Physical, Electronic and Knowledge Connectivity to account for the rise in economic activities with a more capable workforce.

~

A CASE STUDY OF SOCIO-ECONOMIC DEVELOPMENT THROUGH WARANA PURA

In March 2010, we were in the Warana Valley of Kolhapur district in the western India state of Maharashtra, where I interacted with many students, farmers, milk producers, rural entrepreneurs and villagers. I also inaugurated a PURA centre at the Tatyasaheb Kore Institute of Engineering and Technology. The Warana PURA mission demonstrates that the PURA development system requires an integration of initiatives and that capacity-building and economic development are concomitant. The Warana mission began as a sugar cooperative movement in the 1950s—the vision of a great social leader called Tatyasaheb Kore for transforming the Warana region, which was then a backward area overrun by unlawful activities and poverty.

Since then, Warana PURA has evolved into a cooperative framework and implemented sustainable models based on the core competencies of the rural areas covering sixty-nine villages and about 400,000 people. It has more than 60,000 farmers, women entrepreneurs and villagers as its members, to whom it has been able to give a consistent dividend of over 20 per cent per annum.

The Warana PURA programme has succeeded in creating income generation through value addition to sugar and dairy products, innovative agricultural practices and entrepreneurship, striving towards literacy and

---

WARANA PURA MISSION

Sugar Factory
- Warana Cooperative Dairy has more than 20,000 farmers as members
- Has undertaken area development as well
- Has one of the highest sugar recovery rates of more than 12 per cent (almost 20 per cent above the national average)
- Began as a Sugar Cooperative Movement in the 1950s under Sahkarshri Tatyasaheb Kore
- Covers 69 villages and about 400,000 people
- Based on a cooperative set-up, has more than 60,000 members comprising farmers, women and craftsmen
- Has been giving 25 per cent and more returns on investments

WARANA PURA DAIRY

Warana Dairy
* More than 16,000 milk producers are members
* Spread across 60 villages
* Collects and processes more than 500,000 litres of milk from 1,753 collection centres
* Advanced technology and highest quality of value addition; exports to large cities

providing health care for all. The Warana cooperative sugar factory, with about 20,000 farmers as its members, has also taken area development as one of its missions and has helped construct schools, medi-care institutions and libraries. There has been a significant effort to upgrade technology and practices, which has reflected in the consistently high sugar recovery rate of more than 12 per cent which is almost one-fifth higher than the national average. As a result, the sugar cane farmers in and around sixty villages near the factory have been receiving significantly higher revenues.

Warana's economy had to be made inclusive. This meant the creation of income opportunities for the landless and the smaller farmers who were otherwise underemployed. For the welfare of landless villagers, Tatyasaheb Kore envisioned and pioneered the creation of the Warana Poultry and the Warana Dairy which are now a known brand in the state of Maharashtra. The Warana Cooperative Dairy, with

WARANA PURA'S DIVERSE SERVICES

* Warana Bazaar: 58 branches managed largely by women
* Educational Initiatives: schools, engineering college, art and science college, pharmacy college, dental college
* Health Care: Mahatma Gandhi Hospital
* Financial Services: Warana Cooperative Bank with 18,000 members and 24 branches
* Realizing the vision of integrated development and empowerment—next goal to become a carbon-neutral PURA by 2015

more than 16,000 milk producers spread over seventy-eight villages, collects and processes over 500,000 litres of milk every day from its 1,753 collection centres. Each of these collection centres acts as an opportunity for creating more enterprises through the self-help groups (SHGs) that operate them. Generally, there are multiple options in terms of collection points accessible to the milk producers and hence, through competition, the farmers are able to obtain the best price for their products.

Warana sells around 150,000 litres of liquid milk in Mumbai alone. With advanced technologies for value addition and by observing the highest quality standards, the Warana Dairy manufactures and exports many value-added milk products to the Middle East. It has forty-seven stock-keeping units (SKUs) currently in its product portfolio.

Enhanced incomes have led to better living standards for the rural people of the region. The Warana PURA complex has established innovative models in the service and the retail sectors in the form of Warana Bazaar with its fifty-eight stores.

Warana Cooperative has provided its youths with a wide spectrum of education to empower themselves and take the vision of the Warana development further.

The health of the citizens is taken care of by initiatives such as the Mahatma Gandhi Hospital and the Dental College. To inculcate a spirit of saving, the Warana PURA complex opened the Warana Cooperative Bank in 1966. It now has more than 18,000 cooperative members and twenty-four branches across the Warana Valley.

We also visited the Warana Sugar Parliament, which is a mark of empowerment in the democratic framework that the Warana PURA complex has provided to the farmers. I was impressed to see the building which closely resembles the Indian parliament, echoing Tatyasaheb Kore's message of his faith in the democratic, economic, social and educational empowerment of the grass-roots-level rural population.

Today, Warana is a remarkable region which, by keeping in mind a socio-economic objective, has been transformed. It is aiming at becoming a carbon-neutral PURA by the year 2015.

The Warana PURA complex has a message: innovative missions, with focus on better technology and sound management, can fulfil socio-economic objectives of creating a prosperous and happy society emanating from the bottom of the pyramid. The cooperative model, the product diversification, the process innovation and market understanding have all been the hallmarks of creativity of Warana's citizens. We will discuss in more detail the Warana model and its constituents in subsequent chapters.

The authors acknowledge the support of Professor Samar Datta (IIMA), Shri Vinay Kore and Shri Sharad Mahajan who helped in compiling the information provided about Warana PURA.

~

CLASSIFICATION OF PURA

The size, activity and needs of every PURA are affected hugely by the kind of terrain on which it is located. If we were to classify PURAs according to terrain, then we could do a loose grouping as per the core competencies and needs which are often common to a particular type of terrain. For example, most of the coastal- and island-type fishery and other marine enterprise PURAs are prominent income assets, for whom information and market connectivity for perishable goods is an important need. Similarly, most of the desert or, to some extent, even plain PURAs will have to tackle conservation and the creation of water bodies as one of the primary challenges.

Based on this classification, the types of PURAs as in Table 3.3 can be envisaged.

MOVING AHEAD ON PURA

A well-planned PURA would be our tool for the integrated development of Indian villages where three out of every four Indians live. The same concept would be equally applicable towards the empowerment of the 3 billion rural population of the world. It would be a transformation of villages from a subsistence entity to a knowledge and economic powerhouse for the nation and the world. We have already stated that

TABLE 3.3: Types of PURA

Plain PURA	Would cover a population of around 20,000–100,000, spanning around 20–30 villages each. It would be based on diverse competencies depending on the nature and resources of the region. Agriculture and forest products would be a prime focus area in most cases along with non-farm employment opportunities.
Coastal PURA	Would cover a population of around 20,000–80,000 spanning around 20–25 villages each, largely located near the sea. Marine occupations would be a major focal point here.
Desert PURA	Would be established on large stretches of sparsely populated land; each would consist of around 30–50 villages with a population of 7,000–15,000 people. One key challenge which would be common across all Desert PURAs would be the scarcity of water and the need to utilize the available water for maximum economic development.
Hill PURA	Would be similar to the Desert PURA in terms of the size and number of villages. On an average, it would span 30–45 villages with a population of 7,000–15,000 individuals. The rather daunting problem of Physical and Electronic Connectivity would be both a challenge and an opportunity commonly found in these PURAs.
Island PURA	Would be similar to the Coastal PURA in the primary economic assets, but more demanding in establishing connectivity both within the PURA and with the external markets. Typically, it would contain a group of neighbouring islands with a population of 7,000–15,000 people.
Delta PURA	The delta region of the lower Gangetic course in West Bengal is rich in soil fertility and has unique natural resources of bio-medicinal value, especially in the fragile ecosystem where fresh water finds confluence with sea water. It can be a difficult proposition for PURA implementation. The common key issues would be establishing Physical Connectivity and developing a knowledge base. Such a PURA would cover roughly 20–40 villages with 20,000–50,000 people.

we would need 7,000 PURA complexes in India alone, all over the rural regions. This is indeed going to be a challenging task and would be an opportunity for every sector to contribute—the government, industry, entrepreneurs, administration, institutions, citizens and NRIs (non-resident Indians). It would require active participation by all strata of society in an integrated manner.

The realization of PURA would require focus on multiple facets. In the following chapters we will analyse the PURA strategy for different kinds of activities, drawing from existing examples in India and elsewhere in the world.

4

AGRICULTURE AND PURA

THE RELEVANCE OF AGRICULTURE

The agriculture sector is by far the largest employer in terms of human resources in India as well as elsewhere in the world. Ironically, at the same time it is also the smallest sectoral contributor to the GDP of the nation. It is strange that food—the most fundamental requirement of human beings, which also forms the bulk of our agricultural produce—is largely considered an unrewarding sector in the nation.

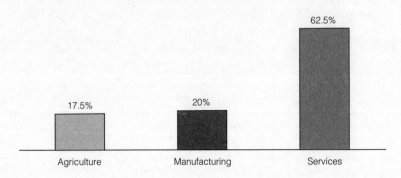

FIGURE 4.1: Sector-wise GDP share

Eight out of every ten BPL families in India reside in villages as depicted in Figure 4.2.[1] Further, three out of every four Indian rural dwellers are dependent on agriculture for their livelihood. It is estimated that any returns on investment in agriculture would be at least four

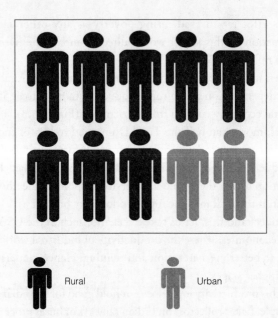

FIGURE 4.2: Distribution of BPL population across rural and urban India

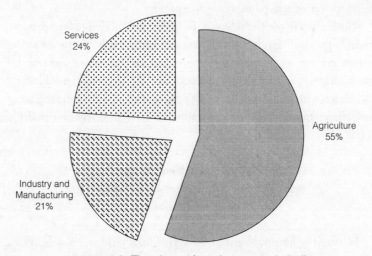

FIGURE 4.3: The share of rural economy in India

times[2] as effective in eradicating poverty as any other sector, and transformation in this sector would directly impact the lives of more than 600 million Indians.

There is still more to the story of Indian agriculture. The rural economy is largely dependent on agricultural produce, with more than 55 per cent of the rural economy coming from agriculture (Figure 4.3).

In fact, more than half the Total Domestic Product of India's rural economy is based on agriculture. Agro-products form the bulk of tradable goods and services emanating from it and thus they act as a benchmark for the valuation of all other goods and services, especially the non-tradable ones, even if they fall into the high-productivity bracket.

To understand this, let us take a scenario, such as the USA or other Western economies, where the productivity of industrial workers is very high due to better mechanization and training. Hence, understandably, they get higher wages.

But, this productivity logic does not hold good for subsidiary services. For example, ticket collectors on Indian railways or buses process a higher number of tickets per hour and hence have more productivity. Despite this, why do ticket collectors in the USA receive much higher wages than their more productive Indian counterparts?

The key lies in the fact that it is the higher productivity of the primary tradable goods or services which acts as a benchmark for the valuation of non-primary or non-tradable goods and services. The reason is also simple: when primary goods or services are marked with high productivity and hence, a high income, the overall purchasing power of the region or nation goes up and people are generally able to pay more for non-tradable goods or services.[3]

Wage or Valuation of Non-Tradable (V_{NT}) =
Function of the Primary Tradable's Productivity i.e.
$$V_{NT} = F (V_T) + constant$$

Hence, any improvement in the agricultural yield will also lead to a consequent rise in market wages and the value of non-tradable services and commodities. Our most effective weapon in our endeavour to eradicate poverty from the nation before 2020 will be targeted and mission-focused

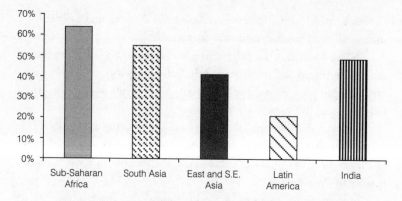

FIGURE 4.4: Agriculture—the largest employer in various regions of the world

Source: Derived from World Bank data

investment in agricultural, financial, managerial and technological sectors.

This situation as regards agriculture is not unique to us, and is commonly shared, in varying proportions, with the rest of the world.

THE INDIAN AGRICULTURAL SECTOR: THE FARM

We have already highlighted the relevance of agriculture, both in terms of rural economy as well as employment. Our dependency on agriculture goes far back in history.

Since Independence, there has been a continuous thrust on reforms and improvements in the agricultural sector—farm-based and not farm-based—which have helped India move away from starvation and severe food

INDIA'S AGRICULTURAL POTENTIAL

- India has 52 per cent cultivable land as compared to the world average of 11 per cent
- All fifteen major climatic regions are present in India
- Forty-six out of sixty soil types are present in India
- India has twenty agro-climatic regions
- There are ten biodiversity regions
- The hours of sunshine and the length of days are ideal for round-the-year cultivation
- India has the largest livestock population

shortage. At the same time, efforts have been made to make agriculture independent of weather factors as far as possible.

Today, India has the largest irrigated land area.[4] With the added usage of fertilizers and researched seeds, India is in a top position in many areas of agro-production. India is also lucky in terms of sunshine, river networks and diversity in climate zones.

However, even though India is in a leading position as regards much of the perishable produce, Indian agriculture is low on yield—low efficiency in terms of water, land usage, the labour employed and the quality of the goods.

This is exhibited in Figure 4.5, which shows the comparative yield of cereals (in rice-milled equivalent) of India, China and Brazil. Notice that all three started at almost the same level of productivity around 1960, all three are known as being among the most promising economies of

TABLE 4.1: India's global position in unprocessed agro-production

Rank	Commodity	Rank	Commodity	Rank	Commodity
1	Lentils	1	Jute	2	Wheat
1	Fruit	1	Buffalo milk, whole, fresh	2	Onions
1	Castor seed			2	Indigenous goat's meat
1	Spices	2	Beans, dry		
1	Chillies and peppers, dry	2	Nutmeg, mace and cardamoms	2	Silkworm cocoons
1	Bananas	2	Pumpkins, squash and gourds	2	Rice, paddy
1	Millet			2	Cotton seed
1	Goat's milk, whole, fresh	2	Cow's milk, whole, fresh	2	Cabbages
1	Indigenous buffalo meat			2	Eggplant (brinjal, baingan)
		2	Groundnuts		
1	Ginger	2	Garlic	3	Cashew nuts
1	Pulses	2	Tea	3	Linseed
1	Chickpeas	2	Vegetables, fresh	3	Peas, dry
1	Lemons and limes	2	Peas, green	3	Potatoes
		2	Cauliflower and broccoli	3	Tobacco
1	Mangoes and guavas	2	Sugar cane	3	Coconuts

Source: Food and Agriculture Organization (FAO)

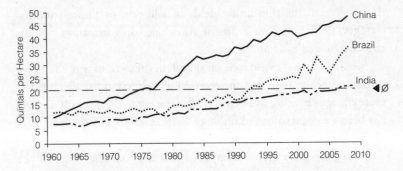

FIGURE 4.5: The yield of India, Brazil and China since 1960

Source: Derived from data available from FAO

the twenty-first century and have been categorized as BRIC.* It shows that China's yield took off during the late-1970s, roughly when India's Green Revolution was finally implemented.† This also corresponds to the time when China removed the tightly controlled system of communes# and gave greater freedom to the farmer in matters of production. This marked a phase of relative liberalization in China's rural, and particularly agricultural, policy. Households were given crop quotas in return for the tools, animals and seeds that were provided. The farmers were given the liberty to put their land to use in whichever way they liked provided

*BRIC was the term coined by the investment banking firm Goldman Sachs to refer to Brazil, Russia, India and China. The investment bank believed that since the countries were developing rapidly, by 2050 the combined economies of BRIC could eclipse the combined economies of the current richest countries of the world. The four countries together currently account for more than a quarter of the world's land area and more than 40 per cent of the world's population.

†India's green revolution began with the introduction of high-yielding varieties of seeds in 1965 and continued through the 1970s. This was also accompanied by the increased use of fertilizers and irrigation.

#In 1958, under the leadership of Mao Zedong, China began a policy of three levels of administration in its rural area. They were production teams, production brigades and the highest level of administration called communes (or People's communes). Typically, a commune was a collection of about 4,000–5,000 households with their small farms, and it represented a shared unit of community ownership. Everything owned by a private family was contributed fully to the communes and the management of communes maintained strict control over its vital resources of labour and land.

they delivered the minimum yield. In addition to these structural changes, the Chinese government also engaged in irrigation projects and encouraged mechanization.

Similarly, Brazil's yield took off sharply at the beginning of the 1990s owing to liberalization and the removal of tight controls, which led to more efficient farming and better yields. The key to the 'take-off' in yield has been mechanization, technology, market access and greater liberty for the farmers.

Analysing on a global comparative scale, too, the surge in the nation's economic growth has not translated optimally into productivity improvements in farming. India's relative position in cereal productivity has been stagnant since the 1990s as shown in Table 4.2.

This may be partly due to the low base in yield with which we started, but with the growth of technology and budgetary allocation, liberalization and reform, we can aim at being among the best in the world.

On the other hand, investment in agriculture, rural development and irrigation has been rising since Independence (Figure 4.6).

Continuously, around 20 per cent of the total Plan outlay has been earmarked for investment in agricultural and rural development,

TABLE 4.2: The relative ranking of nations in cereal productivity

COUNTRIES	1994–96	1999–2001	2005	2006	2007
China	17	19	22	20	18
Egypt	9	5	3	4	4
Germany	10	8	9	9	11
India	**78**	**80**	**90**	**90**	**85**
Brazil	68	59	71	62	52
Japan	6	12	14	14	13
Philippines	72	73	65	63	59
Pakistan	84	82	84	84	77
USA	14	14	10	10	7
Malaysia	42	54	53	56	57
Bangladesh	60	46	42	41	37
New Zealand	12	10	5	7	2

Source: Derived from data available with FAO

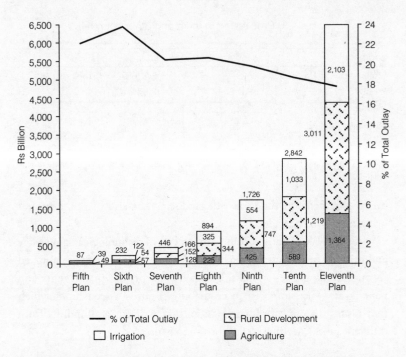

FIGURE 4.6: Planned investment in agriculture, rural development and irrigation since the Fifth Plan

Source: Calculated using data from the Economic Survey, 2009–10

and irrigation and flood control measures—one of the highest in the world.[5] Yet, a growth of merely 2 per cent in agricultural output with about 20 per cent investment indicates poor returns and the need for transformative systems.[6]

There is a similar vast gap as we move up the chain of value addition. While we grow a wide range of perishables on a large scale, the level of processing is far lower than in the West, or even in many Asian countries (see Table 4.3). A low level of processing translates into a lower shelf life for the product and hence, a lower bargaining power for the farmer.

Moreover, it diminishes the prospect of exporting the product over longer distances to places where a higher realization of value could be achieved. At the same time, it significantly reduces employment opportunities beyond production, which translates into more pressure

TABLE **4.3:** Processing in India and other countries

Segment	India	Other Countries
Fruits and Vegetables	2%	USA (65%), Philippines (78%), China (23%)
Marine	12%	60–70% in developed countries
Meat and Poultry	1%	60–70% in developed countries
Milk	37%	60–75% in developed countries

Source: Report on 'India: Food Processing Industry', compiled by Swiss Business Hub India, 2008

on employment on the farm side, reducing the size of the farm and bringing down the yield.

This low value addition comes from a lack of technological knowledge and mismatched investment schemes. Investments are often in a mixed form: various parties—banks, governments, private investments and panchayats—are supposed to contribute towards a seed fund, which may result in an uncoordinated and untimely disbursal of monies from different points, leading to failure of enterprises.

INTERACTION WITH FARMERS AT RASHTRAPATI BHAVAN

I have had a lot of interaction with ground-level farmers from all over the nation. Each meeting brought in some new perspectives and strengthened some known issues too.

Let me share my experiences with you. More than 6,000 farmers from different states and the Union Territories visited the Mughal Gardens at Rashtrapati Bhavan (the Presidential Estate) on 23 March 2007. They also saw the Herbal Garden which includes Jatropha, the biodiesel producing plant, the Spiritual Garden, the Musical Garden and the Nutrition Garden.

The farmers were shown organic farming and the Biodiversity Park and informed about the commercial aspects of various plants and herbs by a panel of experts from leading agricultural universities.

During the interaction, the following suggestions were given to me by the farmers:

- Arrangements need to be made for selecting eligible agricultural farmers from all over the country to go to foreign countries to study their methods and developments; farmers from various states can also be taken to Punjab to see its progress in the agricultural sector.
- Farmers may be given assistance for manufacturing natural agricultural inputs.
- The acquisition of agricultural land for purposes other than agriculture should be stopped in the larger interests of the farming community and the agricultural sector.
- Other alternative biofuels besides Jatropha should be explored, and farmers guided accordingly.
- Agricultural and horticultural techniques should be made available in regional and local languages.

WHAT TARGETS SHOULD SUSTAINABLE PURAS HAVE?

The five points summarized above all point to the one pressing need which Indian farmers experience and express—empowerment. This empowerment has to come through knowledge, technology, investment and decision-making power in the hands of the farmers.

The most pertinent aspect of reforming agriculture through the evolution of a sustainable development system is a focus on the integration of efforts towards well-defined goals. Our challenge is not so much in terms of lack of investment but rather in terms of finding effective returns and outputs on the massive funds being employed.

For an effective output, we need a cadre on the farm with capable skills; we need an environment which promotes an output-oriented entrepreneurial approach; and we need integration in our thinking and efforts. The three distinct segments of the value chain—production, processing and marketing—have to move round one pivot. A summary of the efforts needed in each of these segments is illustrated in Figure 4.7. Especially noteworthy is the need to design systems which are inherently participative and inclusive and which result in the benefits accruing back to the first producer—the farmer. This is essential because farmers will thrive and become innovative only when the benefits

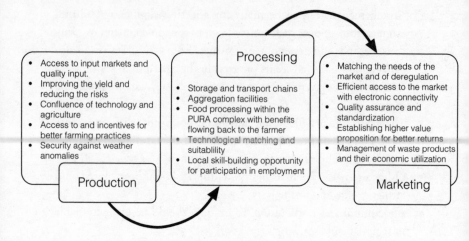

- Access to input markets and
  quality input.
- Improving the yield and
  reducing the risks
- Confluence of technology and
  agriculture
- Access to and incentives for
  better farming practices
- Security against weather
  anomalies

Production

Processing

- Storage and transport chains
- Aggregation facilities
- Food processing within the
  PURA complex with benefits
  flowing back to the farmer
- Technological matching and
  suitablility
- Local skill-building opportunity
  for participation in employment

- Matching the needs of the
  market and of deregulation
- Efficient access to the market
  with electronic connectivity
- Quality assurance and
  standardization
- Establishing higher value
  proposition for better returns
- Management of waste products
  and their economic utilization

Marketing

FIGURE **4.7:** Strategy for sustainable development in the
agriculture sector

really reach them which is often not the case, not even in the most
advanced countries.

For example, in the United States, studies show that from 1990–99
the marketing cost of food rose by 45 per cent, much of which transmuted
into increased food expenditure for the consumer. However, at the
farm gate, the price received by the producer rose only by 13 per cent.[7]
Similarly, in 1990, marketing accounted for 76 per cent of the total
consumer expenditure, with the farm gate value at 24 per cent.

In 1999, when the share of marketing increased to 80 per cent the
farm gate share came down to 20 per cent of the total expenditure.[8]
These numbers point to the need for building systems which are capable
of backward-integrating benefits and forward-integrated processing. In
the rest of this chapter we will discuss examples and challenges that can
fulfil these goals.

TAKING TECHNOLOGY TO THE FIELDS

One of the problems is the failure to take laboratory science to the fields,
or doing so inefficiently. Without the meeting of technology and ground-

level implementation, the benefits of modern technology and science cannot be optimal. This problem may arise due to a variety of reasons, some of which could be:

- Unsuitability of technology given the local agro-climatic conditions
- Unawareness of technology due to a communication gap
- Unwillingness to take unknown risks due to lack of trust
- Improper use of technology at the field level due to lack of knowledge
- Cultural barriers to adoption of modern technology
- Lack of adequate credit or of support investment which is a prerequisite to the adoption of technology

To overcome these barriers, sound management of the technology dissemination needs to be followed. This would require out-of-the-box ideas which, in a cost-effective way, can overcome these issues. We will now discuss some of the examples of how this has been achieved.

EXPERIENCES FROM THE STATES OF BIHAR AND TAMIL NADU

Technology can be a game changer in the agro sector, especially in the developing world. Let us analyse two experiences from north and south India, where technology has been employed instrumentally to reform the productivity and yield of the farmlands.

Bihar: Paliganj

An experiment was carried out by the Technology Information, Forecasting and Assessment Council (TIFAC) team in the north Indian state of Bihar, in RP Channel 5 and Majholi distributary, and later extended to Paliganj and five other distributaries at the request of farmers in the year 2000. The yield of paddy has increased in these villages from 2 tons per hectare to 5.8 tons per hectare, and that of wheat from 0.9 ton per hectare to 2.6 tons per hectare. At present, the paddy and wheat crops are spread over an area of more than 2,500 hectares and involve 3,000 farmers.

This project was carried out by TIFAC in collaboration with a farmer's cooperative society, the Indian Agricultural Research Institute (IARI) and the agricultural university in Pusa, Bihar. By using scientific methods of farming, such as soil characterization, matching the right seed to soil, planting in time, proper selection of fertilizers and pesticides, water management, pre- and post-harvesting methodology, the productivity has been more than doubled.

When I addressed the Bihar Assembly on 28 March 2006, I requested the Assembly to adopt this system-oriented approach in all the thirty-eight districts of Bihar which would enable the state to triple its paddy and wheat crops. The aim should be to increase the rice production from 5.5 million tons to 15 million tons, and the wheat production from 4 million tons to 12 million tons in four years' time. This would make Bihar the Grand Granary of India. Whether we have replicated this success story across the nation is a point for discussion.

Tamil Nadu: Precision Farming Project

Precision Farming or Precision Agriculture—technology adopted in Tamil Nadu—implies doing the right thing, in the right place and at the right time. It has created awareness among the farmers because it has given higher productivity and access to markets, and has turned farmers into entrepreneurs. With this procedure, the collected information may be used to evaluate the optimum sowing density, to estimate fertilizers and other input needs, and to predict the crop yield more accurately. It helps avoid the application of unwanted practices to a crop without taking into consideration local soil and climate conditions, that is, it reduces labour, water, inputs such as fertilizers and pesticides, and ensures quality produce.

The Precision Farming Project was first started in Tamil Nadu in the Dharmapuri district during 2004–05. It was implemented initially on 250 acres, then 500 acres in 2005–06 and 250 acres in 2006–07. The Tamil Nadu Agricultural University was the nodal agency that implemented this project. An amount of Rs 75,000 for the installation of drip irrigation and Rs 40,000 for crop production expenses was given to the farmers. The first crop was taken up under the total guidance of scientists from the university, while the subsequent five crops were taken up by the farmers in three years. In the first year, the farmers were unwilling to undertake this project because of their frustration due to the continuing drought in that area for four years since 2002. But after seeing the success of the first 100 farmers and the high market rate for the produce obtained from this scheme, farmers started registering in large numbers for the second year (with 90 per cent subsidy) and the third year (with 80 per cent subsidy).

The farmlands of the Krishnagiri and the Dharmapuri districts are predominantly rain-fed. Elements of extremism are ripe in the general community—particularly the youths—in certain pockets close to the Andhra Pradesh border and the hills. The government of Tamil Nadu has undertaken the task of implementing the Precision Farming Project on 400 hectares as a turnkey project, with the main focus on a 40–60 per cent enhanced yield and effective market linkage.

One unit is equivalent to one hectare and a farmer is eligible for one hectare only. Under the project, 100 hectares during 2004–05, 200 hectares during 2005–06 and 100 hectares during 2006–07 were covered. Not only the farmers of these two districts, but the farmers of the other districts who were taken to the Precision Farming sites too were amazed by what they saw. The farmer-to-farmer mode added strength to the outcome, and all the other districts of the state made a demand for implementing the project.

Later, the project was scaled up to 40,000 hectares across the state with budget support by the Government of India, under the National Development Project (NADP). The university and the departments of agriculture and horticulture jointly set up the project during 2007–08 and 2010–11. The states of Kerala, Karnataka, Andhra Pradesh, Orissa and Maharashtra have adopted this project on a large scale, and training has been provided for all the farmers and the developmental workers at Dharmapuri in Tamil Nadu.

The processes had been given deep thought, and the products delivered the expected quality. The cluster members were brought together under an association called the Precision Farmers' Association registered under the Societies Act.

The process finally led to the establishment of a farmer-owned producing company called Dharmapuri Precision Farmers' Agro Services Ltd, registered under the Company Act, the first producing company in the Tamil Nadu state, in which 166 farmers of Dharmapuri are shareholders. Later, a second producing company owned by the farmers, Erode Precision Farm Producers' Company Ltd, was established during 2008–09.

The result of this experiment has had multiple effects because it not only focused on maximizing the productivity and enhancing the profitability, but also on empowering the farmers socially, economically and technically. The emphasis was also on social capital through the strengthening of cluster-level associations and district-level limited companies. For example, during an Annual Farmers' Day meeting held in Salem, one of the precision farmers said during his speech, with tears in his eyes that, for the first time, his family had been able to see the 'one lakh currency' bundles. This had attracted the attention of policymakers, bankers and insurance firms, whose frequent visits to the project site brought further economic relief to the farming community. A minimum of Rs 1,00,000 and a maximum of Rs 8,00,000 were the gross returns from one hectare, and this factor has helped every farmer own a project. P.M. Chinnasamy, a farmer, produced 500 MT of brinjals from one hectare in fifteen months, and he has become the resource farmer for hundreds of others who are cultivating brinjal. The precision farmers have doubled the yield in forty-five crops, as compared to the national and the state average.

LONI PURA

One of the most successful initiatives of the Loni PURA* model is the Krishi Vigyan Kendra at Loni. It applies a three-tiered model to ensure that the farmers are a partner in research and that the full impact of agro-sciences reaches the fields.

Loni PURA assists farmers by operating an award-winning KVK or an agro-science centre where it carries out research and trains the farmers in scientific farming practices.

The KVK at Loni has established a unique way of involving the community in the process of agro-innovations. This has not only led

---

* The authors acknowledge the help and support of Dr Ashok Patil and Prof. K.V. Somasundaram in compiling the information given about Loni PURA.

to better knowledge but has also made technology much easier and more acceptable on the ground level.

This has come about through the formation of the Innovative Farmers' Club (Prayog Pariwar) which has a membership of 712 farmers. This is the first tier of the system and it helps identify requirements which need to be addressed. It does a basic scientific analysis at the local level and facilitates the dissemination of the available technology in the villages. They are the first, the ground-level, evaluators of technology and help assess and refine it. They conduct quarterly meetings and share their experiences. The KVK has an incentive structure to encourage farmers to join the Innovative Farmers' Club. Thus, they ensure that the technology offered suits local conditions and that, seeing their enhanced yield due to scientific farming methods, other farmers also start to place their trust in scientific methods.

The next tier of the system consists of the Conventional Farmers' Clubs at the village level. There are 148 clubs with a membership of 2,977 farmers. Once the efficacy of the technology has been evaluated by the Prayog Pariwar, these clubs have the responsibility of disseminating it. They draw up an action plan for technology dissemination within each village and help in the selection and evaluation. They also help in the creation of SHGs, the next level of the system. They ensure that the intended users of the technology are fully aware of how to apply it to their farms and help overcome the communication gap between research and the farms.

KRISHI VIGYAN KENDRAS

Krishi Vigyan Kendra (KVK) or Agriculture Science Centre is an initiative by the Indian Council of Agricultural Research (ICAR) to promote the transfer of technology in agriculture, animal husbandry, beekeeping and many other fields to farms. ICAR is establishing these KVKs across the nation with private partners. Each KVK adopts five to six villages in a radius of 10–20 km around it for upgrading farm technology, agriculture extension services, conducting training courses and live demonstrations, offering advisory services on farm testing, and a wide range of knowledge services in a participative manner. There are, at present, 571 KVKs in the nation with the Eleventh Five-Year Plan envisaging the number as going up to 667.

Source: ICAR website

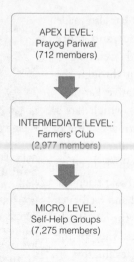

FIGURE **4.8:** Levels of farmer participation

INNOVATIONS IN ORGANIC FARMING

The National Innovation Foundation (NIF) has compiled data about the innovative and progressive farming practices adopted by farmers in different parts of India. Areas where the rainfall is poor, or where the land remains flooded for long periods of time, mountain regions and forest areas are the most suitable for organic farming. These are the areas where farmers should take up organic farming immediately. The NIF has reported over 240 combinations of herbal pesticides being used in different parts of the country. There are many other local cost-effective solutions for the problems faced by the farmers.

For example, planting lady's fingers (bhindi) as a border crop prevents cotton crops from being attacked by pests which are, instead, attracted to the flowers of the lady's fingers, and the cotton crop grows well. This is an important zero-cost solution since 40 per cent of the pesticides in use in the country are for protecting cotton crops. I have come across the successful production of organic paddy in many parts of the country. In one of the districts, 2,400 farmers joined together to cultivate organic paddy in 2,500 acres of wetland in the panchayat areas, and they realized a productivity of 6.25 tons per hectare, which is on par with international standards.

The last tier of the system is the self-help groups of farmers. There are 485 SHGs with over 7,275 members. They help disseminate technology at the field level and undertake the vital task of credit mobilization, to give the farmers financial power to adopt the technology. The SHGs also help in developing entrepreneurship and year-round employment.

Using this three-tier system of employing farmers' clubs at different levels, the Loni KVK and Loni PURA were able to find support for scientific farming in the local community. Moreover, the Innovative Farmers' Club also acts as a decentralized point for generating technological awareness, thereby assisting farmers who have newly adopted methods of scientific farming. The SHG system too helps in accessing markets and hence, the farmers are assured of the saleability of their product.

LIVE DEMONSTRATION FARMS IN CHITRAKOOT PURA

The Chitrakoot PURA* complex in Madhya Pradesh operates two KVKs in Majhgawan and Ganivan, which use an innovative methodology for imparting practical, hands-on training to the farmers. The Chitrakoot PURA operates live demonstration farms of 1.5 acres and 2.5 acres, an area that corresponds to the typical landholding size in the area. The 'demo farm' is a farm-laboratory which shows the farmers how to work on farms of this size, so as to increase both farm and non-farm income through improved sustainable agricultural inputs.

The KVKs calculated the balanced nutritional requirement for a small family, the required income for non-food expenses and other contingencies, and then mapped out a season-wise production plan for the standard farm size. To drive their point further, they started implementing this plan on their demo farm. This helped overcome doubts as regards the suitability of the plan, given the local conditions and, at the same time, gave the farmers the confidence which can be generated by a working model.

* The authors acknowledge the contribution of Shri Bharat Pathak, Mrs Nandita Pathak, Shri Atul Jain and Shri Amitabh who helped in compiling the information given about the Chitrakoot PURA.

Scientific agriculture is further forwarded by ground-level workers in the form of Samaj Shilpi Dampati. We will discuss them in detail later in this book.

SEED CLUBS AT CHITRAKOOT PURA

Small-scale farmers face a huge problem when it comes to purchasing good quality seeds. Besides, there is always a doubt about the performance of particular seeds when subjected to local agro-climatic conditions. Other major issues which the small farmer faces are the increase in the cost of seeds, poor germinating qualities, limited availability of seeds, lack of access to the market and difficulty of transport. It was observed that, as a result, many farmers still rely on the older generation of seeds.

During a baseline survey of some of the villages by the Chitrakoot PURA, farmers repeatedly expressed a desire that seeds of improved varieties should be made available to farmers on a barter basis. However, the Chitrakoot PURA and the KVKs have limited resources and are not in a position to conduct such large-scale seed production. Moreover, it is important to empower the farmers or farmer groups to fulfil most of their requirements independently.

The Majhgawan KVK of Chitrakoot PURA then proceeded to introduce seed production programmes in selected villages. Under this programme, seed clubs at the village level and a seed village in a cluster of villages were developed. The KVK demonstrated seed production technology at its instructional farms (the 1.5 and 2.5 acre demonstration farms). Seed villages and seed clubs are now involved in the production of seeds under the close supervision and guidance of KVK scientists and experts.

These villages are not only meeting with their own seed requirements but are also supplying the surplus seeds to nearby villages, bringing in good income for the growers. A seed exchange has been set up where the innovative farmers can exchange the seeds for grain at an exchange rate of 1.25 kg of grain for every 1 kg of seeds.

This initiative highlights three aspects. First, farmers have been empowered not only as users of technology but also as producers of knowledge. Second, a new value-adding farm technology entrepreneurship has been set up with the focus on quality production. Third, a market-linked incentive to innovate has been nurtured with a 25 per cent mark-up on growing seeds, thereby adopting technology. This is an example of how, even with village-level knowledge and entrepreneurship, a friendly environment can be created through shared investment.

WARANA COOPERATIVE SUGAR FACTORY

We have already discussed the various initiatives which have been undertaken by the Warana PURA complex in Maharashtra (Chapter 3). In the 1950s, most of the sugar cane produced by small and marginal farmers was used for the production of jaggery which requires low investment. The price of jaggery has always fluctuated and, in the early-1950s, its price crashed and brought ruin to small farmers including those in the Warana region. That was when the Warana Mission was set up under the leadership of Tatyasaheb Kore. In 1953, he started to collect money from the small farmers on an equity basis and tried to raise loans from other sources. The mission was supported by many socio-political leaders of the state and, with the help of equipment imported from Buck Wolf Company, the Warana Cooperative Sugar Factory was formed, the first of the twenty-five cooperatives which would later come up in the area.

The Warana Sugar Factory has about 20,000 cooperative farmers as its members and covers around sixty-nine villages with an area of 10,800 hectares under sugar cultivation (2009–10). The factory is an outstanding example of how the collective will of small farmers—with the able guidance of a social leader—was able to overcome obstacles of technology, investment and market mismatch. The factory is a dynamic model with both forward and backward integration for enhancing the benefits to its shareholders, the farmers, to whom it extends credit and subsidy facility so that their productivity is enhanced. This includes subsidies on herbicides (15 per cent), pesticides (60 per cent), micro nutrients (25 per cent) and spray pumps. To further increase the productivity, the Warana Sugar Complex has implemented a three-tier nursery programme to provide quality sugar cane seed. The breeder seed is purchased from the Vasantdada Sugar Institute, Pune, and the Central Sugar Cane Research Station, Padegaon, and then reared on the farms of progressive farmers. Later, it is distributed to the farmers on credit. Similarly, a seedling scheme has been set up, managed largely by women who, over the last two years, have sold more than one million seedlings packed in bags. Once again, we observe how a PURA creates farm workers with knowledge who can derive great social benefit.

Further along in the spectrum of Knowledge Connectivity, the Warana Sugar Cooperative offers free soil-testing facility and recommends optimal fertilizer usage, thereby saving the farmers' money.

Sugar cane is a water-intensive crop. The sugar cooperative also manages eleven big irrigation and thirty-eight small irrigation schemes for its farmers. It has reduced the requirement of water by its drip irrigation assistance which it extends to even the non-member farmers.

To integrate the vertical chain, the Warana Sugar Cooperative has produced innovative products which it is exporting both to other Indian cities and abroad. It has recently come up with processed, packaged and flavoured sugar cane juice which is available in Tetra Pak.

As a result of the cooperative movement to enhance the productivity and income of the 20,000 farmer families, the average yield of Warana cooperative farmers is much higher than that of the state or the nation as shown in Figure 4.9. Over the past decade, the average yield in tons per

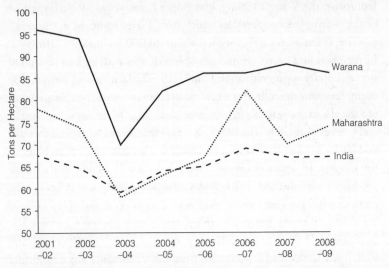

FIGURE 4.9: Yield of sugar cane in Warana as compared with state and national levels

hectare of Warana has been 30 per cent more than the national yield and 20 per cent more than that of the state of Maharashtra. Moreover, since it is a cooperative where the farmers are owners of the sugar-processing plant, the Warana Cooperative is able give one of the highest sugar recovery rates from sugar cane leading to better income and less waste. The sugar recovery rate of Warana is more than 12 per cent which is one-fifth above the national average.

The Warana Sugar Cooperative Factory model highlights the benefits and needs of a vertical integration of systems. It is a unique model, rolling the benefits back to the farmers both in cash and in terms of better inputs for improving productivity at the farm level. It also shows how a vertically integrated model with community participation can lead to implementing better technology and investments through aggregation. Finally, it exhibits the role of ground-level social leadership in development.

Let us now study how, nationally, India has seen some of the great agricultural visions translating into action and what future action is needed.

THE FIRST GREEN REVOLUTION

In the 1960s, the then prime minister of India, Lal Bahadur Shastri, coined the term 'Jai Jawan, Jai Kisan'.[*] One of his first acts as prime minister was to increase the agricultural budget because, at that time, the agricultural output was barely able to keep pace with the population growth. He then appointed C. Subramaniam as a minister with a definite agenda for transforming the Indian agriculture sector.

The first Green Revolution, launched by the visionaries, the minister for food and agriculture C. Subramaniam and his adviser Dr M.S. Swaminathan, in partnership with agricultural scientists and farmers liberated India from the situation of what was called a 'ship-to-mouth existence'.[#] It was supported by renowned scientists from abroad as well, like Nobel Peace Prize awardee Norman Borlaug. The primary focus of the first Green Revolution was HYV (high-yielding

[*] Jai Jawan, Jai Kisan [Hindi] = Hail the Soldier, Hail the Farmer

[#] Ship-to-mouth was a reference by the media to the state of India back in the 1960s when a large number of imports/grants made up for the food deficit in the nation.

variety) crops which absorb nitrogen much faster and whose growth is better. However, it also meant greater usage of fertilizers, water and pesticides.

Through an effort of historical magnitude, India attained near self-sufficiency in food which was important not only from the point of view of food security but also for national self-esteem. As a result of this first Green Revolution, the country has been able to produce over 200 million tons of food grain per year on an average.

AGRICULTURE REFORMS IN THE STATE OF GUJARAT

In October 2009, my team and I met with the professors and researchers at the Centre for Management in Agriculture (CMA) at the Indian Institute of Management, Ahmedabad (Gujarat), to discuss the problems of the agricultural sector and the solutions thereto. While interacting with the experts, I noticed that the agricultural growth rate in the state of Gujarat has been phenomenally high, at 9.5 per cent per annum[9] for the past decade (2000–10), that is, more than three times the 2.8 per cent agricultural growth in the rest of the country,[10] and even significantly higher than the overall national GDP growth for the period. This has also contributed to the above-average total Gross State Domestic Product (GSDP) for Gujarat at 10.2 per cent for the period 2000–10.[11]

I had a discussion with the experts at CMA about the methodology through which such an impressive performance had been achieved. They then prepared a document titled 'High Growth Trajectory and Structural Changes in Gujarat Agriculture' which listed out the reasons for the increased productivity:

PHYSICAL CONNECTIVITY

Water Management

Gujarat is not very rich in terms of water availability; moreover, it has the added problems of a falling water table, irregular rainfall and salination of the soil due to sea water ingress. However, in a typical public–private and community partnership, the state has managed to

NATIONAL AGRO FOUNDATION: THE STORY OF INTEGRATED AGRICULTURAL REFORM

On 15 October 2008, I visited Illedu village in Kancheepuram district, Tamil Nadu, where the National Agro Foundation (NAF) is engaged in improving the quality of life for rural citizens by providing know-how on advanced agricultural practices; characterization of soil; soil upgrading through proper systematic soil-testing; matching seed to soil; a systemic approach to pre- and post-harvesting methodologies; and providing market connectivity. The farmers have achieved an increase in productivity ranging from 40 per cent to 150 per cent in different agriculture produce such as rice, sugar cane, vegetables and other horticulture products. In addition, they have very active self-help group systems which are empowered with knowledge of dairy farming, craftsmanship, making home-made products and selling to the nearby cities and villages. They have also launched a literacy movement and achieved 100 per cent sanitation in one of the villages.

With the help of the National Bank for Agriculture and Rural Development (NABARD), they have created watersheds with inlet and outlet channels for recharging the ground water. NAF enabled an urban garment export company to get relocated in the rural area, and it now provides value-added employment to sixty women from these villages. The members of NAF have also trained rural women to provide cutting and stitching support to garment manufacturers in Chennai and other places, who are engaged in export of garments. This activity has considerably changed the economic condition of the farmers and the craftsmen in the rural areas. There are many such success stories available across the country. We have to take a systematic approach in order to enable a larger number of farmers in the nation to reap the benefits of success.

overcome these problems in one decade and shown remarkable growth rates. This was achieved through an extensive and careful supply-and-demand management of water. On the supply side, massive watershed programmes were executed and check dams constructed. Additionally, farmers were encouraged to construct farm ponds for creating localized and small-scale water reservoirs.

The management of the demand side was undertaken through micro irrigation* schemes, which were readily accepted by the farmers who were

---

* The term 'micro irrigation' is used to describe a network of irrigation systems that supply water through small devices. These devices deliver water to the surface of the soil close to the plant or below the surface directly into the plant root zone. Growers, producers

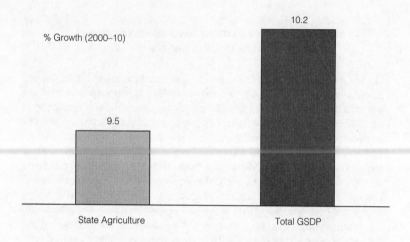

% Growth (2000–10)

FIGURE **4.10:** Agriculture and the GSDP growth rate for Gujarat

**WATER MANAGEMENT
INITIATIVES IN GUJARAT**

- Check dams: 113,000
- Bori bandhs: 56,000
- Farm ponds: 241,000

Source: Data from 'Frontiers
of Agricultural Development in
Gujarat', Centre for Management
in Agriculture (IIMA), 2010

conscious of the falling water levels and also of the sustainability aspect. Within four years (2006–10), more than 180,000 hectares were covered under micro irrigation, which contributed substantially towards managing the demand side of water consumption.

Interlinking of rivers

Under various schemes, the surplus water of the Narmada and the Kandana dams was diverted to seventeen rivers and seven water-starved districts through a 330-km-long canal.[12]

Quality power supply

This was achieved through the action taken by the Gujarat Electricity Board under the Jyotigram Yojana which was started in 2003. Under

---

and landscapers have adapted micro irrigation systems to suit their needs for precision water application.

this scheme, the Gujarat government, which had never before given free power to farmers, now ensured electrical power supply to villages on a 24/7 basis, by segregating the power for domestic consumption from the power for agricultural consumption. This resulted in reduced theft of electrical power and increased its availability to farmers. Moreover, the quality of the power was maintained.

ELECTRONIC AND KNOWLEDGE CONNECTIVITY

Special efforts were made to guide and encourage farmers to produce quality products and organic products. Soil Health Cards were issued to farmers to support scientific farming methods. A World Trade Organization (WTO) cell was set up to increase export-related competency of major agricultural commodities. E-governance was used for programmes intended for the farmers, and credit, insurance and financial support were extended to them. Cattle-breeding was encouraged and efforts made to produce good quality wool from sheep. For the first time, the Krushi Mahotsav, conducted in campaign-mode, helped bring critical stakeholders and service providers to the farmers themselves in their own villages. A mobile exhibition (rath) travelled to every village, and provided an opportunity for the farmers to interact with different government officials and agencies. Even after the rath had passed through the villages, the programmes which were planned under the mahotsav continued to be implemented throughout the month.[13]

ECONOMIC CONNECTIVITY

Agro Export Zones

Across the state, Agro Export Zones have been set up for mangoes, vegetables and onions, and contract farming was encouraged in a big way. The Agro Industrial Policy is set to support agro exports and to process agro products.

Managing investments

The Gujarat Green Revolution Company was established to help the farmers with investments and give them access to technology. The farmers had to contribute 5 per cent of the investment, while 45 per cent of the funds would be made available by way of loans from NABARD. The balance 50 per cent comprised the subsidy component to be borne by the Gujarat Green Revolution Company. At the end of six years, the farmers' agriculture income was doubled and it has been continuously growing. While the national average of agriculture exports was recorded as 3 per cent, Gujarat achieved a record growth of 12 per cent agricultural export growth.

To sum up, what does this imply? The fact that Gujarat should have achieved 9 per cent growth, while the rest of Indian agriculture was recording a 2 per cent growth, is due to its vision and its system-oriented approach, enabling irrigation and power infrastructure. Proper management of natural resources is vital not only for increasing agricultural yield and income, but also for mitigating adverse impacts of water scarcity in a state. Integrated land and water management activities, improved farming practices and appropriate market and credit linkages have the potential to increase the productivity of natural resources in a sustainable manner, and to ensure the nurturing of the local economy which would ultimately translate into national growth.

NATIONAL WATER BALANCE: THE CHALLENGE

India gets approximately 4,000 billion cubic metres (BCM) of water every year from all natural sources. Out of this, 700 BCM are lost by

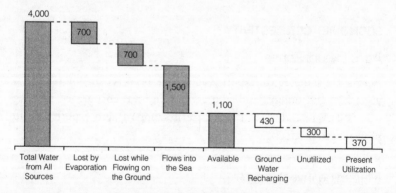

FIGURE **4.11**: India's water balance

Demand Side	Supply Side	Flexibility
• Reducing the consumption of water by management and technology • Recycling	• Preventing run-offs into the sea • Managing the rivers and water bodies	• Storage and linkage • Smart waterways and connectivity

FIGURE **4.12**: Required strategy for water management

evaporation and another 700 while flowing on the ground. Also, a large quantity of water—1,500 BCM—flows into the sea during floods. Thus, the remaining available water is only 1,100 BCM. Out of this, ground water recharge accounts for 430 BCM per year, while the present utilized surface water is 370 BCM. The balance unutilized water which can be harnessed is 300 BCM.

Sustainable development systems of 2011 and beyond will have to develop the management of the water resources of the nation with regard to supply and demand, and to promote flexible ways and means of making water resources available over time and location.

LOW WATER EFFICIENCY IN AGRICULTURE

With over 70 per cent[14] of the developed water sources being used exclusively for it, irrigation is the largest consumer of water resources in the nation. India has the highest area of irrigated land and the second-highest area of arable land in the world. For long-term sustainable development, the PURA model has to evolve a judicious action plan to study how expansion of irrigation facilities and water management can work in synchrony.

On the demand side, our sustainability has to focus on how to reduce the consumption of water per unit crop generated. The water efficiency of our current crop generation is a matter of concern. Every cubic metre of water consumed produces 300 gm of crops in India, while the same amount of water can generate 1,300 gm of crops in a developed world nation like the United States, giving them a four-fold advantage in

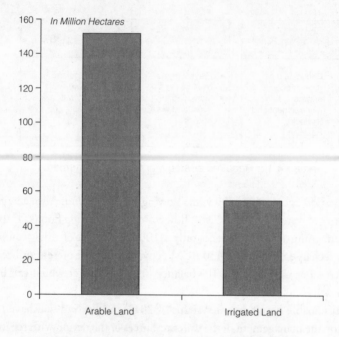

Figure **4.13:** Arable and irrigated land in India

the water efficiency of crops. This situation is reflected in most of the developing and underdeveloped world.

Every plant generally requires the same amount of water for its growth irrespective of location. The fact that India receives abundant sunlight—due to which there is more evaporation—can account for, perhaps, not more than 10 per cent extra water usage. PURA's sustainable system has to deliberate on how this can be improved. The competitive advantage lies largely in productivity. While about 600,000,000 litres of water is diverted every year per hectare, the land would yield 2.3 tons of cereals in India but more than 6.6 tons in the United States.

Secondly, and closely related, is the need for scientific cultivation using less water and less land and, instead, using methods such has drip irrigation. Technology can definitely play a major role in water management if it is able to customize itself according to the needs and constraints present at the field level.

AGRICULTURE SUSTAINABILITY: THE EPCOT EXPERIENCE

In October 2009, my team and I visited the Experimental Prototype Community of Tomorrow (EPCOT) located in the Walt Disney World Resort, Florida, USA, where actual experimentation is taking place in agricultural technology, in 2.5 million square feet of greenhouses.

The entire agro-tech research centre area has been rebranded in the name of sustainability, and now includes a public exhibition on agricultural technology and global ecology called 'Living with the Land'—an amazing exhibit on organic farming and agricultural innovation which takes a 1950s-like position that humanity can solve its food shortage and environmental problems by improving agricultural technology.

When the required mineral nutrients are introduced artificially into a plant's water supply, the plant no longer requires soil to thrive. Crop yields can ultimately be limited by factors other than mineral nutrients, like light. Soil-less culture is a broader term than hydroponics; it only requires that no soils with clay or silt be used. Tomatoes, harvested by these techniques from a single plant in one year, weighed 522 kg. Similarly, greenhouses can be built in rural areas with the help of SHGs, cooperatives and enterprises, and plants grown using drip irrigation with organic farming practices and hydroponic techniques.

This would reinvigorate rural economy by creating a sustainable alternate farming ecosystem from seed to market. These technologies, if taken properly under well-established alternative farming ecosystems, will certainly bring about a transformation in the agricultural economy of India. It will help reduce our dependence on water and, more significantly, will also assist in reducing our dependence on natural forces especially rainfall. For sustained growth, agriculture has to be transformed. For agriculture to be transformed, technology has to be matched with farming in an entrepreneurial manner.

ADVANCED RESEARCH AND DEVELOPMENT AND MARKET MANAGEMENT IN AGRICULTURE

On 9 November 2006, I inaugurated the GFAR (Global Forum on Agricultural Research) Third Triennial Conference, in New Delhi, with the theme 'Re-orienting Agricultural Research to meet the Millennium Development Goals'. I met with researchers and agriculture scientists from over eighty countries around the world. I highlighted the strong linkages between science and agriculture, and suggested the following

WATER USAGE EFFICIENCY

Across the world, water engineers use Water Usage Efficiency (WUE) as a parameter to evaluate the proportion of irrigation water to the amount of water which reaches the crop root zone.

WUE is broken down into two terms, Conveyance Efficiency (CE) and Field Efficiency (FE), where,

$$WUE = CE \times FE$$

CE refers to the amount of water from the irrigation system which reaches the fields, and FE is the amount of water applied to the field which actually reaches the root zone. Worldwide, the quest for higher water efficiency has to begin with efforts to improve Conveyance and Field Efficiencies, in a balanced and cost-effective way.

We need a focused approach to address both these components. CE, for example, has been improved in various parts of the world through measures like lining canals to reduce seepage (CE improvements were up to 10 per cent). The use of pipes instead of earth canals improved CE by about 30 per cent in the North China Plain. It must be understood that much of the CE improvement would take place over aggregated levels and hence would require policy action with public and private partnerships.

FE or Field Efficiency improvement, on the other hand, is pertinent to the action at the field level. It includes better irrigation equipment and technology, and the cultivation of plants which consume less water. For example, in Israel, drip irrigation has been extensively applied to bring down water usage per acre by 33 per cent. Reducing field evaporation is being developed as an alternative to the traditional method of flooding rice fields to further improve the FE.

Improvement in CE and FE to impact the Water Usage Efficiency requires technological development. It would also require an understanding of the available resources, needs and the costs involved, which would be specific to local conditions. For example, a region with high labour costs would probably find investing in drip irrigation more feasible than a region where cheap labour was available. Community awareness and action are vital for activating measures for WUE improvements, and managing and maintaining the development measures.

Source: IFAD (International Fund for Agricultural Development), *Report on Rural Poverty, 2001*, and FAO

seven areas for research missions which, by using scientific tools, would ensure a bright future for agriculture:

HIGH-YIELDING VARIETIES

The productivity of current varieties has reached a plateau. We have to develop high-yielding varieties with more quality characteristics, namely, more vitamins and minerals, which will help reduce nutrition-dependent health problems. For example, lack of vitamin A in food leads to night blindness. To overcome this problem, rice and other stable foods must possess adequate quantities of vitamin A. Research in genetically modified plants, such as the Golden Rice programme, needs to be speeded up.

TISSUE CULTURE AND CLONAL PROPAGATION

There are many variations in productivity. Wherever possible, micro propagated plants which have high-yield capabilities and are free of disease should be used.

GLOBAL WARMING

This has resulted in an increased CO_2 percentage in the atmosphere. It favours the cultivation of C_3 plants (rice, wheat), which has to be oriented towards enhanced yield by absorbing more CO_2 from the atmosphere.

RADIOISOTOPES

Research and Development (R&D) can be focused on the use of radioisotopes to diagnose nutritional deficiency in plants and soils for the precise application of fertilizers.

PRECISION FARMING AND AUTOMATION

R&D should concentrate on precision agriculture. Mechanization has to be resorted to for providing the right quantity of water and nutrition to the crops.

ENERGY FARMING

1. Wastelands have to be fully utilized for energy crops (sweet sorghum, sugar beet and cassava for ethanol production). Appropriate technologies have to be developed for making these crops economically viable.
2. R&D has to be applied to power generation through biomass which has extensive application in agriculture.

ASSISTIVE TECHNOLOGIES FOR FARMS

Out of consideration for the environment and to reduce the usage of fossil fuel, we have to design farm vehicles and farm equipment which can run on 100 per cent biofuels or can be electrically operated. Researchers must focus on developing intelligent farm machines. For example, a harvester should record the yield per unit area while harvesting. Intelligent mechanization— like removing only weeds and not plants—has to be developed.

I further highlighted the necessity of carrying out market research to have a market focus for maximizing the returns of the agriculture sector. It is necessary to examine the products that are in demand due to the changing lifestyles of the modern generation. For example, a special type of corn is required for making cornflakes and a special kind of potato for making chips. Hence, farmers should take into account the demand for the end processed product when selecting the seed. Government agencies should facilitate the dissemination of such information to enable farmers to get better value for their increased output.

The agro-processing industry across the world has to consider the retention of nutritional value; possible side effects from the use of additives and preservatives for increasing storage life; and aesthetic, eco-friendly and cost-effective packaging. In addition, agriculture and the agro-processing industry have to observe many new standards and perceptions for cleanliness, generally described as phyto-sanitary requirements. Scientists have to reorient their research projects to achieve these goals.

NATIONAL MILK VISION FOR INDIA

India is the largest producer of milk in the world.[15] As an industry, the Indian dairy industry contributes 13 per cent in terms of employment and 5 per cent in terms of its share in the national GDP. Much of the milk production is concentrated in the rural regions of the nation. Roughly, in India, about 45 million full-time employees are engaged in producing milk, which makes it the largest sector across the world in terms of employment. Also, India has more cattle—numbering about 283 million—than any other country. With such a huge human and animal capital, the opportunities in the Indian dairy sector as a contributor to the national GDP are immense. Cooperative milk product brands like AMUL have become household names, both in the rural and the urban areas. But the challenge to the milk industry still remains to be tackled in terms of the productivity per animal, which is currently about one-tenth that of the United States. There is also a need for organized processing and marketing at globally competitive standards.

I have interacted with various milk producers, processors and milk production support organizations in the last two decades. In March 2010, I addressed the Convocation of the National Dairy Research Institute in Karnal where we evolved the National Milk Vision.

As envisaged in India Vision 2020, we need to launch a 'National Milk Vision' in an integrated manner in the following areas:

1. Cattle breeding
2. Feed and nutrition
3. Cattle health care
4. Farm management
5. Improved production of clean and good quality milk
6. Milk procurement and transportation

CATTLE BREEDING

It is essential to have a progressive breeding policy on the national level and to draw up consistent policies at the state level for increasing the input-to-output (feed-to-milk) ratio. The major technologies implemented and tried are cross-breeding through Artificial Insemination (AI); Embryo Transfer (ET); and the development of transgenic animals. It is necessary to enhance and enrich the number of semen banks; to have properly trained human power; an infrastructure for monitoring the blood levels of cross-bred cows; and good quality-proven mates. Also, we need to add more than 30,000 AI centres before the Eleventh Five-Year Plan period. In order to accelerate the progress, the policy may be implemented in the public–private partnership mode and, through the Knowledge Connectivity of the PURA platform, efficient, quality breeding services may be provided at the farmers' doorstep. Embryo Transfer has to be commercialized and made into an economically viable proposition. Patenting of cross-breeds through DNA markers for adoption may be considered in the short term.

FEED AND NUTRITION

Feed accounts for almost 60 per cent of the cost inputs for milk production and has a direct bearing on the yield of cattle. At present, the primary feed for cattle is crop residue and seasonal fodder because of which the yield—particularly that of cross-bred animals—is low in lean seasons. The area under cultivated fodder production is only 4.6 per cent of the total cultivable land, and it is essential to increase it to 12 per cent. Here, too, there is a need to carry out research for producing quality fodder from dry land.

Research and innovations carried out by various agencies may be studied and introduced, depending on the suitability of their adoption to the Indian environment, such as straw soaked in urea water; appropriate feeding systems for buffaloes and cows; medicated urea-molasses blocks (UMBs) for parasite control; agro-forestry systems of livestock production; the use of herbal anthelmintics for cattle; genetic characterization of livestock; laboratory-based feed evaluation systems (in vitro and nuclear techniques); feeding systems using unconventional low-cost feed and integrated rice; and forage production.

Besides this, appropriate management intervention has to be focused on increasing the average milk production per cow per day. Increasing the lactation period, decreasing the age to first calving and decreasing the calving interval, could be expected to triple the yield and the average income. The utilization of grassland and wasteland for fodder cultivation is expected to take place only in medium- to long-term because of social factors associated with the development of such lands.

Apart from that, a large quantity of oil cakes is being exported. Consequently, the prices of groundnut cake, soya extraction, rapeseed extraction and sunflower extraction have increased by 60 to 66 per cent between 2009 to 2010. This has resulted in an increase in the cost of feeding and maintenance of milch cattle which, in turn, has added to the cost of production. Recently, I came to know that there is an effective method of removing toxicity from Jatropha oil cake, after which it can be used as cattle feed. According to the International Dairy Federation (IDF), farmers in India are paid the lowest price in the world for their produce. A critical situation is already developing because dairy farmers find it more profitable to sell off buffaloes since, due to the export initiatives by the government, the export of meat is fetching good prices. We need to implement policies which will help enrich the feed and nutrition for cattle at an affordable price. The most pressing need is to empower dairy farmers.

CATTLE HEALTH CARE

India has the largest number of cattle in the world—283 million. It occupies the first position in the world in respect of milk production and the fourth position in egg production. But, a comparative analysis in various countries shows that the yield of milk per head of cattle in the major milk-producing countries is six to twelve times higher than that in India. This is largely due to the presence of a large number of unproductive cattle and a scarcity of feed resources. In this connection, it is beneficial to study the model created by Baba Shri Bhadariya Maharaj in the desert area of Pokhran. His ashram has provided shelter for nearly 20,000 stray cattle, reared them and converted them into milk-yielding cows. He provides free milk and buttermilk to those travelling through the desert.

The most fundamental factor behind low productivity is ill health, lack of nutrition and the poor stock of a large number of cattle. High yield per cattle, which is the function of its breeding, feed and nutrition, health care and farm management are the essential requirements. It is essential to inform farmers of effective breeding programmes; of the availability of veterinary drugs and antibiotics;

and of the need to ensure satisfactory hygiene conditions for housing cattle. Providing better accessibility to veterinary services at the village level is also essential.

FARM MANAGEMENT

Farm management is one of the factors that affect the productivity of cattle and thereby, milk production. Currently, there are very few organized dairy farms in the country. Most of the dairy farming is undertaken by small farmers whose primary activity is agriculture. They have small landholdings and a few heads of cattle. They need proper education and training so that their cattle are housed in hygienic conditions, provided with a feed of increased nutritional value and adequate water and given good health care; and so that the milking process is automated at the central level.

AN EFFICIENT MILK-BASED ECONOMY IN WARANA PURA

During the visit to the Warana PURA in Kolhapur district in Maharashtra we witnessed a sugar factory, banking and retail services. It also operates the Warana Milk Cooperative which has about 20,000 milk producers as its members spread across eighty-nine villages. Formerly, it used to take at least three to four hours for the milk to reach from the producer to the Warana Dairy processing facility. This presented the risk of the milk getting spoilt or the bacterial count increasing, thereby reducing the hygienic quality of the final product. The Warana Milk Cooperative is implementing a unique method for improving milk procurement from individual milk producers.

Each village has formed one or more primary cooperative societies where farmers can 'deposit' the milk. The milk producers are free to select the primary cooperative of which they wish to be a member. That way, there is an incentive for the primary societies to give the best price to the producers and also to handle the milk in a way in which it is preserved best.

For every five to six villages, the Warana Dairy is setting up micro chilling plants with capacities of about 5,000 litres, where all the primary milk societies in the cluster deposit their milk. When the micro chilling plant is full, a tanker takes the milk to the Warana Dairy for processing. In this way, the exposed time for the milk is reduced to about thirty to forty-five minutes, allowing the milk to be unspoiled by keeping down the bacterial count, lengthening its shelf life and hence improving the final quality of the product.

IMPROVED PRODUCTION OF CLEAN AND GOOD QUALITY MILK

In order to boost the yield of clean and good quality milk, it is important to improve the productivity of dairy livestock. This can be achieved by following clean and hygienic practices during manual milking and also by mechanized milking. By doing so, the bacterial quality of the milk can be maintained. This has been demonstrated by TIFAC milk projects in Punjab, Karnataka and Andhra Pradesh and should be applied in other states too. With these favourable conditions, we should be able to target, per animal, the annual milk yield at 1,000–1,200 litres in the short term, 1,500–2,400 in the medium term, and 2,400–3,000 in the long term.

MILK PROCUREMENT AND TRANSPORTATION

We also need to concentrate on milk procurement and transportation by empowering the village cooperative societies to take up this task with the participation of private entrepreneurs. They should have local quality-testing centres as in Anand, Gujarat, to create awareness among the farmers of the desirability of a minimal microbial count and a low degree of contamination.

PROCESSING AND MARKETING

It is essential to make farmers realize the importance of producing bacteria-free milk. However, this needs the setting up of adequate chilling plant facilities, proper maintenance of equipment and the provision of venture capital loans for periodic enhancing of processing capabilities. The level of processing is expected to be around 15 per cent in the short term, 20 per cent in the medium term and 30 per cent in the long term. We need to inform the farmers so that large and modern, commercially viable units are encouraged to enter into the field of manufacturing indigenous dairy products; and to introduce improved quality standards, commercially viable technologies, nano technology-based packing and refrigerated transportation systems for hygienic distribution and an increased shelf life.

WORLD TRADE

Today, India is not a major player in the international milk trade. India's share of dairy products in world trade is negligible (0.2 per cent),[16] and in meat and poultry too it is very low (0.5 per cent).[17] The global export from India of dairy products (in milk-equivalent terms)* was projected at 40.4 million tons (2008–09), up by almost 3 per cent from the previous year. The export during 2008–09 was worth around US$224 million.[18] In the long term, we should aspire to exports of over US$4 billion, at least 15 to 20 per cent of our production. For this, it is essential to concentrate on (1) improving the quality of raw milk; (2) high standards of dairy hygiene; (3) maintaining the consistency of supplies; (4) improving the packaging systems; and (5) formulating a consistent and clearly enunciated export policy for dairy products which could include incentives for exports, particularly in view of global competition.

LAUNCH OF NATIONAL MILK VISION

When we launch National Milk Vision II, as a variant of the White Revolution, we will enable the farmers by implementing the above missions; we will put India on the high-yielding milk map; we will bring sustainable development in the rural areas, enriching agriculture, animal husbandry and food processing; we will create value-added employment opportunities for 60 million families. The second Green Revolution will be accelerated by this National Milk Vision, because it will act as a feeder channel and result in an economic multiplier for the nation, especially during these times of recession.

There are already many inspiring initiatives in the milk sector which can be emulated across the nation. We have a number of success stories which have made a difference in the life of rural citizens, such as the Gujarat Cooperative Milk Marketing Federation Ltd (GCMMF) pioneered by Verghese Kurien; the Bharatiya Agro Industries Foundation

---

* This is a standard measure of the quantity of fluid milk used in a processed dairy product. It is measured in terms of milkfat. For example, one kilogram of butter will be equal to about 21 kg of milk-equivalent.

(BAIF); the JK Trust Gram Vikas Yojana; and other successful models operating in various states.

THE FISHING INDUSTRY IN THE COUNTRY

India is the third largest fish harvesting country in the world. The sector has immense potential for rural development, domestic food security, employment generation, women empowerment as well as earning through export. The Indian fisheries sector has been witnessing a steady growth, and the annual fish production has risen to over 7 million tons.[19] The rate of growth of the inland sector has been faster than that of the marine sector. The inland fish production is close to 4 million tons and has almost doubled in the last decade.

At present, fisheries and aquaculture contribute to nearly 1 per cent of the GDP and 5 per cent of the agriculture and allied activities. Considering the output of the sector, it can provide livelihood for over 10 million citizens at a subsistence level of annual income. To achieve a rapid growth for this sector, we have to address the problems of seed, feed and capacity-building of the fishing community, promotion of the latest technological practices, administrative skills and disaster management. We need to carry out a full-fledged study for increasing the output of the fishing industry to a minimum of 10 million tons by the year 2013.

One of my suggestions for improving the industry is to create a Ministry of Fishing and Fish Products at the Centre and corresponding departments or ministries in the states. Some of the methods by which marine fishing can be improved is by the use of large trawlers, high-sea processing, packaging and marketing. Value addition to fishing and fishing products by using high technology is indeed an important mission.

CHALLENGES FOR THE INDIAN FISHERIES SECTOR

The fisheries sector in our country has to overcome many challenges. The industry is still dominated by 'capture fisheries', that is, by creating a 'property rights' problem, which subsequently becomes a threat to the sustainability of not only the aquatic species harvested but also the

THE BHARATIYA AGRO INDUSTRIES FOUNDATION (BAIF) MODEL FOR TRIBAL REHABILITATION AND DRY REGIONS

I saw the integrated village cluster development programme during my visit with Narayan G. Hegde, an IIM graduate and an expert in farming and dairying. Chonda and Lachakadi, two village clusters in south Gujarat, have a population of 5,000. The tribal people from these villages migrate to nearby towns every summer. The BAIF model was installed here with the cooperation of the people and the participation of state authorities. First, water harvesting was undertaken to make water available to all. Every home was provided with livestock and a market for the milk produced by them.

DAIRY HUSBANDRY

BAIF members demonstrated the possibility of producing high-yielding cows by cross-breeding uneconomic, nondescript cattle with exotic dairy breeds while conserving the elite native breeds. Unemployed local youths were trained to undertake livestock breeding, pregnancy diagnosis, vaccinations for preventing disease, primary health care, forage production, feeding and other technical aspects of livestock development in rural areas. Each para-veterinarian assistant was assigned twelve to fifteen villages. This programme has enabled needy farmers to regain their self-confidence and produce good quality cattle. Door-to-door service has helped them avail of timely assistance and to develop faith in adopting technology. This programme has also helped conserve community pastures and forests, and promoted organic farming, women's empowerment and food security through the easy supply of milk and the enhanced agricultural production.

CATTLE-BREEDING CENTRE

BAIF runs nearly 1,850 cattle breeding centres which they propose to increase to 5,000. The country needs over 30,000 cattle breeding centres in order to generate the cattle needed by 50 million families. This requires a replication of the BAIF type of organization in different parts of the country and simultaneously, additional input to BAIF, so that it can train and empower the local people to undertake the tasks involved in cattle breeding, cattle care, milk processing and marketing.

The BAIF model of integrated economic development with knowledge empowerment is an ideal example of the approach we need to take in order to empower the 3 billion rural population of the world through the PURA platform.

fishermen engaged in this activity. In marine fisheries, there is a decline in the catch rates along with a rapid increase in the mortality rates of fish. Slow-growing and low-fecundity species like lobsters, sharks and catfish have started showing signs of vulnerability. The number of marine species that recorded reduced landing between 1994 and 2005 is significantly high, and the landing of some traditional, indigenous inland species has also gone down considerably during the same period. We need to pioneer strategies by which the biodiversity of the Indian marine species can be nurtured and conserved. Satellite observation can be used for generating database and mapping.

In order to facilitate the seamless movement of fisheries products—fresh fish—from harvesters to the ultimate consumers, an effective and efficient cold supply chain management, interlinked with a value chain management, has to be put in place. It is noteworthy that in 2004 about 83 per cent of the Indian fish catch was marketed fresh, a significant and steady jump from 1977, when the proportion of fish sold fresh was a little less than 66 per cent of the total catch.[20] We need to spearhead the development of cost-effective and efficient technologies which can promote fish processing and storage. Regarding the efficiency of fishing vessels, the cost of fuel and clean fuel are important factors and have to be considered and developed.

A CASE STUDY: ICELAND'S FISHING INDUSTRY

In 2005, I visited Iceland, a small-sized island nation in the northern Atlantic Ocean. There, my team and I studied its unique fishing industry. Iceland harvests 2.13 million tons of fish every year. Deep-sea fishing on a large scale has become possible for Iceland mainly due to its large fleet of 330 mechanized boats. Also, its population of 290,000 is largely seafaring and capable of using modern fishing vessels, state-of-the-art fish processing and marketing methods for servicing the European markets. It has a strong fisheries management system and control over the total fleet through the well-networked Iceland Defence Agency. There is an annual quota system for individuals based upon the total permissible catch. What is most remarkable is the fact that the entire cycle of catch–storage–process and market is managed at sea, on the trawlers. The developing parts of the world can learn from this experience and empower the coastal-region PURA systems to use this technology.

TOWARDS INDIA'S SECOND GREEN REVOLUTION

Our discussions so far clearly indicate what the agenda for the Indian agricultural sector has to be for the next decade and beyond. India now has to embark on the second Green Revolution which will enable it to further increase its productivity in this sector. Above all, it has to be designed keeping in mind the needs of the small farmer as well: the success of the next agricultural revolution will be more proportional to the benefits it delivers to 5-acre farms than the 500-acre farms.

By 2020, India will be required to produce over 340 million tons in view of the population growth, and the increased purchasing power will mean a further demand for food per capita. The increase in production will have to surmount many impeding factors. The requirement of land to satisfy the needs of the increasing population as well as for more afforestation and environmental preservation activities will bring about a situation where the present 190 million hectares of arable land will not be fully available. It might shrink to 140 or even 120 million hectares by 2020. In addition, there will be a shortage of water due to competing demands and a reduction in the agricultural workforce. We have already seen that with the current availability of water, it would be very difficult to double the output in a sustained fashion.

India has to work hard to increase the average productivity per hectare: from about 2 tons to more than 4 tons per hectare of the available land for cultivation, with less water. The

**FIRST GREEN REVOLUTION
(1960–70)**

- Seed
- Fertilizers
- Water management
- Training farmers
- Cultivation management
- Harvest and post-harvest
- Output = 200 MT Grain

**SECOND GREEN REVOLUTION
(2010–20)**

- Soil characterization
- Matching the seeds
- Fertilizer management (organic farming)
- Water management
- Drip irrigation: halving water consumption
- Training
- Cultivation
- Post-harvesting (silos)
- Output = 400 MT Grain
- Food processing (value addition)
- Marketing

technologies needed would be in the area of developing seed varieties that would ensure a high yield even under constraints of water and land.

Support infrastructure, too, has to be ensured. We have to get rid of the typical picture of low-cost, low-productivity agriculture and, instead, have a vision of integrated technology and value-added agro-business. Farmers will have to graduate from being agrarian to becoming agro-technicians and agro-businessmen. For that, we need research of the highest order, technology transfer to the fields, and better access to credit with quality in terms of timeliness and accountability. Farmers will have to be encouraged to integrate vertically into storage and processing, but only when proper access to markets has been ensured. For that we need a competitive storage network and processing facilities, which can ensure a fair price at the farm-gate level. This will give the farmers' products a longer shelf life which, in turn, will help them have greater bargaining power. These facilities can be owned by the farmers themselves in a cooperative or can be a network of enterprises.

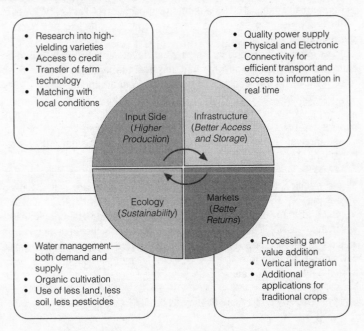

FIGURE **4.14:** The focal areas of the second Green Revolution

EFFICIENT INNOVATIVE TRADITIONAL METHODS

It is indeed important to use science and technology as a tool to reform the agriculture sector in India and the world. But while we focus on science, it is also necessary to assess the efficacy of certain traditional methods, and study how carrying out innovations in them can lead to convergence with technology for enhanced returns. India and the rural world are rich in traditional methods which have been passed from one generation to the next, often limited to local application. Let us discuss one such innovation which has brought large areas of barren land under cultivation in Burkina Faso and Niger where the soil was sealed by a thin crust that prevented the entry of water. The innovation used to reclaim the land was simple, cost-effective and yet efficient, through Tassas.

Tassas are 30-cm holes which are filled with manure as the soil is dependent on organic material. This environment promotes the growth of termites, which increase infiltration by air and moisture. In the rainy season, these holes get filled with water and the farmers plant millet in them. In Yatenga (Burkina Faso), about 10,000 hectares of land have been thus treated. They are yielding about 1,000 kg of cereal per hectare per annum as against 150 kg without the application of Tassas. Wherever fertilizers were also used, the yield went up to 1,400 kg per hectare per annum.

The International Fund for Agricultural Development (IFAD) Report on Rural Poverty (2001) highlights that 'the average family in Burkina Faso and Niger, using these technologies shifted from an annual deficit of 644 kg (6.5 months of food shortage) to a surplus of 153 kg'.

Every village in the world has some unique skills in agriculture learnt over generations, often purely based on experience and the test of time. These innovative technologies are vital as they are customized to local conditions. Two important steps are needed in this area.

First, we need to create an open source and multilingual directory of all the traditional innovations and technologies which are being applied across the world.

Second, there is a need to find out the environmental conditions to which they are applicable, and the active ingredient in the technology. This would help identify how a particular technology from one part of the world can find application in suitable conditions in another village, miles away from the place of origination.

Source: *IFAD Report on Rural Poverty, 2001* and FAO

The second Green Revolution will indeed be a graduation of knowledge: from characterization of soil to the matching of the seeds with the composition of the fertilizer; water management; and evolving pre-harvesting techniques for such conditions. The sphere of a farmer's work would expand from mere grain production to food processing and marketing. While doing so, utmost care would have to be taken for various environment- and people-related aspects leading to sustainable development.

THE LOW VISION TRAP

I have seen and interacted with rural regions in India throughout my life. I know how an Indian fisherman works at sea and I have watched an Indian farmer toiling in the field. I am aware how difficult it is for their families to meet the basic human needs for food, medicine and shelter. The problem is that we have set a low vision for our agriculture sector—one of low cost, low technology and low value production. It is a precarious outlook to have for a sector on which more than half of India depends directly as the primary source of food, especially as India has the second highest number of people to feed in the world.

PURA's sustainable development system has to be given a new vision in all sectors of growth, especially that of agriculture. It has to be an infusion of technology with the participation of the community; an improvement of yield with regard to its impact on the environment; and integrated action for value addition.

Our agriculture sector has to graduate from a mere low-value employment provider to a vertically integrated chain which will provide employment and opportunities for entrepreneurship at all levels of the value chain, including the services in the rural sector. Excessive employment pressure on limited land, water and other resources has led to smaller-sized holdings which suffer from the disadvantages of small scale. While it is a fact that agriculture—especially the growing sector—employs more than 70 per cent of rural Indians and about half of the overall population, this system will have to change in the long run. Compared to some of the developed nations of the world, we find that the

USA employs about 1.7 per cent and the European Union about 4.3 per cent of the total workforce in agriculture[21] (Figure 4.15). This also means that each farmer is able to support roughly fifty-eight non-agriculture people in the USA and twenty-three in the European Union, while the ratio for India is around one.[22]

In India's context, it is true that given the large population and demographics it would not be feasible for us to reach similar figures, but in the long run we could definitely see around 25 per cent of the total population engaged in agriculture, many of whom should be employed in value addition rather than just production. This would mean that every farmer would be able to support three non-agriculture jobs. This does not mean that it would lead to mass rural unemployment with jobless farmers. The agricultural sector with value processing would lead to higher income levels, create more demand and increase the paying capacity for services and other production in rural areas. This effect, coupled with the creation of connectivity, which would aggregate the

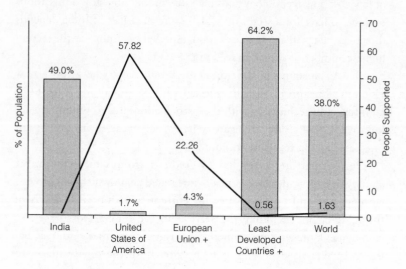

FIGURE **4.15:** Employment and dependence ratio in agriculture

markets, and the effect of creating amenities as envisaged in PURA, would be able to spur non-agro sector employment and entrepreneurial opportunities in rural areas. In the following chapters, we will discuss how non-farm and service sector employment opportunities can be created and nurtured for achieving a good balance between sectors, achieving economies of scale and promoting sustainable growth in rural India.

5

EFFECTING A SOCIAL TRANSFORMATION

A NEED FOR SOCIETAL FOCUS

The aim of a sustainable development system is not confined merely to generating higher incomes and a better economic growth. The evolution of such a development is complete only when the monetary benefits can translate directly into human development; be reflected in literacy and health care; and result in the reduction of poverty and eliminating other conflicts in a society. Such a planned system, with close integration between incremental income and capacity-building, is the key to creating happy and prosperous societies.

THE GAP IN RURAL–URBAN AMENITIES

Across the world, whether in developing or developed nations, rural areas lag in terms of providing basic amenities with quality and consistency. Most public and private employees in India—as in most of the world— find rural postings equivalent to a reprimand, with leading doctors and engineers doing their best to remain in cities. This lack of amenities has its effect first and foremost on rural talent itself, when the search for education or skill-building is often the first step towards migrating to urban regions. Table 5.1 shows the divide in literacy levels across a select group of nations around the world, while Figure 5.1 graphically represents how sharp the rural–urban divide is with respect to access to basic sanitation facilities. A similar divide would exist in any amenity that one might consider.

TABLE 5.1: Literacy levels in urban and rural areas

Country	Rural	Urban	Country	Rural	Urban
Bangladesh (1991)	30.4	62.3	Brazil (1991)	68.9	89.3
China (1990)	73.8	88.0	Morocco (1994)	20.7	58.9
India (2001)	59.4	80.3	Pakistan (1998)	33.6	63.1

Source: UNESCO Statistical Yearbooks

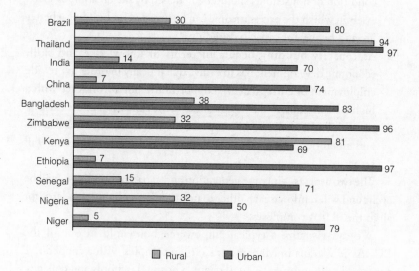

Rural   Urban

FIGURE 5.1: Access to sanitation facilities in rural and urban areas

Source: International Fund for Agricultural Development (IFAD) *Rural Poverty Report 2001—The Challenge of Ending Rural Poverty*

It is a well-known fact that the basic human amenities of health care, education, sanitation and access to goods and services are the fundamental building blocks for empowering rural regions. Their coexistence with augmented income levels through enterprise or job creation is paramount to the sustainability of the initiatives. Skill and talent cannot be sustained in rural complexes without creating social assets.

THE LINKAGE BETWEEN ECONOMIC AND SOCIAL ASSETS

The concept of a PURA is fully achieved only when there is a dynamic linkage between economic development and social and cultural transformation in real time and in a seamless manner. What this means is the realization of the following two dynamic scenarios:

1. All income-generating activities which lead to the better economic condition of households should be matched by the creation of social assets in which the excess income can be invested for building a better life and hence, for capacity-building.

2. As capacity-building occurs in terms of knowledge and skill, economic development has to evolve dynamically in order to provide employment or entrepreneurial opportunities for a workforce with a higher set of skills, and to accommodate the expansion of the existing set of skills. With economic empowerment and access to social assets and amenities, a gradual cultural change and moral upgrading will set in.

The two aspects—income generation and capacity-building—will be cyclic and will reinforce each other to promote better living standards for all in the PURA complexes.

We can visualize a typical empowered household in one of the PURAs at Warana in Maharashtra.* It is a complex with a cooperative sugar and milk industry, a retail chain, a hospital, schools and colleges. I visualize a joint family household owning about 10 to 12 acres of land where sugar cane is being cultivated and then processed in the cooperative factory. The women of the house are active and skilled members of the cooperative network which manages the various retail outlets across the region. The children receive quality education in the Warana schools and the youths of the house are students of advanced learning available locally in the Warana engineering, medical or commerce colleges. Through the local retail outlet, the household has access to all the best quality products available in any of the cities and to health care in the hospital. Since the household is technologically

---

* We have discussed details of Warana PURA in Chapter 3.

empowered through the network of cooperative enterprises, it is economically independent and able to avail of the services. It has access to clean drinking water and nutritious food; the children use modern technological tools for e-learning, through the Internet; and the farmer-parents practise advanced methods of agriculture for improving the yield and sustainability. Every member of the family is empowered, knowledgeable and productive.

This is the goal of sustainable development through PURA. Every rural household in the world needs to be propelled into becoming an empowered household on the lines of Warana or any other PURA. Let us analyse at the macro level the relationship between economic activity and social transformation which would be the basis for developing a strategy for integrated growth.

Beginning with the scenario of a typical rural complex, the economic empowerment would have to be initiated in such a way that it is inclusive of the marginalized sections of society who participate in it. The economic empowerment and additional income will spur the demand for better nutrition, better education, better health care and other amenities and services. This will create a demand for service industries and capacity-building. Carefully planned, this new demand will start creating more value-added jobs. The pace of social transformation will keep on accelerating and will match the economic development. Due to the economic and social empowerment, there will be a gradual cultural shift—towards respect for women and their empowerment, as also that of the economically and socially marginalized sections.

Up to a certain point, there is a need for external investment and support, but after that PURA's rural complex becomes sustainable, both in terms of economy and the augmentation of capacity and services. Furthermore, the development of skills and the augmentation of knowledge become sufficiently stabilized for high income value addition and enhanced yield production and services. Also, there will be a significant increase in opportunities for employment beyond mere agriculture, with more than two-thirds of the jobs in areas of value addition, knowledge, technology and services. This would be the state of a self-sustained society, where the society's culture would be further refined to a state of spiritual growth and moral upgrading, and lead to

TECHNOLOGY FOR LOW-COST EXTENSION OF HEALTH-CARE SERVICES

Technology can be a great tool for the extension of vital services to those who have still not been reached. *Businessweek* has highlighted an invention by an Indian company, Neurosynaptic Communications, that has the potential for bringing about a convergence of IT and health care, and which can act as a tool for extending health-care services at marginal costs to remote regions. This is done through a small and portable medical diagnostic kit which would cost about $300 (Rs 14,500) and is capable of carrying out vital tests like taking temperature, pulse, blood pressure and electrocardiograms. It can then almost immediately transmit the results from remote regions and villages back to the main hospitals using modern IT. All this can be achieved at a marginal cost, from $0.38 (Rs 18) to $0.66 (Rs 32), about one-tenth of what it would cost if done in a regular clinic.

This is one example of how technology can bring down costs and greatly increase the scope of basic services. If about five such units were mapped—through a network of health workers—to a centrally posted doctor, the reach of a single doctor could be increased manifold. Such a device can also increase the speed of extensive health insurance, preventive health care and the primary-impact assessment of initiatives—the benefits of which would vastly help the needy across the world. When we are dealing with the issues of half the population of the world, low-cost technological extension of existing services has to be a focus area.

Source: 'A Rural Health Clinic in a Box', Special Report, *Businessweek*, November 2007

the emergence of enlightened citizens who will strive for a conflict-free society with peace and prosperity for all.

INDIA'S CURRENT AMBIENCE: CREATING SOCIETAL AMENITIES

It is often assumed that economic growth eventually trickles down to the needy, leading to their uplift. This assumption, in many cases, may fall apart as the needy are left with little capacity-building and a low level of skills to fend for themselves, to have increased incomes, even to obtain the basic necessities of life—food, medicine and clothing. In the absence of avenues to convert additional income into measures for capacity-building, the growth of the family is not sustainable. Let us analyse this typical situation, the 'low-capacity trap', as depicted in Figure 5.2.

Let us take the situation of an impoverished family with low skills, poor education and vulnerable health due to the lack of amenities, and all this will almost certainly translate into a low income. A low income and vulnerability to disease mean severe obstacles to savings, which may be compounded by a lack of finances. A lack of amenities like water, a lack of harmony in society and a lack of access to energy result in a disproportionately high time being spent in daily, mundane activities to provide food, shelter and other necessities to the family, thereby lessening the number of economically productive hours, especially for the women of the household.

The combination of lack of amenities and the inability to pay for them makes the family vulnerable to a variety of sufferings, especially those caused by poor weather or disease. This leads to the creation of 'have-nots' who can potentially be trapped for generations in the low-capacity trap.

Add to this the severely restrained access to sources of information, which is also a consequence of poverty—because information comes at a price, both monetary as well as in terms of time. In a dynamic world, poor access to information can permanently put one in the first gear, left far behind from progress, prosperity, technological benefits and deprived of even one's basic rights as a citizen to perennially grapple with problems whose solutions are perhaps only a 'few clicks away'.

In a multidimensional problem, single-focused solutions do not work. To avoid the trap, and to achieve the objectives of sustainable development, it is necessary to have an integrated, spontaneous and synchronized solution.

One of the commonest answers to poverty and deprivation has been a regrettable regime of subsidies and free handouts, which may be as wide-ranging as foodgrains and colour televisions. The schemes are due to political as much as to social considerations.

Subsidies, in whichever form, are merely relief measures—quick fixes and temporary measures to settle pressing issues. But subsidies and freebies can never offer solutions that will ultimately empower citizens, especially the needy. They only succeed in creating dependency on external sources, beyond one's means and controls. The goal of sustainable development is to create empowerment as a solution, and this demands thinking and planning beyond subsidies—direct or indirect. That is the only way to create empowered citizens, empowered villages, empowered cities, empowered states and, ultimately, an empowered nation.

This approach to sustainable development has to cover aspects far beyond that of creating income alone. It would encompass capacity-building through quality education and health care which enable better usage of entrepreneurial opportunity or employment as a skilled workforce. It would simultaneously include the setting up of better services like banking to boost the saving potential, and retail for better access to modern products. Furthermore, amenities at the doorstep, like clean drinking water, nutrition and basic health care have to be provided, access to information be improved and a sense of social agreement has to be fostered. The result would be more productive hours per day, leading to a higher income and savings. An increase in savings—accompanied by financial tools like insurance—would give greater stability and eliminate the vulnerability, with sustained prosperity and a better life.

The opportunity that beckons India is to make optimal use of technology, management, entrepreneurship and investments to overcome the challenges of this decade and beyond. Yesterday's goals cannot be a benchmark as India contemplates graduating to the company of the developed nations of the world. Our targets must be higher, our coverage more inclusive and above all, the methods to achieve must be unique.

Since Independence, India as a nation has indeed made massive progress in almost every social and economic field. But, as we strive to have an economically developed nation by 2020, each incremental step opens up new vistas before us. After every few pages, we mark our place in history, heading for a new chapter of challenges not experienced earlier.

Following a steady decline in world income—from about 33 per cent in 0 CE to around 25 per cent in 1600 CE—India's share declined even further during the British Raj, falling sharply from about 16 per cent in 1820 CE, to less than 4 per cent at the time of Independence (see Figure 5.3).[1] Since Independence, there has been a steady rise in income, and the per capita national product has increased by more than five times, from

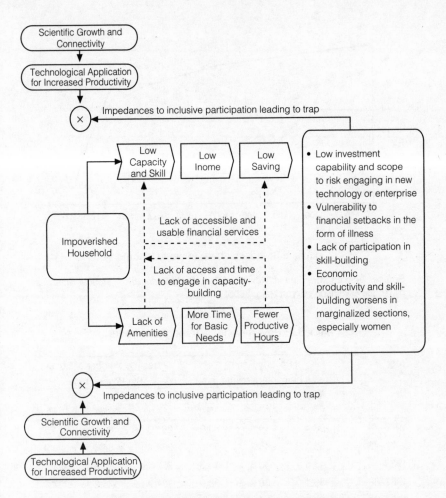

FIGURE 5.2: The low-capacity, low-income trap

Rs 5,700 in 1950 to about Rs 32,000 in 2008,[2] and today, India's share in world income—purchasing power parity (PPP)—stands at about 6.3 per cent.[3] But while the economy has been growing steadily and poverty, as a percentage, declining steadily, the absolute number of people below the poverty line has been constant. In fact, as Table 5.2 shows, from 1973 onward, the percentage of people living in poverty has reduced to half—

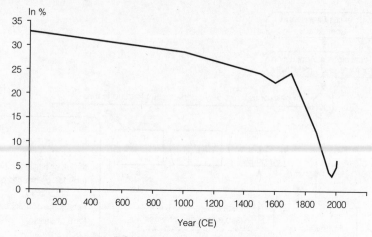

FIGURE 5.3: India's share of world income

Source: Derived from data in 'Review of *The World Economy: Historical Statistics* by Angus Maddison', Bryan Haig, 2005.

TABLE 5.2: Poverty in India through the years

Year	Poverty Ratio (as a percentage of the total)			Absolute Number of Below the Poverty Line		
	Rural %	Urban %	Total %	Rural *Million*	Urban *Million*	Total *Million*
1973–74	56.4	49	54.9	261.3	60	321.3
1977–78	53.1	45.2	51.3	264.3	64.6	328.9
1983	45.6	40.8	44.5	252	70.9	322.9
1987–88	39.1	38.2	38.9	231.9	75.2	307.1
1993–94	37.3	32.4	36	244	76.3	320.3
2004–05*	28.3	25.7	27.5	220.9	80.8	301.7

Source: The Planning Commission of India[4]

from 55 per cent to 27.5 per cent—but the absolute number of BPLs has been more or less constant at around 300 million. The problem has been a lack of integrated amenities, which could empower the households and propel them sustainably into higher income levels and capacity.

* Using a uniform reference period hence comparable to the 1993–94 estimates.

Literacy rates increased almost fourfold, from 18 per cent in 1950–51 to 64 per cent in 2001[5] and to 74 per cent in 2011.[6] India has a larger English-speaking population than any other nation in the world[7] and, depending on this segment, industries like BPO (business process outsourcing) are flourishing. But the stark reality presents a disturbing picture when it comes to the quality of education, especially in rural regions. The ASER (Annual Status of Education Report) 2009 reports on the performance of Indian rural children in linguistic and mathematical abilities show some alarming results. The report states that, out of rural students in class five, as many as 47.2 per cent are unable to read the texts of class two, and 62 per cent are unable to divide two numbers.[8] As we target at 100 per cent enrolment of children in schools, the quality of education will remain a focal point. The purpose of education is reflected in the children's learning and not the act of teaching. Moreover, there needs to be additional focus on vocational and higher education and the acquiring of skills that are of international quality. As a nation develops, it requires more scientists, more technologists, more doctors and more workers with multiple dimensions. With half of India's population still young, and one-third in education, this is a great opportunity that the twenty-first century presents to us and other developing nations—an opportunity we cannot afford to miss.

We have stated these issues in the context of India. However, the fundamental concerns are shared, in varying degrees, by almost all the nations of the world. PURA's sustainable development system would have to face these challenges and harness the opportunities for building stronger societies and economically developed rural regions across the world.

CREATING A SOCIETY BASED ON KNOWLEDGE AND SKILLS

At present, India's university education system contributes more than 2 million graduates and postgraduates every year,[9] while students seeking employment after completing class ten and 10+2 total about 7 million per year. Thus, nearly 10 million youths enter the employment market every year. In the twenty-first century, India needs a large number of talented youths with higher education for acquiring, imparting, creating and sharing knowledge. There is a vast gap in the availability of employable skills.

To bridge the gap, an interface is needed between the school curriculum and the needs of the three sectors of the economy. Moreover, with 70 per cent of youths[10] residing in the rural areas of the nation, it is important to focus on opening avenues for developing skills at the rural level.

At present, India has 550 million youths under the age of twenty-five, and this number will continuously grow till the year 2050. Keeping this resource in mind, universities and educational systems should create two cadres of personnel, both at the rural and the urban levels:

1. A global cadre of skilled youths with specific knowledge of special skills
2. A global cadre of youths with higher education

These two cadres will be required not only for powering the manufacturing and services sectors of India but also for fulfilling human resource requirements of various countries. Thus, universities and the secondary school education system will have to work towards increasing the output of the higher education system from the existing 11 per cent to 20 per cent by the year 2015; to 30 per cent by the year 2020; and to 50 per cent by the year 2040, with quality education centres spread across the nation.

The population not covered by the higher education system

NUTRITION IS A MATTER OF CONCERN

The National Family Health Survey (NFHS)—3, released in 2007, points out the fact that even now, almost 46 per cent of the children born in India, that is, every second child, is malnourished. The Global Hunger Index of 2009 ranks India at 65th position in terms of nutrition.

Country	GHI Rank (2009)	% in Hunger (2009)
China	5	5.7
Morocco	7	5.8
South Africa	14	7
Thailand	22	8.2
Ghana	28	11.5
Sri Lanka	35	13.7
Mali	52	19.5
Sudan	53	19.6
Kenya	56	20.2
India	65	23.9
Bangladesh	67	24.7
Rwanda	70	25.4
Zambia	72	25.7

Source: 'The Challenge of Hunger: Focus on Financial Crisis and Gender Inequality', Global Hunger Index, 2009

should have the opportunity to acquire world-class skills in areas such as construction and carpentry; maintenance and repair of electrical and mechanical systems; fashion designing; paralegal and paramedical services; accountancy, sales and marketing; maintenance and servicing of software and hardware; and ensuring quality assurance in software and hardware. No youth should be without either world-class higher education or without world-class skill sets. This is the mission that must be undertaken by the sustainable development model for the twenty-first century.

CHALLENGES IN HEALTH CARE AT THE RURAL LEVEL

We see life expectancy reach sixty-three years now. A newborn today can have a life twice as long as that of a child born in 1950.

The top end of Indian health care carries an international stamp of quality at minimum cost. It has seen a continuous double-digit growth in the medical tourism sector, and is expected to reach $2 billion (about Rs 9,600 crore) by 2012.[11] But the challenges of this decade are, more than anything else, to reach the goal of 100 per cent access to

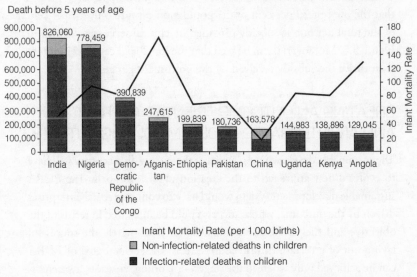

FIGURE 5.4: Rate and causes of infant mortality

the basic amenities of sanitation, clean water and nutrition, and of bringing down the Infant Mortality Rate (IMR) and the Maternal Mortality Rate (MMR) to less than one-third of the present rate. In absolute numbers, even today India sees more infant deaths than any other nation (Figure 5.4), a situation that has to be tackled with determined action by all stakeholders. The realization of an economically developed nation will be complete only when we are able to set up development systems which guarantee access to preventive and curative health care for all.

There is a need to ensure that all forms of service are carried out in an entrepreneurial manner, which would not only ensure job creation but also ensure that the benefits reach the intended targets without leakages. Only then will the investments made by the public or the private sector have a meaningful and measurable impact.

Now we will discuss the new approach needed which would become the hallmark for achieving the goal for sustainable development in this decade and beyond.

Above all, there is an oft-cited issue of lack of coordination and synchronous delivery. This has to be overcome by an improved supply mechanism and the empowerment of the intended beneficiaries.

Let us take the case of health care. It is estimated by research groups that the poorest 20 per cent of the population capture only 10 per cent of the total net public subsidy provided by clinical services as shown in Figure 5.5. Moreover, it can be seen that the top 20 per cent receive more than thrice the subsidy received by the bottom 20 per cent.

CREATING AN OUTCOME-ORIENTED APPROACH AND AN INTEGRATED PROBLEM-SOLVING OUTLOOK

The sustainable development systems of the twenty-first century will have to evolve a new approach to the creation of societal goals. The PURA sustainable development system would have to comprise social enterprises driven by the outcome, whose success could be measured in terms of the objective and the visible parameters, rather than merely the successful laying out of a certain infrastructure. Thus, the societal goal of PURA can be achieved only when all the stages—planning, creation, awareness, usage and feedback—are completed.

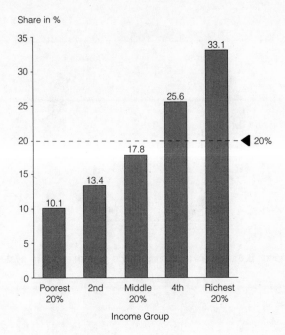

Share in %

<figure>FIGURE **5.5**: Share of public subsidy for health care according to income group</figure>

Source: Derived from World Bank data, 2001

There is a decidedly higher level of challenge in this approach of shifting our categorization from the outlay to the issue. Most of the challenges posed by a societal transformation are not elementary in nature but a mixture of many different fundamental social amenities. As a societal system, those who implement PURA will have to act as social engineers rather than mere creators of assets. They will have to generate a sound understanding of the linkages within the various issues and evolve strategies which will take into account all the underlying causes. The linkages between social problems go deep and sometimes may not be that apparent.

Let us take an example. Figure 5.7 plots the IMR, that is, the number of deaths per 1,000 new births, with the fertility rate for women (the number of births per woman) for 175 countries from around the world (figures for 2005).[12] Notice the significant linkage between the two

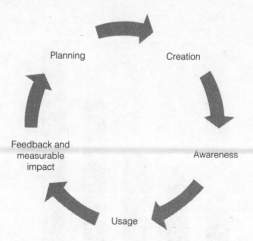

FIGURE **5.6:** Stages in achieving the goal of a PURA system

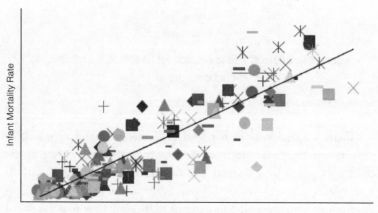

FIGURE **5.7:** IMR and fertility rate (global)

aspects of society. It arises out of the fact that when the IMR (and the child death rate) is high, there is a pressure on women to give birth to more children to cover the risks of child deaths.

Those implementing PURA need to take this up as a societal mission and give deep thought to it. There is also a logical linkage between the fertility rate, the population growth rate and the family size. A big family with a limited income means less money to spend per child which, in turn, leads to poor education, possible malnutrition and disease, especially for the girl child. The family has to ration its resources for education and health care, which leads to more dropouts in schools and chronic illnesses at later ages.

Figure 5.8 is specifically in the context of India. The curve plots the fertility rate vis-à-vis the female literacy rate in India after Independence. Notice that there is a direct and unambiguous correlation between the rise in female literacy and the reduction in fertility. The purpose of pointing such data is to highlight how our societal challenges are associated with each other. When our challenges are interlinked, the solutions to them too have to be integrated.

The cycle would naturally be interlinked and would encompass many aspects. The societal mission of PURA would be based on this social re-engineering and an understanding of the underlying causes. So, if there is a pressing need to reverse the number of dropouts, the short-term plan would be by way of giving incentives, while the long-term solution would lie in re-engineering a host of societal assets. Of course, this would have to done in an order of priorities.

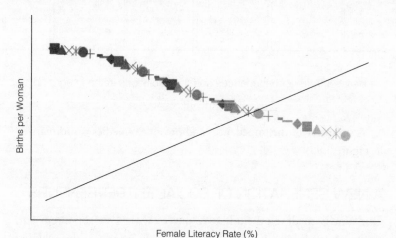

FIGURE **5.8:** India: Female fertility rate vis-à-vis female literacy rate

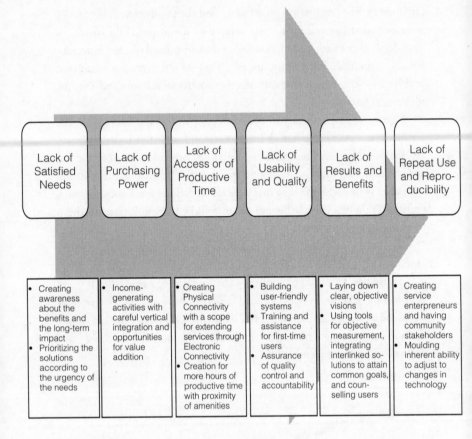

FIGURE 5.9: Major impedances and their solutions in the integrated solution approach

A summary of the impedances and possible remedies is summarized in Figure 5.9.

A NEW GENERATION OF SOCIAL ENTREPRENEURS

Our aim is to develop human resources with a value system and entrepreneurial skills and, at the same time, ensure affordable amenities of a minimum quality standard for all. The question is: Who can do it?

THREE BROAD APPROACHES TO DEVELOPMENT

The world over, agencies have been engaged in many different methods of development, in the government, the private sector or a combination of both. These initiatives have met with varying degrees of success and failure.

What makes them work? How do they differ from each other?

Let us try to analyse some broad outlines. We will categorize them into three distinct classes.

Illusory approach: At times on purpose and at other times inadvertently, many initiatives taken around the world in the name of social transformation are completely tangential and poorly coordinated, but the expenditure incurred on them gives the illusion that efforts are being made. Besides being quite expensive, they are also futile in view of the fact that little is being achieved at the ground level. There is hardly any relationship with the receiver—who is extraneous to the system—and the initiatives themselves are highly hierarchical in their structure with little accountability.

Quick fixes: Quick fixes are probably the commonest and the most frequently applied approach—they are like firefighting measures for instant relief from a particular problem or issue without much being done about the real causes and stresses. They are often makeshift measures to hide the problems temporarily, often at a huge cost which cannot continue over a long term. While they do, to some extent, touch people's lives, they rarely empower and can almost never lead to economic independence. Quick fixes are not completely undesirable, though, and sometimes may be required in issues which deal with relief work but certainly not with a long-term objective. The receiver is a mere short-term beneficiary here. Generally, the control structure is bureaucratic with a rigid 'one-size-for-all' model.

Sustainable solutions: Sustainable solutions are the need of the hour across the world. They require a careful study of the underlying aspects of the problems or issues, and a customizing of solutions according to local competencies and conditions. They demand an innovative approach in order to deliver the best at the lowest cost, and so, a sustainable solution is often also the most cost-effective. Sustainable solutions empower and create local leadership in planning and execution, and hence have a long-term, objectively assessed goal. The receiver is a stakeholder in such initiatives, and the structure of such initiatives is entrepreneurial, flat and participative.

There is a need for initiatives to move to the third category—sustainable solutions. This would require six key elements: ingenuity in thinking, depth in understanding, integrated solutions, community participation, technology and creative leadership.

Of course, there is a role which governments and corporate bodies will have to play as a part of social responsibility. But even enthusiastic individuals with bright ideas can bring about a tremendous societal transformation, in a sustainable way, entirely by virtue of their own capabilities. This new and fast-growing set of entrepreneurs who—through their education and acumen—hold the promise for the nation's future transformation, are called social entrepreneurs. Their role in developing a sustainable growth model would be paramount as they would be the interface between people, technology, investments and solutions. Let us discuss some of the social entrepreneurs whom I have come across.

FROM LOS ALAMOS TO PEDA AMIRAM

The life of Dr M.R. Raju is a shining example of an internationally known nuclear scientist working in the Los Alamos National Laboratory, USA, who decided to transform his native village, Peda Amiram, in the state of Andhra Pradesh, and the surrounding area. With the support of his wife M. Subhadra Devi Raju, a well-known social service worker, and other family members, he set up the Mahatma Gandhi Memorial Medical Trust in that village. Within a decade, he and his team, supported by volunteers from various institutions from India and abroad, have brought about a great change in the lives of the people. They have particularly targeted character-building and uplifting the child population in the age group of three to five years. This has totally transformed the village atmosphere and the dropout rate of the children in schools has come down from 70 per cent to less than 30 per cent. Due to the creative learning that is being imparted to them in a harmonious atmosphere, a self-confident young population is emerging in the village.

In addition, two hospitals—one for cancer diagnosis and treatment, particularly of cervical cancer in the tribal people, and the other for treatment of eye diseases—have been commissioned in the village. I myself have visited Peda Amiram and seen the development and the progress of the project. Dr Raju and his team are silently carrying out an important and noble mission in Peda Amiram with the cooperation of state government officials.[13]

EQUITY IN EDUCATION

In June 2010, I visited Teach for India, Pune, a non-profit organization, where I met many bright young teachers who are passionate about spreading the mission of education. This is a unique movement of college graduates and young professionals who commit two years to teach full-time in under-resourced schools (English-medium primary schools with a fee structure of less than Rs 300 per month) in Pune and Mumbai. These well-qualified youths are contributing to the process of bringing equity in education starting at the grass-roots level.

In 2010 alone, 150 young professionals from leading companies and fresh college graduates chose to give two years of service to the mission. These young and dynamic teachers are called 'Fellows', and they are engaged not only in classroom teaching but also in transforming schools, evolving innovative educational patterns that address the students' needs and building their creativity. The inspiration the talented youths can provide and the transformation that such a mission can achieve will help kindle the light of knowledge in the lives of many children.[14]

REACHING THE UNREACHED THROUGH SOCIAL ENTREPRENEURSHIP

In the present circumstances and environment, it is inspiring to see the manner in which Dr H. Sudarshan, for the last thirty years, has put all his efforts into the integrated development of the Soliga tribal people of Karnataka, through the Vivekananda Girijana Kalyana Kendra (VGKK), at BR Hills. When I visited the area in 2006, I saw the new tribal hospital, and the societal transformation of which he is the architect. Karuna Trust, affiliated to VGKK, has as its areas of focus education and livelihood improvement, along with health care. The trust runs twenty-five primary health-care centres (PHCs) in Karnataka and nine in Arunachal Pradesh. VGKK also has a vocational training institute where sixteen crafts are taught. Due to its efforts, 60 per cent of the tribal people now get a minimum 300 days of employment.

When Dr Sudarshan was just twelve, his father passed away in a village without any medical help. This event, followed by his reading

Dr Sudarshan says the greatest joy he has experienced was when he resuscitated a patient whose lungs had given out and whose heart had stopped. Also, whenever he sees a smile on the face of poor patients who have come to the hospital with cataract in both eyes and who walk out with full vision after the cataract surgery.

the biography of Dr Albert Schweitzer who worked in Africa, motivated him to take up the medical profession and work in tribal areas in India. Dr Sudarshan derives his philosophy of work from Swami Vivekananda's teaching, which states 'they alone live who live for others, the rest are more dead than alive'.

Dr Sudarshan starts his day at 4.30 a.m. with yoga, meditation and prayer with the tribal schoolchildren. From 9 a.m. to 1 p.m., he goes around the wards and sees the patients individually. He has lunch with the tribal students between 1 and 2 p.m. Later, till 7 p.m., he is busy in the clinic where he conducts minor surgeries, and he visits the tribal complex. He spends a large part of his time in clinical and laboratory diagnosis and treatment, in addition to supervising, monitoring, teaching and carrying out research with his team members.

He pays particular attention to the typical problems of the Soliga tribal people such as cases of snake bite, mauling by bears, pneumonia, tuberculosis and acute respiratory infections. They also suffer from sickle cell anaemia and Dr Sudarshan has developed a low-cost electrophoresis machine for diagnosing the disease. He has built up a health-care system based on the strengths of the traditional knowledge available in the tribal areas. The secret of his mission is that he is empowering the people to manage their own health problems through the provision of knowledge. He has trained tribal girls as auxiliary nurses and midwives (ANMs) and posted them in the tribal sub-centres. Thus the rural areas have become self-sufficient in nursing resources. He has also developed a low-cost management system for epilepsy and set up dental care and cancer control measures in the PHCs.

He is providing quality health care to the people by the introduction of low-premium health insurance for all the people living below the poverty line. He suggests that medical colleges should inculcate in their students sensitivity to the suffering of patients. The medical education system should aim at facilitating the application of medical technology to provide the poor with the best care at the most affordable price.[15]

All these social entrepreneurs are well-qualified individuals with a mission to change society in a sustainable way. The nation, to attain its full development and prosperity, needs many such inspired youth powered with education and talent who would take up the challenge of being the transformers of today and the architects of tomorrow.

FOCUS ON UNDERLYING CAUSES: RESEARCH BEFORE EXECUTION

Societal development is similar to scientific missions. They both need a 'research first' approach. Unfortunately, many well-funded initiatives around the world are also the most poorly researched, often based merely on perceptions. Just as many scientific expeditions owe their success to understanding the hidden and the significant, social development has to be based on knowing and mapping the concealed factors. Much like technological missions and operation management, social development has to follow a solution broken down into a time-bound order of precedence for initiatives—to clearly outline which step precedes and follows which initiative in order to achieve the objective.

Let us take the very simple case of addressing the problem of dracunculiasis, also known as Guinea worm disease, that used to affect millions in Africa and Asia. Today, without any vaccine or cure, the disease has been greatly controlled and is now endemic in four African countries. There is a high likelihood that the disease will be the first parasitic disease to be eradicated and the first disease to be eradicated through behavioural changes alone. The disease is caused by the consumption of water contaminated with water fleas (copepods) containing the *Dracunculus* larvae. The larvae develop for about a couple of weeks inside the water flea and during this stage it can infect a person if ingested. Once inside the body, the water flea is digested but not the Guinea worm larvae which burrow deep into connective tissues or joints. The worm grows to a length of two to three feet and then, after about a year, emerges out of the skin of the afflicted person, causing a lot of pain and a burning sensation. This leads the person to immerse the affected part in water, into which the new larvae pass. Often, in poorer regions without access to filtered water, these contaminated sources are used for drinking purposes, leading to fresh infections. It is surprising that there is no way the parasite can survive without passing through humans, and yet, the disease has continued for over 3,500 years, even found in calcified Egyptian mummies. It has begun to reduce greatly only in the past two to three decades. (*Contd*)

FOCUS ON UNDERLYING CAUSES: RESEARCH BEFORE EXECUTION (CONTD)

The fundamental solution for dracunculiasis was to base it on the lines of sustainability and search for the underlying causes than just symptomatic relief. For ages, people had tried everything—from burning the affected parts to finding vaccines and medicines—with no success. But, solutions need not always be from the laboratory, sometimes they require ingenuity in thinking.

The point of interception in the modern initiative was to ensure that the worm did not get to breed in one cycle and, given its inability to survive outside the human body, its eradication was assured. Thus the solution lay in preventing the water flea from entering the human body, and if this were done for just one year, the cycle would be broken forever. All it took to eliminate an age-old killer disease was a very low-cost instrument coupled with health practices. Villagers were given special nylon cloth to filter the water. They were advised to obtain drinking water from wells wherever possible. Besides, 'pipe filters' were widely brought into use. They are basically drinking straws fitted with a water purification system and are especially useful for those travelling away from home. They work on the energy due to suction by the mouth and cost a little over $1 each.

The Carter Center reports that, in 1986, there were about 3.5 million cases of Guinea worm disease in twenty nations. By 2009, the number had reduced by more than 99 per cent to about 3,190 cases across four countries. Totally eliminating Guinea worm disease—which should be completed within a few years—would perhaps be one of the most cost-effective and innovative solutions ever achieved. We need such innovative thinking and understanding to tackle the many issues and problems in not just health care but also education, societal biases and economic stagnation.

Source: The Carter Center and World Health Organization web resources

---

CREATING A VALUE-BASED SOCIETY

We are witnessing a new situation throughout the world. Economically prosperous nations with their mighty security forces are under various forms of threat. Developing countries with certain value systems are in fear for their future.

I have met over 1 million children below seventeen years of age and I have also met thousands of young students in thirteen countries. All the youths, during my interactions with them, unanimously shared with me their dream of living in a happy, prosperous and safe nation. Giving our nation and the world a sustainable development system with a focus on creating value-based citizenship must be considered an important mission. To achieve this, I have evolved a three-dimensional doctrine: (i) Education with a value system; (ii) Religion transforming into spirituality; and (iii) Economic development for societal transformation. All these three components have to be tackled in an integrated way throughout the world.[16]

Let us discuss the relevance of education with a value system. The best part of a person's life is childhood, and the learning period in school, which is between five and seventeen years of age. Of course, at home a child receives love and affection, and values are imparted. A student spends approximately 25,000 hours on the school campus and roughly three times that with parents. Hence school and home both have to be focused towards learning and need the best environment and mission-oriented learning with a value system. During this stage, they need value-based education in school and at home for them to become good citizens. This echoes a great teacher's saying, 'Give me a child for seven years. Afterwards, let God or the devil take the child. They cannot change my child.' For parents and teachers, the school campus and the home must have an integrated mission, that is, education with a value system. They must inculcate moral leadership in their children, which involves two aspects. First, it requires the ability to have compelling and powerful dreams or visions of human betterment; a state in which human beings would be better off in the future than they are now. Second, moral leadership requires a disposition to do the right thing and influence others, too, to do the right thing.

The Chitrakoot PURA, in central India, focuses specifically on promoting value-based learning and value-driven societies as its fundamental goals, which is being implemented through its gurukuls.* The Deendayal Research Institute (the implementing body of the Chitrakoot PURA) has established gurukuls on the ancient educational pattern. Children of all social strata, without any discrimination, live and

---

* Gurukul (Hindi): It is a traditional Indian education system where the students live with the teachers and also help in managing the day-to-day activities of the school.

learn in the gurukuls. There are ten such gurukuls (six for boys and four for girls) with the capacity to accommodate twenty students each.

The novelty of this system is that one retired elderly couple, along with two attendants, has been assigned to every gurukul, so that each has a family of twenty-four. The vision of the gurukul system is that since students spend three-fourths of their time in a hostel, it is the best opportunity for imparting values to them. This inculcation of the value system is the responsibility of the elderly couple. The school also acts as a point where the experience of the elderly is utilized to nurture the young.

Gurukuls also focus on teaching the children lessons in self-reliance. Each gurukul has its own land where the students grow vegetables for their own consumption. Each gurukul also has a cow. Besides academic studies, the students are given training in different trades in the Udyamita Vidyapeeth,* the entrepreneurship development centre of the Chitrakoot PURA.

The gurukul system is an excellent example of how value-based learning can be facilitated and how the retired and elderly population of the nation can be meaningfully, and with respect, utilized in the task of building the nation and generating enlightened citizens. A sustainable development system, to be truly inclusive, has to find such opportunities for elders.

ACHIEVING AN INTEGRATED HEALTH MISSION FOR THE LONI PURA COMPLEX

Let us now move to the western part of the nation. The Loni PURA is located in the Ahmednagar district of Maharashtra. It has a participative model of integrated rural development which has come up among 235 villages with a population of 500,000 people. The seeds of the Loni PURA were sown back in 1948 with the setting up of Asia's first cooperative sugar factory at Pravaranagar by the late Padma Shri

* Rural education complex
* Rural medical complex
* Industrial complex
* Sahakari Bank
* Rural and agricultural development complex

---

* Udyamita Vidyapeeth (Hindi) = Entrepreneurial School

Dr Vithalrao Vikhe Patil, who mobilized the local community into creating this income asset. This economic reform at the regional level was transformed into a social movement and, over a period of time, Loni saw the creation of many other social assets such as schools, colleges and hospitals, which led to a better development of the local population.

The health services at the Loni PURA are being managed by the Pravara Medical Trust with the help of its constituent health-care colleges and various other international development agencies like the Swedish International Development Cooperation Agency (Sida) and Pathfinder International (a USAID Mission). The Loni PURA has a large tribal and remote area under its management, and has had to face the challenges of poor connectivity, a high incidence of malnutrition, poverty, poor child and mother health and the problem of the spreading HIV infection.

The health-care mission for the Loni PURA evolved as an integrated and outcome-oriented mission with a special focus on improving the much neglected mother- and childcare. The multi-pronged mission for health care had the following components:

AWARENESS

One of the first steps towards implementing preventive health care was to generate an awareness of hygiene, prevention and diagnosis. The primary problems of the area were identified as HIV, childcare and female foeticide, as well as the necessity to promote general health and hygiene. Institutional workshops were organized for conveying the concept of a clean village. Training was organized specifically for schoolteachers, with more than fifty workshops for more than 3,000 nodal teachers and educators, covering eighty-five secondary schools in the area. Involving teachers was an important measure and it had a cascading effect, as it was observed later that more than 70 per cent of the trained teachers included the issues that had been discussed in the workshop in their teaching schedule. They also empowered the students to act as watchdogs against the observance of blind faith and unhygienic practices.

One of the serious problems that had to be tackled was the falling female-to-male ratio. Out of the 235 villages, thirty-eight had a gender ratio of fewer than 900 females to 1,000 males, and villages like Rahata

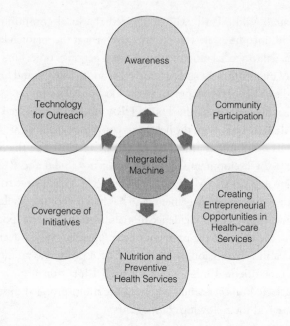

FIGURE **5.10:** Components of the multi-pronged health-care mission at the PURA Complex

had 638 females to 1,000 males in the age group of zero to six years. To improve this situation, the health-care mission undertook a multi-pronged approach of awareness and empowerment of the women. Using multimedia tools on mobile platforms, short movies and posters were prepared and exhibited in the villages. The community was also made aware of the alarming situation and urged to take action.

A total of 14,000 books, along with posters and handbills, on seven different local problems and local entrepreneurship opportunities, are there in all the villages of the Loni PURA to promote healthy living and empowerment of the people.

COMMUNITY PARTICIPATION

One of the major tools for promoting health care is making a sustained effort to create an awareness of it as a common goal owned and shared by the community. The Loni PURA's health-care mission promoted the concept of a 'healthy village'. It was accepted by the state government and included in the activities of the National Rural Health Mission (NRHM). The national-level 'Nirmal Gaon' (Clean Village) programme and the state-level 'Sant Gadge Maharaj Puraskar' for villages, where 100 per cent households have access to quality sanitation, are being actively implemented in the PURA complex areas. As many as 196 villages were recommended for the Nirmal Gaon Award for 2007 from Ahmednagar district—the highest number of villages from a single district in the country, since the scheme was launched by the Government of India. Out of these 196

'NIRMAL GAON' AWARD

The Nirmal Gaon Award was launched by the Government of India under its Total Sanitation Campaign. The award is given to district blocks and villages on total elimination of the practice of open defecation. To qualify for the award many parameters have to be ensured, like the entire village (or block) has the provision for modern lavatories with the facility of water. Besides, the village should also have provisions for providing safe drinking water to its residents.

---

villages, fifty villages were from the Loni PURA area. The total number of villages from the Loni PURA that have received the award now stands at sixty-eight.

Another major problem which formed a thrust area for the Loni PURA health mission was the rehabilitation of and improvement in the lives of widows, especially those who were without family support on account of their husbands—usually the primary and sole earning members of the family—having died of AIDS. Many of these women were minors with children, who had been married off early, and were most probably infected by HIV. They were often economically deprived and socially marginalized. Moreover, most of them were not even aware of the HIV they had acquired and its implications. The issue was not only of health but also of social equity, justice and human rights within the community. The challenge was to screen the cases and at the same time empower them enough to guarantee them a livelihood. The operations began in 2006 with focused group discussions (FGDs) and informal surveys in thirty-five villages; these were extended to 100 villages in 2007 to identify the HIV Seropositive cases. After special screenings and tests, many cases of positive HIV infection, especially in widows, were identified and referred to the district hospital for free antiretroviral (ART) treatment.

But that was only a part of the effort; the ultimate aim was the empowerment of the widows. Hence, a socio-economic rehabilitation programme for 102 HIV/AIDS-identified widows, imparting training in self-employment to make them economically independent, was drawn up through individual, family and community counselling sessions. Self-help groups were formed for the HIV/AIDS widows identified in the Loni PURA, and they were trained in self-employment schemes such as, growing Spirulina, making fortified foods, screen-printing and manufacturing detergent powder.

CREATING ENTREPRENEURIAL OPPORTUNITIES IN HEALTH-CARE SERVICES

One of the unique aspects of Loni PURA's health-care mission is the evolution and empowerment of women entrepreneurs in the field of delivering health-care services. They are called female health volunteers (FHVs), and are usually in the age group of twenty-five to fifty years with a basic education. They generally operate as part-time health extension and monitoring agents in their own or nearby villages. Each FHV is responsible for a variety of tasks, including disseminating knowledge, assisting at the health camps in the villages, and maintaining and monitoring general health and hygiene at the village level.

> **SHAKTHI+ FACTS**
>
> The special supplementary diet is made using locally available cereals and pulses—wheat, rice, ragi, soyabean, black gram, Bengal gram, green gram, yellow gram, almond and sugar.
>
> 100 gm of Shakthi+ provides 463 calories, 39.4 protein gm, 17.5 fat gm and 16.6 mg iron.

Besides the FHVs, there were a number of traditional birth attendants (TBAs) and traditional healers (THs) in all the villages. While their skills might be worth scrutiny, there was no doubt that they had a micro-level reach deep into the villages. Instead of rejecting and replacing them, the Loni mission embarked on a programme of value addition and quality enhancement for them, banking on their competence and knowledge of the villages and their inhabitants. In 2007, 117 TBAs and sixty-seven THs were trained in modern methods of health care. Thereby, their ability as modern providers of health care was developed and their enterprise potential enhanced. To encourage the adoption of new health-care practices, there is a policy of paying the TBAs Rs 50 as an incentive for conducting a successful and safe home delivery using a freely supplied DDK (disposable delivery kit) worth Rs 40. On an average, each of the 200 trained TBAs is earning Rs 400 per month on this account.

NUTRITION AND PREVENTIVE HEALTH SERVICES

For a result-oriented societal mission, it is important to widen the field of action with a careful analysis of all the problems that need to be addressed to achieve the objective. One of the primary obstacles which the Loni PURA mission faced in its goal of bringing down the IMR and the MMR and guaranteeing a healthy life for all was anaemia and lack of nutrition. To address the urgent problem of quality food, an innovative supplementary nutrition diet called Shakthi+ was started. This supplement is locally manufactured by women SHGs, and has converted nutritional rehabilitation into a social entrepreneurial opportunity for them.

At the same time, about 200 exhibitions involving local volunteers, on food and nutrition, were held in schools, rural health centres and project offices. Women were encouraged and trained to develop community-level nutritional gardens so that access to nutrition was available at the doorstep.

CONVERGENCE OF INITIATIVES

To realize the mission of providing quality health care and ensuring a healthy life for all, the Loni PURA mission also strives towards a convergence of different initiatives, from international agencies, the community and the government. Loni PURA has built up a consortium of local NGOs, medical institutions and an international development fund under the Sida.

On the field level, the services provided by the mobile clinics of the project were synchronized with the government clinics of the same village in order to strengthen the overall service delivery to the community. The Loni PURA's project staff have been contributing to the district-level medical and public health and other services by training nurses under the NRHM, the ASHA (Accredited Social Health Activists) scheme for tribal areas, and the International Regulatory Development Partnership (IRDP) training programme and implementation.

The Loni PURA health-care mission is an integrated effort for identifying health problems and their underlying causes, and then embarking on a task of preventive health care; social empowerment; electronic extension of services; mobility in health care; and the development of social entrepreneurship and societal employment. The integrated health-care initiative has had a colossal impact on the target health indices in a very short span of about two years. The most immediate impact was shown in the MMR and the IMR of the area. Annual reports of the Loni PURA show remarkable results of these efforts in the reduction of maternal deaths and infant mortality. This has made Loni, which is largely a tribal area, emerge as a trendsetter in the health-care domain for the nation and a guiding principle for the development of sustainable development systems in all indices including Crude Birth Rate, IMR, MMR and vaccinations as shown in Table 5.3.

TABLE 5.3: Comparative performance of the Loni PURA

Description	Unit	India	Maharashtra State	Ahmednagar District	Loni PURA Region
Crude Birth Rate[17] (rural)	Per 1,000 population	24.7	18.7	17.3	14
Infant Mortality Rate (IMR)[18]	Per 1,000 births	61.0	41.0	35.6	25
Maternal Mortality Rate (MMR)[19]	Per 100,000 births	450	380	290	180
Fully Immunized Children[20]	Percentage	37 (rural)	77 (rural)	52.3	85

TECHNOLOGY FOR OUTREACH

Since the Loni PURA is operating in a tribal and difficult terrain, it is necessary to 'reach the unreached' through the application of technology and mobility.

To achieve better coverage in the PURA complex, and to empower the people with better information on health and hygiene, seven e-health centres were set up in partnership with the local community. The latter contributed by providing some of the physical infrastructure and by paying part of the IT operator's salary, thereby making the staff and the centre socially accountable to the community. The other fixed expenditure such as equipment and running expenses is managed by the Pravara Medical Trust. Each e-health centre, using its seamless and fast access to the Pravara Institute of Medical Sciences University (PIMS), is able to reap the benefits of Electronic Connectivity for creating health-care facilities in the remotest regions.

First, each e-health centre acts as a consulting point for the capacity-building of the regular medical staff employed by Loni PURA and the private practitioners operating in the rural region. Electronic Connectivity with experienced doctors and experts at PIMS provides the facility for consultation in complicated cases and obtaining a second opinion, thereby upgrading the health-care services from the existing medical set-up. Besides this, patients can connect directly with the doctors at the Pravara Institute for their specific queries without having to travel all the way to the hospital. This facility is, at present, benefiting over 100 villages. Even in cases where a physical examination is required, patients can consult with doctors at the PIMS through e-connectivity. All the medical records and information of patients under treatment are electronically available through the e-health connectivity.

Besides, medical treatment and consultation, the centres also constitute a place for offline and online health education and awareness programmes on pertinent topics like HIV, environmental health and hygiene through a direct connectivity available at the doorstep.

The e-health centres are, in fact, well-managed points of fast Internet connection and multimedia situated in the heart of the village, and hence, with innovative thinking, some amount of additional resource utilization was a definite possibility. Keeping this in mind, the e-health centre tapped further into the Electronic Connectivity and started interacting directly with the Krishi Vigyan Kendra, Loni (discussed in detail in Chapter 3). The centres are also used for obtaining information on the quality of seeds, pesticides, scientific farming, weather and current government schemes. Market connectivity was also set up using the centres, whereby farmers can get online information about the prevailing market prices of different products in at least ten different city markets.

Students, unemployed youths and women's SHGs can avail of the offline and online guidance and counselling on career and self-employment opportunities through the same e-health centres. Finally, they also offer free web-surfing facility to the Internet users of the villages.

The success of the e-health centres at Loni has three important lessons. First, it shows how, using Electronic Connectivity, an economically feasible model can be established, where the knowledge capital available at a central point—in this case, at the PIMS—can be shared for the benefit of a larger audience and also empower other private health-care givers in the area. The second lesson is the design of the e-health centre itself. Since the gram panchayat provides the space for the centres and pays part of the salary of the IT operator who is a trained, computer-literate local person, the community enjoys ownership of the product. This type of community ownership contributes to the sustainability of the project. It is also significant to note that, by the innovative sharing of the pre-existing

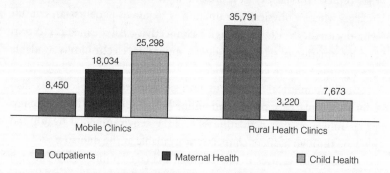

FIGURE **5.11:** Number of patients served by the mobile and the rural health clinics in 2007

Electronic Connectivity, the e-health centres are slowly graduating to e-community centres by providing value-added services well beyond the field of health and towards integrated empowerment of the local population.

In order to extend the outreach even further, the Loni PURA's health-care mission has introduced five mobile clinics and eight rural health centres (RHCs), located strategically across the villages. The mobile clinics are equipped with two trained nurses and a paramedic, equipment for diagnosis and the monitoring of health, and facilities for basic treatment and medicines. Each mobile clinic follows a schedule where it covers two villages every day in morning and evening shifts. Many of the villages covered by the mobile vans are far-flung tribal villages and settlements with no connecting traversable road and no access whatsoever to medicinal facilities till the mobile clinics started providing the first-of-its-kind health services through special smaller vehicles. The mobile clinics are assisted by local women health volunteers who help inform the local population about the services offered and bring the sick to the mobile clinic camps. Every year, about 3,000 health camps are conducted across the Loni PURA complex, with a special focus on mother and child health care. The RHCs run special health clinics for children twice a week and a general clinic every day for the villagers. They also use the e-health centres for long-distance consultation with the specialists in the PIMS, and transport the more serious and critical cases to the hospital at Loni.

SETTING BROADER GOALS WITH OBJECTIVITY: CHITRAKOOT PURA

The Chitrakoot PURA, in Madhya Pradesh, lends a unique meaning to development and sets an integrated target for the measurement of development, which has a combination of parameters including economic status, poverty, education, health, women's empowerment, harmony, physical connectivity and environmental aspects. The Chitrakoot PURA strives to go beyond development and reach a state of self-reliance on economic, social, cultural and environmental levels.

It has devised an objective way to measure, monitor and assess the progress of each village based on multidimensional criteria that include the parameters listed and defined in Table 5.4.

TABLE 5.4: Parameters to measure progress in the Chitrakoot PURA

Parameter	Definition	Measurement
Unemployed	A person in the age group of 18–35 (not pursuing education) without the means to generate income to fulfil his needs	The number of unemployed persons (should be employed 180 days out of 365 days).
Poor	A family that cannot fulfil its basic needs	An income below Rs 18,000 per annum for the whole family
Illiterate	A person who is unable to read or write, or understand his or her responsibilities, and does not have decision-making powers	• Children in the age group of 6–14 years should have a school education • The family should be aware of matters that concern the village • Every village should have a primary school • The head of the family should participate in gram sabha meetings • Those in the age group of 15–35 years should be able to read and write through adult education
Healthy	A person who is mentally and physically fit, and willingly performs the responsibilities of the family, society and the nation on the basis of physical and mental abilities	• The number of people suffering from chronic disease • The number of infants suffering from malnutrition • Vaccination • Birth and death rate • The number of families with access to clean drinking water • The number of families aware of family planning
A Clean and Green Environment	Management of home and its surroundings; plantation of multi-purpose trees. Consciousness and conservation of the environment	• After finding the number of members in a family, to determine the number of compost pits required • Whether a drainage/soak pit system is available or not • Access to clean drinking water • Cleanliness of the houses and nearby areas

(contd)

Parameter	Definition	Measurement
		• A signboard in every village displaying matters related to cleanliness • A system of sanitation to be evolved by the villagers themselves according to their local situation • A nutritional or kitchen garden with tulsi plants at every home, and panchvati (pipal, banyan, neem, anola, ber trees) in every village
Societal Harmony and Conflicts	Cases that are registered with the panchayat, in police stations and courts. Villages should become completely dispute-free.	• The number of cases registered in the panchayats • The number of registered cases (in police stations and courts) • Registration of new cases
A Self-reliant Family	The family should have its basic needs met with, and should save a part of its income	• The family should save a minimum of at least Rs 2,000–3,000 per annum • Children in the age group of 6–14 should have a school education
A Prosperous Family	Education, social recognition and moral values in the family and in society	• The family should be aware of and be knowledgeable about village matters • At least one person in every family should be a graduate • Children in the age group 6–14 should have a high school education • The family should be in a position to give employment opportunities to others • The family should save at least Rs 7,000–10,000 per annum
Public Amenities	Guidance and assistance in constructing public amenities, and creating awareness of the need to maintain the common facilities available	The facilities should include, depending on an assessment of the needs, a playground, a school, a panchayat bhavan, wells, ponds, hand pumps, a post office, a public telephone and roads. Maintenance of existing facilities would also be considered within this parameter.

(contd)

Parameter	Definition	Measurement
Social Consciousness	A society in which the people are aware of and conscious about their social duties, and do not rely blindly on others	• The number of encroachments • The practice of child marriage • The number of dowry cases • The number of child labourers • The number of divorce cases • The number of religion-based disputes • The number of widow remarriages (this is considered a positive sign) • The number of community functions • The number of families still believing in superstition

The Chitrakoot PURA assesses the state of self-reliance based on these parameters and has realized this model in eighty villages of Chitrakoot in 2005 with the vision to expand it to the nearby 500 villages. This was realized and in February 2011, I inaugurated the self-reliance model for the 500 villages of Chitrakoot.

BRINGING QUALITY GOODS TO PURA THROUGH COOPERATIVE SUPERMARKETS

We have already seen in Chapter 3 that the Warana cooperative movement is a model of integrated development. One of its prominent features is the Warana Bazaar (supermarket). By the 1970s, the Warana region had made good economic progress due to the cooperative sugar and milk processing enterprises which gave the local farmer families a reasonable disposable income. The leaders of the Warana movement then realized that the incremental income was translating into a demand for better products, but there was a lack of market connectivity for consumer goods. This led to the birth of the Warana Consumer Cooperative Movement in 1976. Since then it has become a highly successful enterprise managed by the womenfolk of the villages. It has been audit Class A since its inception, and its sales and profits have been rising steadily. It pays dividends at the rate of 26 per cent per annum against investment in both cash and kind.

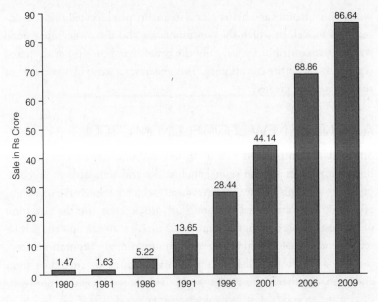

FIGURE 5.12: Sales of Warana Bazaars

Besides the high returns, in 2003, the Warana Bazaar issued bonus shares at a 1:4 ratio—a sure sign of its success as a business enterprise.

Today, it has more than 16,000 members, 80 per cent of whom are women with fifty-eight rural stores. The sales of the Warana Bazaars have crossed Rs 86 crore (Figure 5.12) starting at less than Rs 1.50 crore in 1980. It directly employs more than 500 individuals, besides sourcing most of its products from local micro entrepreneurs. Since most of the members are also consumers, the quality of the products sold and the customer-friendly attitude are strictly maintained. For example, Warana Bazaar offers its consumers regular discounts and other value-added services like free insurance policies and mobile consumer-awareness vans. To remain competitive, it emphasizes the training of its employees, and many of the current managers were sent abroad to study the working of consumer cooperatives and to adapt the best practices in rural Warana. A wonderful inspiration and idea, indeed, learning from the best in the world and adopting it in an Indian village setting.

The long-term growth and sustainability of the Warana Bazaar model highlights the possibility of harnessing the latent demand in rural regions with rising incomes and better access to quality products to build a socio-business model, in which the consumers are also the owners in a small cooperative contributory way, and the benefits and profits are all shared equally by the entire community. This generates a sense of ownership of the social assets created.

ADVENT OF NEW SOCIO-ECONOMIC TOOLS

Since PURA's mission is one of socio-economic transformation, it is important to set up the right benchmarks and standards for societal obligations. In this chapter, we have already seen how closely the social and economic goals are linked and how both are necessary for the evolution of any sustainable development model. We have also seen how the private sector, individual entrepreneurs and multinational corporations, too, can play a significant role in taking the PURA mission across the nation and even to other parts of the world. This is significant as the reach of consumer goods, fast-moving consumer goods (FMCG) and food companies is immense and today, most of the remote villages have access to soft drinks and packaged foods, branded toiletries and toothpastes and basic medicines—all coming through the distribution channels owned and operated privately, often by the large companies themselves. The point here is, if distribution channels can be set up to carry these goods efficiently and regularly to the common man, how this procedure can be synergized as a shared vehicle to achieve education, health care and better employment for the rural masses. There are five challenges here:

1. How can social and economic goals be integrated so that both become sustainable? It is evident that certain societal projects are not economically beneficial, so how can this problem be overcome?
2. How can large companies and the private sector be incentivized to undertake societal missions?
3. How can a convergence of private and public initiatives be achieved for common societal missions?
4. How can people at the local level be empowered to articulate their needs? This will help ensure that the societal assets being delivered are pulled by demand and not pushed by supply, and help match investments with the required interventions.

5. How can transparency be maintained during the process over a sustained period of time?

The answers to these questions are complicated because a fine balance is needed between a centralized and a decentralized approach. One key aspect would be to objectively link social and economic goals through a 'virtual credit system'.* We will term this new 'virtual credit' as 'P_S' or social credit.

Consider P_S as a form of appreciation given to any initiative, whether private or public, which has a societal consequence. This social credit, P_S, will be linked to objective capacity-building or any measure providing an amenity in the rural complex. For example, the value of social credits can be assigned for:

1. Every child for whom the societal mission, say a school, would be able to provide quality education with full amenities at the premises.
2. Every additional hospital bed which could be availed of by the local people at an affordable price.
3. Every family which is able to access clean drinking water without any discrimination.
4. Every BPL family which would get sustained and respectable employment and would thus be able to come out of poverty.
5. Every extension in health-care delivery due to the extended services would be provided through a tele-centre.
6. Improvement in yield (in percentage) or in area under cultivation (in acres) which happened as the result of a new water conservation initiative.
7. Every family which is insured against illness or loss of farm or livestock, and the expected number of families which will be saved from falling back below the poverty line as a result of added capacity to absorb shocks.†

In fact, a societal development radar can be evolved with different contributions and objectively measurable parameters for each of the segments, as shown in Figure 5.13.

---

* Later in the book, we will add another variable to this—the environment.

† In this chapter, we will keep environmental initiative out of the picture as we will introduce it separately, later.

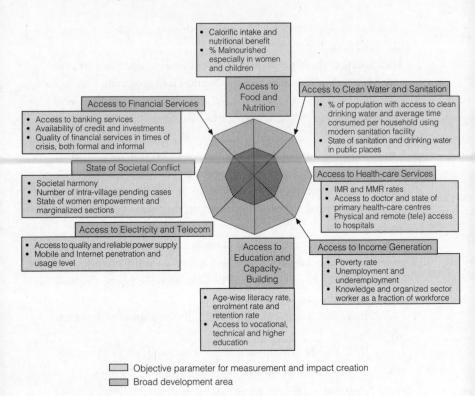

Objective parameter for measurement and impact creation

Broad development area

FIGURE 5.13: Societal development radar

The value of credit for each initiative would need to be evaluated separately, but in a joint manner where some part of the value would be judged by experts based on its perceived impact on a general scale. The remainder would be decided by local-level bodies by profiling the community demand. This would give the requisite weightage to those societal initiatives which are on a local priority basis.

All socio-economic missions by the private sector, academic institutions, NGOs or other organizations, which satisfy the criteria of the social credit system, would lead to an accumulation of social credit, P_S, with the implementer. This credit system of P_S can be reapplied in a variety of forms:

- It can be linked with priority lending and development-focused soft loans and aids.

- It can be a measure for a new class of products and services which are also in some way linked to the betterment of society. Corporate bodies can position themselves on this brand proposition.
- Institutions which generate social credit may be given priority for undertaking economic missions in the region. This can be done by assistance offered through the existing panchayati raj scheme or by dovetailing government-sponsored development schemes to create a package of capital and labour for the creation of social assets (for example, NREGA,* the Total Sanitation Campaign, Sarva Shiksha Abhiyan†). This will help incentivize projects with the highest priority and the most impact.
- The same social credit can be used to promote social entrepreneurship in areas where it may be needed but where it is not economically feasible in the immediate future.
- Specific social credits—for example, water or health-care credits—can be used to generate a demand. This can be done by giving credits for different human development exercises to the needy, and social entrepreneurs and cooperatives can be promoted to work towards such goals.
- Over a period of time, a market for social credits may also emerge on a wide scale. This will enable large enterprises to outsource the work of societal development to those who have developed expertise in the field of creating social assets. Thereby, it will lead to a new cadre of large-scale social enterprises.

Over time, each PURA complex may evolve a social credit exchange which can be managed cooperatively by the locals or through the

---

* NREGA: The National Rural Employment Guarantee Act was enacted in 2005. Under it, every rural household in the nation is eligible to 100 days of employment as a right at a stipulated wage of Rs 100 per day. At least one-third of the workers are women. NREGA work can be done in the area of the creation and maintenance of water bodies, check dams and roads, afforestation and levelling land. It is now known as the Mahatma Gandhi National Rural Employment Guarantee Act (MGNREGA).

† The Sarva Shiksha Abhiyan (Hindi: Education for All) is a flagship programme for achieving the universalization of elementary education in a time-bound manner, as mandated by the 86th Amendment to the Constitution of India, which makes free and compulsory education of children aged between six and fourteen a fundamental right. The programme had aimed to attain this goal by 2010.

panchayati raj institutions. With the help of experts, it can determine what is needed most for the development of the village through public appraisal.

Depending on the identified needs, a portfolio of social credits can be extended. For example, if a village needs access to clean water on priority for the development, then they can be given water credits. A group of such credits can be mapped on to some concessions which can help facilitate the setting up of societal credit. It may be in the form of land, labour or investments. This social credit can be fulfilled by enterprises, NGOs or through corporate social responsibility.

Similarly, there may be enterprises or initiatives that seek concessions or permission to use the resources of the village. Ordinarily, this can potentially lead to a hostile situation which would be detrimental to the economic growth and social goals of all the stakeholders.

If the system of the PURA complex social exchange is followed, then such an industry would be mapped against a negative social credit which

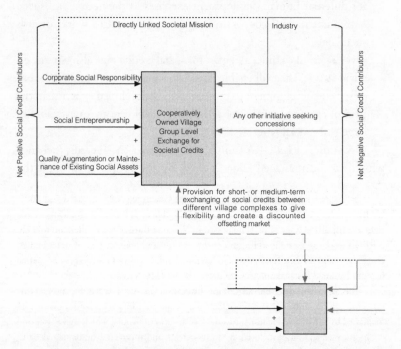

FIGURE 5.14: A Typical working plan for the social credit system

it would either have to offset itself—in a form dependent on what the village needs—or, alternatively, sponsor positive social credits, which would then be realized by another social entrepreneur or organization, or through a village cooperative.

Over a period of time, these social credits could be exchanged between villages, so that negative social credit could be used to ensure automatic selection of the best possible alternative for a particular initiative. A typical working plan is shown in Figure 5.14.

MEENAKSHI MISSION PURA

In May 2010, we visited a remote village called Thonugal in the Virudhunagar district of Tamil Nadu and inaugurated the Meenakshi Mission PURA pioneered by the Super Specialty Hospital and an IT institute of Madurai. The unique feature of this PURA is that several institutions have come together with the people's participation to focus on health, education, employment generation and water.

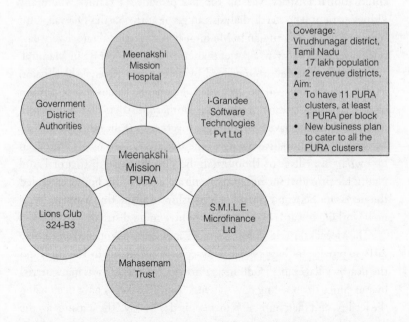

FIGURE 5.15: Meenakshi Mission PURA: Partners, coverage and aim

A tele-medicine centre has been set up with adequate medical modalities. By February 2011, more than 2,000 patients had been treated, ten free medical camps conducted and more than 3,000 people have benefited. Microfinance has been provided for creating entrepreneurs in over 500 small and micro enterprises: 600 women's SHG members have been identified and given small and micro loans for enhancing their livelihood possibilities and creating employment potential. Rural e-BPOs have been created for providing services to the BPO industry: unemployed youths in the region were selected and are undergoing training to do telemarketing for organic food items in the USA, and for digitizing the medical records. An e-learning centre for primary and secondary school students and a reverse osmosis (RO) water purification plant for providing clean drinking water to school students and villagers, to the tune of 250 litres per hour on a daily basis, have been installed.

Apart from this, a unique service I saw for the first time is the Mobile Dialysis Van on call basis which goes to the doorstep of the villagers suffering from kidney disease and who are immobile. The Lions Club International District 324-B3 too has provided a facility where any kidney patient who needs dialysis can get it at the Sastha Dialysis Unit managed by Dr Palanirajan in Madurai at a concessional rate. Every day, on an average, twenty-five patients are treated at this centre in Madurai.

All these schemes are managed by the unified Meenakshi Mission PURA system and will be expanded, in phases, to cover a minimum of thirty villages in each of the three southern districts of Tamil Nadu. Many institutions have been brought together to realize this Meenakshi Mission PURA initiative owing to the initiative taken by V. Ponraj, in his own native village of Thonugal in the Virudhunagar district of Tamil Nadu. He provided the necessary facilities, a part of his home, extended the necessary help and provided leadership to make this happen. He is now working towards expanding it to three more districts.

The Meenakshi Tele-Care/Tele-medicine Centre was opened on 19 May 2010 to provide the local people with access to health care in Thonugal and the nearby villages in Virudhunagar district. The centre was inaugurated by me. Since the opening day, patients from six villages have been using the facility, and their number is increasing day by day. The statistics for the Thonugal centre as in August 2010 are depicted in Figures 5.16 and 5.17.

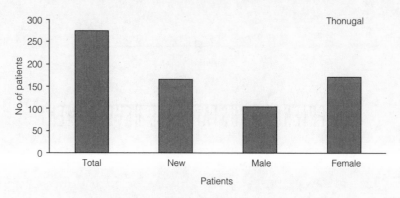

FIGURE **5.16:** Number of patients in August 2010

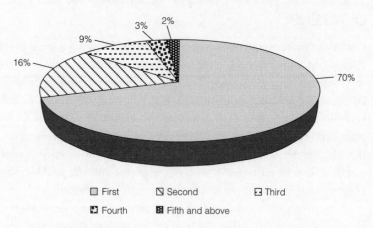

FIGURE **5.17:** Number of visits by patients in August 2010

The authors acknowledge the help and support of Mr V. Ponraj in compiling the information about the Meenakshi Mission PURA.

ECO-FRIENDLY SUSTAINABLE DEVELOPMENT

THE GLOBAL ENVIRONMENTAL SUSTAINABILITY CHALLENGE

One of the most pertinent challenges for sustainable development in the twenty-first century is the impact of developmental initiatives on the environment. Global warming and climate change are worldwide issues and have far-reaching consequences that will be felt by every human being in times to come. It is a challenge whose outcome will affect the sustainability of the earth and its ecosystem for future generations. In this chapter we will try to understand the problem of environment sustainability, its relationship with development and the possible ways of integrating development and environmental conservation.

A term which is exclusively associated with the environment is greenhouse gas (GHG). GHGs are gases that absorb and emit radiation into the atmosphere. Carbon dioxide, water vapour, methane, nitrous oxide and ozone are some of the primary GHGs in the earth's atmosphere. In our solar system, Venus, Mars and Titan—the largest of the many moons of the planet Saturn—all have greenhouse gases in their atmosphere.

GHGs lead to the phenomenon of greenhouse effect in the earth's atmosphere. As we all know, the sun heats the earth by the process of radiation. About 50 per cent of the energy radiated by the sun is absorbed by the earth's surface while the rest is reflected back into space. This reflected energy is absorbed by the GHGs and then re-emitted in all directions and on to the earth. Thus, the lower atmosphere and the surface get heated much more than they would have been by solar radiation alone. In fact, it has been established that in the absence of greenhouse gases the earth's temperature would have been about $-19\,°C$ which is about $33\,°C$ below the current average surface temperature.[1] At this temperature, most of the oceans would have been frozen, and most of the life forms that inhabit the planet would not have been possible. Thus, per se, the presence of naturally occurring GHGs is a necessity for life to exist.

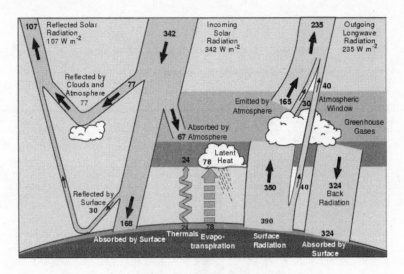

FIGURE **6.1:** Global heat flows

Source: J.T. Kiehl and K.E. Trenberth, 'Earth's Annual Global Mean Energy Budget', 1997

The earth has both natural sources and sinks for the GHGs, which are delicately balanced. The natural sources of GHGs are volcanic eruptions, decaying vegetation, releases from oceans and land—all due to natural processes. These are balanced by the natural sinks of GHGs like ocean absorption, plants and soil. But it is now evident that human activities since the Industrial Revolution have been systematically altering this thin balance.

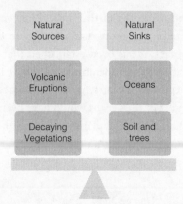

FIGURE **6.2:**   Natural sources and sinks of GHGs

Source: *Climate Change 2007*, IPCC Report 2007

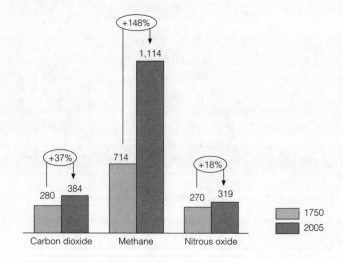

FIGURE **6.3:** Increasing levels of GHGs

Source: *Climate Change 2007*, IPCC Report 2007

As of 2007, the human-generated, or anthropogenic, annual carbon dioxide emission worldwide stood at roughly 30 billion tons (30 trillion kg) or 30 gigatons,[2] while the total GHG emission (including carbon dioxide) stood at 41 billion tons (measured in carbon dioxide equivalents).[3] Out of this, around half is absorbed by the natural sinks

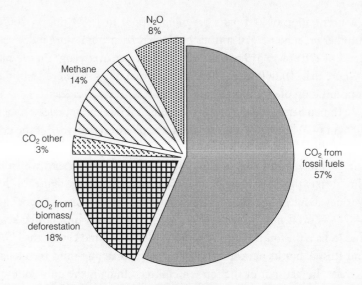

FIGURE **6.4**: Contributors of human-generated CO_2

Source: *Climate Change 2007*, IPCC Report 2007

of oceans and soil. This means around 15 gigatons of additional CO_2 is released into the atmosphere. Different scientific calculations show that one part per million (1 ppm) roughly corresponds to about 7.8 billion tons of CO_2. This means that we are adding about two parts per million of carbon dioxide every year. Such imbalances have been more significant since the Industrial Revolution. Analyses show (see Figure 6.3) that the CO_2 concentration has risen from the pre-industrial figure of around 280 ppm in 1750 to about 384 ppm in 2005.

Carbon dioxide is not the only greenhouse gas which has risen significantly. Methane, which is another greenhouse gas with a warming effect four times that of CO_2, has risen from

EMISSIONS FROM SOME DAILY ACTIVITIES

1 KW-h (kilowatt-hour) of power
= 1.27 kg of CO_2
1 kg of coal burnt
= 2.87 kg of CO_2
10 km by car
= 2.10 kg of CO_2
1 litre of diesel burnt
= 2.70 kg of CO_2
10 km by two-wheeler
= 0.70 kg of CO_2

a concentration of 714 parts per billion (ppb) to 1,774 ppb in 2005. Another greenhouse gas, nitrous oxide, has risen from a pre-industrial figure of 270 ppb to 319 ppb in 2005.[4] When seen over a large time frame of more than 10,000 years, there is clear proof of a massive surge in the concentration of greenhouse gases in the recent few decades.

Human beings, by the process of biological respiration, release about 900 gm (450 litres) of CO_2 into the atmosphere every day.[5] But the net carbon dioxide footprint is many times this figure. An average American releases more than 50 kg of CO_2 equivalent emission per day, which is almost sixty times the biological requirement. The average figure for the world is about 12 kg per day, while an average Indian emits about 3.7 kg of CO_2 equivalent per day into the atmosphere.[6] It is worth noting here that India is the fourth-largest emitter of GHGs, behind China, the USA and Russia, but its per capita emission is less than one-third the global average. In fact, out of the top ten emitters, India is the only country whose per capita emission is below the world average.

We need to consider why we human beings have become such high-intensity GHG-emitters. Let us take a few examples. The mobility of human beings has gone up exponentially over the last half a century, which is a burden on the usage of fossil fuels.[7] Take air travel, for instance. A return journey from New Delhi to New York burns more than 260,000 kg of fuel. Each kilogram of fuel yields about 3.1 kg of CO_2. The release of water vapour into the dry stratospheric conditions and the emission of NOx (nitrogen oxide) add to the GHG effect. The net amount of CO_2 equivalent added per person for the return journey would be around 12,000–24,000 kg.[8]

From where does this carbon emission come? As in Figure 6.5, energy supply is the highest contributor and is responsible for around 26 per cent of the overall emissions, largely due to the burning of fossil fuels to generate electricity. Industries have a share of more than 19 per cent of the global emissions, while deforestation contributes another 17 per cent.[9]

Agriculture, too, is responsible for about 14 per cent of the global GHG emissions. The entire transport sector put together is responsible for

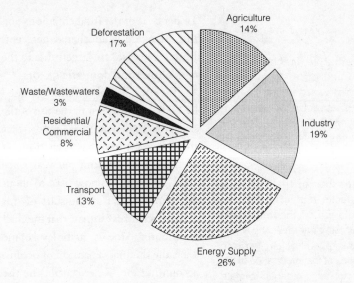

another 13 per cent. The rest of the emission comes from the residential and commercial sectors, waste and wastewaters.[10]

This increase in the concentration of GHGs translates into an increase in radiative forcing (heating power) of +2.3 watts per square metre[11] as estimated by the Inter-governmental Panel for Climate Change (IPCC) in 2007. Besides GHGs, human activities have also led to an increase of aerosol content in the atmosphere, which occurs in the form of sulphates, black carbon, nitrates and dust. The combined effect of this aerosol—both directly and indirectly—is atmospheric cooling at the radiative force of about −1.2 watts per square metre. Putting together all the effects, the net human-generated global warming, as measured in radiative forcing, is about +1.6 watts per square metre. Even if this rate were held constant at the current levels, it would translate into a rise of 0.1°C of temperature every decade during this century.

In terms of the gases, CO_2 from fossil fuels is the largest contributor (see Figure 6.4), with a share of about 57 per cent, to the overall GHGs emitted. Another 18 per cent of the GHGs is the CO_2 coming out of decomposition of biomass and deforestation. Methane constitutes about

RADIATIVE FORCING

Radiative forcing, often measured in W/m², is a typically used scale to measure the impact of a particular factor or GHG in heating the atmosphere. IPCC defines radiative force thus:

'Radiative forcing is a measure of the influence a factor has in altering the balance of incoming and outgoing energy in the earth-atmosphere system and is an index of the importance of the factor as a potential climate change mechanism. In this report radiative forcing values are for changes relative to pre-industrial conditions defined at 1750 and are expressed in watts per square meter (W/m²).'

In simple words, radiative forcing is the rate of energy change per unit area.

14 per cent of the total emissions and nitrous oxide is another 8 per cent. Both these gases are largely due to the agricultural and domestic sectors.[12]

The effect of global warming caused by GHGs is also seen in the rise of the sea level. Expert agencies report that the global sea level has been rising at an average of 1.8 mm per year since 1961. This rate has now risen to about 3.1 mm per year at the start of this decade. Scientists estimate that the chief contributor to the rise in the level of the sea is the thermal expansion of oceans, accounting for 57 per cent of the rise (see Figure 6.7). Another 28 per cent of the rise is due to the melting of glaciers, and the rest comes from loss of polar ice sheets. This rise is accompanied by a decreasing ice extent. Satellite data shows that the Arctic Sea extent has been shrinking by 2.7 per cent per decade since 1978.[13]

The rising sea level is a global threat, especially to low-lying deltas, smaller islands and coastal areas across the world. This is even more critical as today nearly half the world population lives within 200 km of the sea, and this number is expected to double by 2025.

To offset the carbon emission there are many natural sinks of carbon. One sink of CO_2 is trees which essentially lock up the CO_2 present in the atmosphere as carbon within their trunks and also in the soil. The forests that are still standing have about 4,500 GT (gigatons) of carbon stored in them. By contrast, the total remaining oil has only about 2,400 GT of carbon equivalents. Even the atmosphere on an average has about 3,000 GT of carbon stored in it.[14] But by

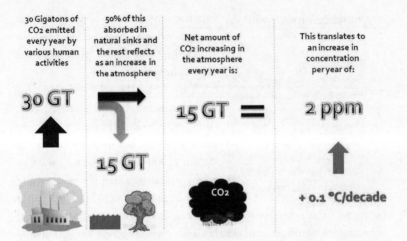

FIGURE 6.6: The greenhouse budget

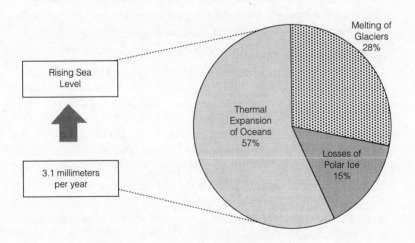

FIGURE 6.7: Causes of the rising sea level

METHODS OF REDUCING EMISSIONS

- Reforestation
- Energy independence
- Renewable sources for power generation
- Use of biofuels
- Reducing waste and converting it into wealth
- Reducing emission by intelligent building

far, the largest sinks of CO_2 are the oceans, which dissolve almost fifty times the CO_2 that is present in the atmosphere itself.

The challenge posed by environmental change is indeed real. There may be debates on the intensity of the problem, but the fact that the last decade (2000–09) was the warmest one so far in the recorded history[15] of the world is proof that, while we cannot be sure of the rate of associated threat, one thing is certain—global warming is a significant and clearly visible phenomenon. Any sustainable development system has to be integrally linked to environmental considerations.

Now we will discuss some of the factors which can be instrumental in bringing down the GHG emissions and in realizing a sustainable development system that would have global significance. Later we will discuss some prominent small-scale—often village-level—initiatives from

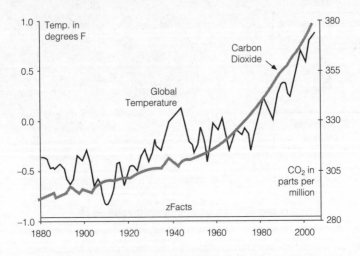

FIGURE **6.8:** Temperature rise and CO_2 emission

Source: *Climate Change 2007*, IPCC Report 2007

across the world which can be the building blocks for any sustainable development system in the form of a PURA complex.

Of course, the GHG emissions from human activities come in many forms and hence the approach to solving the problem also needs to be multi-pronged, covering many areas.

REFORESTATION

We had earlier discussed how oceans are a sink for GHGs. But there is a problem. Oceans are essentially liquids that contain dissolved gases. But the capacity of any liquid to absorb gases decreases sharply with a rise in the temperature. Hence, with rising temperatures, oceans are able to absorb less and less GHGs. Forests are the most stable carbon sinks because their ability to absorb—unlike that of oceans—is affected less by heating. Each tree, on an average, removes 20 kg of net CO_2 every year by the process of photosynthesis. Besides this, each tree provides shade and protection from the wind which, by conservation of energy, can indirectly cause reduction in the emission of CO_2 equal to fifteen times its absorption by the tree itself. Of course, this value varies from tree to tree, and tropical trees are far more effective in absorbing CO_2. Every acre of trees is thus capable of removing CO_2 generated by burning 3,700 litres of gasoline in a year and providing oxygen to about twenty-two human adults.

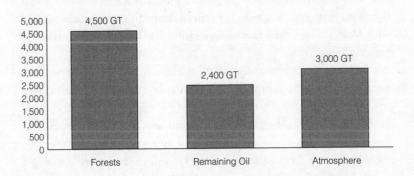

FIGURE **6.9:** CO_2 stored in forests, oil and the atmosphere

Source: Video titled 'A Convenient Truth', FAO

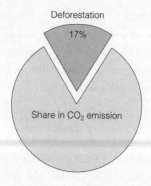

Deforestation

17%

Share in CO₂ emission

- Globally, the deforestation
  rate (1990–2005) has been 13
  million hectares every year—
  area equivalent to Greece
- Since 1850, deforestation has
  released 120 gigatons of CO_2
  in the atmosphere

FIGURE 6.10: The results of deforestation

Source: Video titled 'A Convenient Truth', FAO

However, when forests are cleared, they release the carbon back into the atmosphere in the form of CO_2, methane and other gases.

In fact, deforestation accounts for 17.4 per cent of CO_2 emissions and is a larger source than the entire global transport sector. Eight thousand years ago, nearly 50 per cent of the earth's surface was covered with forests. Over the years, deforestation has brought it down to 30 per cent now.[16]

Today, we are destroying forests at the rate of 13 million hectares every year, which means we are annually removing forest cover equivalent to the size of Greece.[17] Most of the deforestation has occurred in the least developed regions of the world, especially in the equatorial forests of Amazon, Africa and Indonesia. During the period 1990–2005, there has been a decrease of more than 5 million hectares in Central and South American forests and about 4 million hectares in Africa.[18]

This trend can be reversed by a thrust on reclaiming the lost forests by replacing the lost trees and creating new ones.

The Indian government has promoted the plantation of new trees under the Mahatma Gandhi National Rural Employment Guarantee Act (MGNREGA), which mandates 100 days of guaranteed employment to every rural family. Similar efforts are being made by many state governments across the country.

India has a unique strength in the 130 million young school-going children. If each student were assigned the responsibility of planting and taking care of ten trees, we could plant more than a billion trees in the country during the next ten to twelve years. Schools need to participate actively in such environment-friendly ventures.

An important aspect in this context would be the choice of trees for replanting. In such initiatives, we should focus more on fruit-bearing trees or trees with medicinal value. Further research should be conducted in the development of fast-growing varieties which are more resistant to climate changes and pests.

MGNREGA AND TREE PLANTATION

Tree plantation is one of the activities promoted by the MGNREGA, a flagship programme of the Indian government. This was successfully carried out in Bihar under the leadership of a civil servant, S.M. Raju. Every village council has now been given a target of planting 50,000 saplings. A group of four families has to plant 200 seedlings and to protect them for three years till the plants grow sturdier. Depending on the survival of the trees, funds are released. One proof of the success of this initiative was clearly seen on 30 August 2009, when 300,000 villagers from over 7,500 villages in northern Bihar were engaged in a mass tree-planting ceremony, which had the potential for breaking the record for the highest number of trees planted by a group in one day.

Source: A BBC report

ENERGY INDEPENDENCE

Energy is the lifeline for modern societies. But today, India has 17 per cent of the world's population and just over 1 per cent of the world's known oil and natural gas resources, including the petroleum and natural gas reserves in the Krishna–Godavari (KG) basin and the Barmer (Rajasthan) region.[19] We might be able to extend the use of our coal reserves for some

GLOBAL ENERGY VISION 2030

Global Energy Vision 2030 has to be three-dimensional. First, it has to ensure that quality energy is made affordable and accessible for all. Second, it must ensure that dependence on depleting fossil fuels is minimized, thereby giving stability to the energy supply. Third, it has to be balanced against the environment aspect, by stressing the development of greenery, thereby adding cleanliness to our energy. The energy independence vision has to be global in its implementation and a priority for all nations.

Five objectives for achieving Global Energy Vision 2030:

1. Improving energy efficiency in industrial, transport, residential and commercial sectors and reducing by 50 per cent the growth rate of energy demand.
2. Dependence on fossil fuels as the primary energy source to be brought down to under 50 per cent.
3. Replacing petroleum as a primary fuel source for transport by renewable fuels that emit less carbon or are completely carbon-neutral.
4. Enforcing methods for development of green energy through a seamless flow of ideas and technologies with international collaboration.
5. Reducing the net emission per unit of energy consumption to 25 per cent of the current rate.

time but that too at a high cost and by facing environmental challenges. The climate of the globe, as a whole, is changing.

We will first discuss energy security, which rests on two principles. The first is, using the least amount of energy to provide services and cutting down energy losses. The second is, securing access to all sources of energy including coal, oil and gas supplies, before the end of the fossil fuels era, which is approaching fast. Simultaneously, we should access various technologies to provide a diverse supply of reliable, affordable and environmentally sustainable energy.

Energy security, which means ensuring that our country can supply energy to all its citizens at affordable costs at all times, is thus a very important and significant need, and an essential step on the path to progress. But it must be considered as a transition strategy, to enable us to achieve our real goal—energy independence—an economy that will function effectively with total freedom from oil, gas and coal imports.

Hence, our highest priority has to be achieving energy independence. We must make a tremendous effort to attain this within the next twenty-one years, which means, by the year 2030. For carrying out this mission, a proper policy must be formulated, funds guaranteed and leadership entrusted without delay, as a public–private partnership, to our younger generation—now in their thirties—as a lifetime mission in a renewed drive for nation-building.

Let me now explain the pattern of energy consumption in India. We have to look critically at the need for energy independence in different ways in its two major sectors: the generation and the transportation of electric power. At present, we have an installed capacity of about 180,000 MW (megawatts)* of electricity, which is 3 per cent of the world capacity.[20]

A forecast of our energy requirement by 2030—when our population may be 1.4 billion people—indicates that the demand from the power sector will increase from the existing 180,000 MW to about 400,000 MW. This comes to a growth rate of 5 per cent per annum.

In India, electric power is at present generated from four basic energy sources: fossil fuels such as oil, natural gas and coal; hydroelectricity; nuclear power; and the renewable energy sources—biofuels, solar, biomass, the wind and the oceans.

Fortunately for India, 89 per cent of the inputs for power generation today is available indigenously: coal, 55 per cent; hydroelectricity, 21 per cent; nuclear power, 3 per cent; and renewable, 11 per cent. The solar energy segment contributes just 0.2 per cent to our energy production.

It can be seen that only 11 per cent of electric power generation is dependent on oil and natural gas, most of which is imported at an enormous cost. Only 1 per cent of oil (about 2–3 million tons) is being used every year for producing electricity. However, power generation to the extent of 10 per cent is dependent on high-cost gas supplies. With the recent discoveries of oil and natural gas, this will come down,

---

* 1 megawatt = 1,000 kilowatts. When 1 kilowatt is consumed for 1 hour, it constitutes 1 kilowatt-hour (KW-h) of energy, which is also typically known as one unit of energy for metering purposes.

but only marginally. India is making efforts to access natural gas from other countries.

Let us discuss coal, another fossil fuel. Even though India has abundant quantities of coal, it is constrained by regional locations, a high ash content that affects the thermal efficiency of our power plants, besides which there are also environmental concerns. Thus, a movement towards energy independence would demand accelerated work in the production of energy from the coal sector through integrated gasification and a combined cycle route.

In 2030, the total energy requirement of the nation is expected to be 400,000 MW. By that time, if we were to follow the present route, the power generated from coal-based power plants would increase from the existing 80,000 MW to 200,000 MW. This would demand a significant build-up of thermal power stations and a large-scale expansion of coal fields, leading, naturally, to much higher levels of pollution.

The hydel capacity generated through normal water sources and by the interlinking of rivers is expected to contribute an additional 50,000 MW. Numerous large-scale solar energy farms with a capacity of hundreds of megawatts could together contribute around 55,000 MW. The nuclear power plants should have a target of 50,000 MW of power. At least 64,000 MW of electrical power should come from wind energy. The balance 51,000 MW has to be generated through conventional thermal plants, through coal and gas, and renewable sources of energy such as biomass, through burning municipal solid waste and solar thermal power. The most significant aspect, however, is that the power generated through renewable energy technologies has to be increased to 28 per cent from the present 5 per cent.

We also depend on crude oil to the extent of 192 million tons every year, of which about 83 per cent is imported and used almost entirely by the transportation sector.[21] The resources known at present and the future exploration of oil and gas may give mixed results. The import cost of oil and natural gas for 2009 was almost Rs 400,000 crore ($80 billion).[22] Petroleum prices are highly volatile and steadily rising, going as high as $147 per barrel in 2008.

Electricity production is the single largest source of man-made GHGs with a share of 25.9 per cent in the overall emission of CO_2. This is largely due to the fact that more than 41 per cent of overall world electricity[23] depends on coal-based plants, which are highly polluting. This trend is yet to start reversing with many countries still rapidly putting up coal-based plants.

RENEWABLE SOURCES FOR POWER GENERATION

Against this background, any move towards sustainability would be fruitless without altering our methods of generating electricity. One of the ways out of this problem is to focus on green and non-emission processes of electricity generation, at both the local and central levels. We shall discuss some of these ideas.

Solar energy

At sea level on a clear day, any part of the surface of the earth which is perpendicular to the sun's rays receives about 1,000 watts of solar energy per square metre. The total solar energy absorbed by the earth's atmosphere, the oceans and the land masses is approximately 3,850,000 exajoules (EJ) per year. Thus the solar energy absorbed by the earth in one hour is more than what the entire human population uses in one year.[24]

Such a huge source of energy holds tremendous possibilities for mankind. Solar energy, in particular, has the potential for massive application in the agricultural sector, where farmers need electricity exclusively in the daytime. This could be a primary demand-driver for solar energy. Shortages of water—both for drinking and farming operations—can be met by large-scale desalination of sea water and pumping it inland, using solar energy supplemented by biofuels wherever necessary.

Wind energy

Experts have estimated that the potential of wind energy in India is around 45,000 MW.[25] Intense research and development is required for reducing the investment per MW through improved designing and the application of newer technologies. The generation cost at present is between Rs 2.50 to Rs 3.50 per unit, depending on the site, and should be brought down to Re 1.00. Autonomous wind-generating units can be established in islands and remote areas if the site has wind potential. Feasibility studies have to be conducted to determine the economic size of wind energy plants, which can be used for lifting water from a 30-metre depth and can serve the needs of farmers with small holdings in a region with an average wind speed of 8 to 10 km per hour.

Such integrated actions will enable the realization of 64,000 MW of wind power against the present ceiling.

Energy in the transportation sector

The transportation sector in India is the fastest-growing consumer of energy. As discussed earlier, the import cost for India in 2009 of oil and natural gas was almost more than $80 billion, which is much more than the budget allocation for any other sector in the same period, as compared in Figure 6.11. Moreover, every time we import petroleum products we indirectly import GHGs, as each litre of petrol burnt produces about 2.7 kg of CO_2.

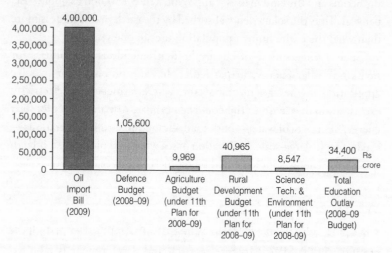

FIGURE **6.11:** Oil import budget versus other allocations for India (figures are in Rs crore; 1 crore = 10 million)

Source: Indian Budget 2008–09, Indian Economic Survey

This has to be carefully addressed as a large fraction of our net imports consists of only petroleum and hence, major fluctuations in the international prices of oil and gas have the potential to destabilize our balance of payments situation. This highlights the need to explore the next-generation alternative fuels which are economical, fast to produce and safe to use. In the future, India has to take immense strides to achieve energy independence, which means satisfying its energy requirements by a combination of unconventional energy sources like wind, solar, nuclear, tidal and geothermal. One very promising clean fuel is in the form of biodiesel from a variety of agricultural initiatives. This form of energy can be the answer to the energy needs of the 1.6 billion people worldwide who lack access to electricity, and about 2.5 billion people who rely on traditional biomass fuels to supply their energy needs.

> **PETROLEUM IMPORT AND ECONOMIES OF THE WORLD**
>
> Petroleum import is a major burden on most of the developing and underdeveloped economies of the world. Of the fifty poorest nations of the world, thirty-eight are net importers of petroleum, and out of these, twenty-five are totally dependent on imports to meet with their requirements. This means that their already-fragile economies are made even more vulnerable by fluctuations in oil prices. A United Nations report highlights the fact that some of these nations were spending six times more on fuel than they do on health. A sustainable development system—whether on a national or an international scale—cannot be realized without achieving energy independence.

Initially, biofuels were obtained from edible crops like corn and gave rise to apprehensions of biofuels creating a gap in the food supply. But now, there are a number of advanced 'second-generation' biofuels that are made from inedible plant material. What is most significant is the fact that, lately, many special energy crops are coming up which can be grown in poor soil conditions, with less water requirements. Hence, they will not enter into a 'resource competition' with the much-needed food crops.

USE OF BIOFUELS

In June 2006 we held the Conference on Biodiesel: Towards Energy Independence in Rashtrapati Nilayam, Hyderabad, in which various stakeholders—farmers, entrepreneurs, marketing agencies, researchers, policy-makers and NGOs—actively participated. The conference suggested the following actions to be taken up in mission mode:

1. Achieving the production of 60 million tons of biodiesel per annum by 2030 (this would be 20 per cent of the anticipated oil consumption in 2030).

2. As a first step towards reaching this target, drawing up a coordinated plan for achieving a 6-million-ton production by 2010, which would be 5 per cent of the present import of oil.

3. Improving, through research, the productivity of seed and extraction techniques and expanding the area under crops capable of yielding biodiesel in order to obtain 30 million tons of oil by 2020, and 60 million tons by 2030.

There are many kinds of biofuels.

Jatropha

One such type is the biodiesel obtained from Jatropha, whose success I have seen near a cluster of villages in Allahabad district in north India. The Jatropha plant, which can be grown in non-arable and fallow lands, has the unique property of transforming alkaline land into cultivable soil. Also, where land has to be reclaimed from the sea, it has been done in less than two years' time with the Jatropha plant. Another property, unique to this plant, is that after it is cultivated it takes only two years to bear fruit. When the seeds are crushed, the resulting oil from them can be processed to produce a high-quality diesel oil with less carbon content than fossil fuels. It is estimated that each hectare under Jatropha plantation can yield 2,500 plants and offset 20 tons of CO_2 per year for forty years. Moreover, there is the economic gain from the sale of the biodiesel.

The biggest advantage of Jatropha lies in the fact that it can be used to reclaim wastelands with little input and yet give good results. India has about 33 million hectares of wasteland allotted to tree plantation. This land can be gainfully used to produce biodiesel and create energy independence. Let us see how.

ECO-PRENEUR WITH A BIOFUEL MISSION

The country has been engaged in cultivating Jatropha for the last decade, but the real momentum for it began only in 2005. Based on the present estimates, as of June 2008, over 560,000 hectares are under Jatropha cultivation. Out of this, nearly 84,000 hectares are in the state of Chhattisgarh and 10,400 hectares in Allahabad (Uttar Pradesh), where the impetus has been provided by Dr D.N. Tiwari, a former member of the Planning Commission, Government of India. Under his leadership, an NGO has been working near Allahabad and has converted 735 hectares of wasteland (infertile, marginal and abandoned land) into Jatropha-producing land, capable of earning Rs 50,000 per hectare.

Originally, this land, which was alkaline in nature, was given to the farmers of Allahabad district. Many of the farmers started using the mud from the land for producing bricks. Others gave it up and went to the cities for work. When the special characteristics of Jatropha were realized through the work of Dr Tiwari, the villagers undertook its cultivation on that land. Since then, these villagers have realized energy independence through the use of biofuel. They do not use kerosene for cooking, or petrol and diesel for running their generators and vehicles. Not using kerosene has resulted in better health for women in rural areas. Jatropha is also planted on fertile land as a shield against heat for the banana plantations during summer.

Owing to the planting of Jatropha, the soil from being alkaline has become neutral, and it has reduced environmental pollution. Seeing the success of 735 farmers, over 10,000 farmers have taken to planting Jatropha in the Allahabad region. In addition to the upgrading of soil, the Jatropha plantation has enabled water retention and an enhancement of the water table in the neighbouring areas. Dr Tiwari and his team are now engaged in research and development to make Jatropha a more feasible source of biodiesel. This includes increasing the yield from seed to 35 per cent (oil content); the use of oil cakes; and using the residue as fertilizer and pesticide.

On an average, one hectare of land under Jatropha plantation gives about 5 tons of Jatropha seeds a year, from the third year after planting. This can generate about 0.75 to 2 tons of biodiesel depending on the conditions. If we take a rough average of about 1.4 tons per hectare, then the wastelands of the nation have the potential to generate more than 43 tons of diesel oil every year, which roughly matches our current demand. With improving technology, this quantity can only move upwards and biodiesel can be the mission for energy independence and economic returns. Can we employ our wastelands to meet our energy demands?

The government of Chhattisgarh in central India is actively pursuing a biodiesel mission based on Jatropha. The state has already planted 160,000 hectares with Jatropha and, with further cultivation it hopes to extract 2,000,000 tonnes of biodiesel annually. Interestingly, one of the users of biodiesel is the chief minister of the state himself.

Algae oil

One clean fuel is in the form of biodiesel from algae. Recently, I visited Eastern Kentucky University in the USA where they have set up the Center for Renewable and Alternative Fuel Technologies to carry out research for making algae fuel production commercially viable. Algae can be easily grown in low-lying, shallow areas near the sea. It is later used to extract algae oil which can act as a supplement to the conventional petroleum derivatives. Algae oil is far superior in terms of yield per hectare. Compared to conventional biofuel crops like corn—which generates about 172 litres per hectare—algae oil can generate more than a hundred times that yield. The challenge is to develop better technologies which can bring down the cost of generating algae oil. Also, the sequestration process of algae means that, for every 100 kg of algae produced, almost 180 kg of CO_2 is absorbed from the atmosphere, during which process about 22 litres of algae oil is also produced.[26] The residual algae mass can be used as an organic fertilizer that can economize the process.

At the international aerospace exhibition, ILA 2010 in Berlin, the world's first algae-oil-powered aircraft, a Diamond DA42 powered by two Austro Engine AE300, was exhibited. The test showed that with minor modifications to the engines, a biofuel-powered flight is possible. In fact, the reports further highlighted that due to the higher energy content in the algae oil, the fuel consumption was actually lower than that of the standard JET-A1 fuel. The amount of CO_2 released during the flight was equal to that amount of CO_2 absorbed by the algae during its growth—leading to a carbon-neutral flight. For the entire transport industry, this is indeed a promising development.[27]

Other biofuels

Biofuels are being generated from various sources around the world. They include a wide variety of edible and non-edible crops like maize, soyabean, potato, wheat, rice, sunflower, sugar beet, willow and sugar cane.

Coco biofuel is also one of the highest-yielding land-based varieties, with an output of up to 700 gallons per hectare. It is a promising option for the coastal and island areas and their PURA complexes.

REDUCING WASTE AND CONVERTING IT INTO WEALTH

Generating electricity through municipal waste

Residential and commercial areas contribute about 8 per cent to the total GHGs, a large part of which is due to untreated waste. Increased urbanization has further led to another serious problem—that of the accumulation of municipal solid waste. The efficient and environmentally clean disposal of this waste has always been a major technological challenge. Although it is a threat to the environment, mounting garbage is also a rich source of energy. The potential for converting this waste into usable energy—which would, at the same time, eliminate a major source of urban pollution—was realized by one of our innovative organizations, the Technology Information, Forecasting and Assessment Council (TIFAC) of the Department of Science and Technology. The department helped by developing a completely indigenous solution for the processing of waste into fuel which could, in turn, be used for generating electricity through mini plants.

Two entrepreneurs in Andhra Pradesh have adopted and refined the technology and established two independent plants in Hyderabad and Vijayawada, generating over 12 MW of electricity which is being supplied to the state grid. India needs thousands of mini power plants using municipal waste in small towns and urban areas. The banking sector, with the collaboration of small- and medium-sized enterprises, can provide the thrust for promoting such power plants in major municipalities.

Recently, I was introduced to the Plasma Enhanced Melter (PEM), which offers a revolutionary method of dealing with two pressing needs of today's society: disposal and treatment of waste, and clean sources of energy. The PEM can convert almost any kind of waste material into 'syngas'—composed of 40–45 per cent hydrogen and 30–35 per cent CO_2—that can be used to power a turbine generator. The PEM is superior to competing methods because of its economic and environmental advantages and its potential to be used across a wide range of applications.

Converting fly ash into a wealth-generator

The use of coal for generating power results in an increased quantum of fly ash production, which has reached about 100 million tons per year. All-out efforts are needed to utilize this fly ash, not only out of environmental considerations, but also to avoid using land for dumping it. It is reported that when fly ash is mixed with soil, the agricultural increase of grains is around 15 per cent, that of green vegetables 35 per cent, and root vegetables 50 per cent, without any risk of toxicity. Fly ash can become a wealth-generator by using it for agriculture and producing 'green' building materials. Its usage can also be an employment-generator and, at full utilization, it can provide a business volume of over Rs 4,000 crore ($8 billion) per year.

REDUCING EMISSION BY INTELLIGENT BUILDING

The emerging trends of intelligent and 'green' building entail the use of modern technology, smart materials and eco-friendly designs. The building environment and comfort conditions could be monitored and altered to suit specific requirements, using new processing tools like neural networks and fuzzy logic. The future holds a lot of promise as new concepts in nano technology, smart materials and design software will open fresh avenues and unleash an era of efficient and sustainable buildings.

DEVELOPMENT AND ENVIRONMENT: ARE THEY COMPATIBLE?

There have been significant discussions on how development can be compatible with non-linear developmental goals. Development is

GREEN BELT MOVEMENT

Professor Wangari Maathai is passionate about environment and biodiversity, and is actively contributing to the sustainable development and growth of planet Earth. Wangari Muta Maathai was born in Nyeri, Kenya, in 1940. She is the first woman in east and central Africa to earn a doctorate degree and to become chair of the Department of Veterinary Anatomy and an associate professor. Wangari Maathai was active in the National Council of Women of Kenya and was its chairperson from 1981 to 1987. While she was on the council, she introduced the idea of community-planting of trees and has continued to develop it into a broad-based, grass-roots organization whose main focus is the planting of trees by women's groups in order improve the quality of their lives and to conserve the environment. This led to the birth of the Green Belt Movement, through which Professor Maathai has evolved a movement with 600 community networks across Kenya and in twenty countries, resulting in the plantation of 40 million trees.

She and her movement have received numerous awards, most notably the 2004 Nobel Peace Prize.

Professor Maathai gives a new meaning to the important act of planting a tree by extending it to life itself, when she says, 'The planting of trees is the planting of ideas.' She highlights the qualities of patience and commitment in planning and realizing a future, which is what we learn when we plant trees and wait for them to yield fruit. India honoured her contribution to the furthering of the relationship between India and Kenya, and awarded her with the Jawaharlal Nehru Award for International Understanding (2005).

She concluded her Nobel Lecture in 2004 thus: 'As I conclude, I reflect on my childhood experience when I would visit a stream next to our home to fetch water for my mother. I would drink water straight from the stream . . . I saw thousands of tadpoles: black, energetic and wriggling through the clear water against the background of the brown earth. This is the world I inherited from my parents.'

closely linked with energy consumption, and increase in the demand for energy is both a prerequisite for development and a consequence of it. Mechanization is required for rapid development, which is an additional burden on energy needs. Moreover, development, in the end, leads to better incomes for people who then have more purchasing power and consequently, there is a further increase in the demand for energy. As long as our primary energy continues to be supplied largely by fossil fuels and their derivatives, development will come at the cost of the environment.

The new generation development models of PURA, with sustainability as a focus, have to evolve mitigating strategies to avoid falling into the vicious development–environmental degradation trap as shown in Figure 6.12. They have to use technology and innovation as a bridge between the environment and ecology.

AN ENVIRONMENTALLY CONSCIOUS SOCIETY

First and foremost, it is important to create a society which is sensitive and committed to the cause of environmental conservation and enhancement. For this purpose, it is necessary to make environment a part of the education system and engage the youth in the mission for conserving the environment. There are more than 550 million youths in the nation, and if each youth could be motivated to plant and nurture ten trees, then we could achieve a cumulative target of planting more than a billion trees for the nation.

It is also important to link environmental conservation with economic and social benefits. If people can be persuaded that their wealth and health are inseparably associated with their care of the environment, a significantly eco-conscious society can evolve. This is proved in the case of the Mudiali Fisherman's Cooperative Society that shows how successful and sustainable initiatives can be undertaken, which are also environmentally beneficial.

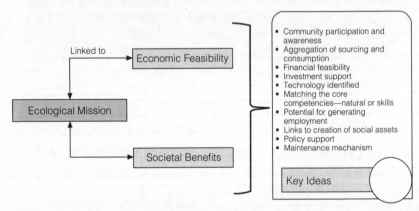

FIGURE 6.12: Building ecological missions

LINKING ECOLOGY AND ECONOMICS

The Mudiali Fisherman's Cooperative Society is located on about 80 hectares of wetlands leased from the Kolkata Port Trust (KPT), in a densely populated area about 10 km south-west of the heart of Kolkata (West Bengal).

The local people, largely fishermen, leased this unused marshy wetland, cleared it of not only natural weeds and debris, but also of anti-social elements, and used it for wastewater fisheries. In the process, it cleansed the water by natural means and converted the area into a nature park, which has become quite a popular attraction in the city of Kolkata.

The park accepts the domestic sewage and industrial waste-laden water as input, and employs a series of cleansing processes to remove the heavy metal from the wastewater. This water, laden with organic material, is used to breed quality fish and manufacture fish food, thereby significantly improving the income levels of the fishermen. The park, which sees thousands of visitors every day, is also an income-generating source for the women of the households that run small restaurants and other enterprises in the park.

While this experiment is relatively smaller, it is a great inspiration in the way a community, through its innovative spirit and entrepreneurship, has linked an environmental mission with economic goals, and demonstrated how wastewater can act as a significant source of income.

ECO-PRENEURS AND INNOVATION

The new generation of sustainable development can give rise to a new form of entrepreneurship that would be a bridge between environment and business—eco-preneurship, which would generate green jobs.

The PURA complexes—especially those located in regions with forest cover and unspoiled natural conditions—can find the possibility for such eco-preneurship opportunities. These may be run independently, such as an ecotourism centre; or they could be a part of an existing model like the value addition of green energy sources to enterprises, solar cookers to homes, water conservation and treatment measures; or the installation of bio-gasifiers in the animal husbandry sector to cut down on the methane emissions that are dangerous for livestock. Let us understand this with a real life example from Siwa in Egypt.

Siwa is an oasis in the western desert of Egypt (about 550 km from Cairo, the capital of the nation). It is an isolated settlement of Berbers

THE ECO-PRENEUR WITH A TREE MISSION

In May 2010, while in Gujarat, I met with Premjibhai who has made a remarkable contribution to tree-planting in certain areas of Gujarat. Starting his mission in 1987, he would set out every morning with a small spade in hand and a bagful of seeds, which he would plant on the bunds of fields. Later, at the age of fifty-five, he bought a motorcycle and added mobility to his mission. He began approaching individuals and institutions for voluntary service and motivated them to engage in ecological restoration. He also brought schoolchildren into the fold of the mission by contacting local schools. He travelled more than 140,000 km during his first five years on the motorcycle. Later, he and his team invented a unique petrol-driven mechanical blower that could be mounted on the back of a jeep and which could blow the seeds to a distance of 15 metres.

In 2009, using this invention, he 'broadcast' 10 tons of tamarind seeds in the villages around Ahmedabad. It is estimated that about 45 billion seeds have been distributed by him. Even if 0.25 per cent of them survived, Premjibhai is responsible for planting more than 10 million trees. This is equivalent to nearly 200 million kg of CO_2 removed every year which, in a typical carbon market, would be worth about Rs 20 crore per year.

and has a dense landscape of trees, natural springs and salt lakes. It is an important stopping place for caravans travelling in the desert from the Nile Valley towards Libya. It is home to the Oracle of Amon and it is also believed to have been visited by Alexander the Great. Thus, Siwa has significance as a trading point and also possesses heritage value. It has a small population of about 25,000 people and, given its core competencies, it had the potential for a sustainable development system with a multi-pronged integrated development focus.

It was only in 1977 that the Government of Egypt established some physical connectivity to the place by providing roads from other parts of Egypt. In 1998, Environmental Quality International (EQI), the Cairo-based environmental service and consulting firm, began to invest in the area of Siwa Oasis, by implementing the Siwa Sustainable Development Initiative (SSDI). This project was done in partnership with the Canadian International Development Agency (CIDA), which supported it under its initiative for generating employment, and the

International Finance Corporation (IFC), which provided the necessary financial assistance.

The objectives of the SSDI were to make Siwa Oasis a natural heritage site; to preserve and enhance the fragile ecosystem of the Oasis; to generate employment for the local people; and, at the same time, to establish a business utilizing the core competencies of the Siwa region. The initiatives chosen for implementation included temporary lodging facilities; women's artisanship development initiative; sustainable agriculture; renewable energy for the region; organic farming and other development projects for the community.

The materials used for constructing are entirely traditional, comprising palm beams and olive wood. In this way, it preserves the culture and the environment and also establishes an attraction value proposition for its customers. Under the renewable energy initiative, the SSDI is implementing twenty-five bio-digesters that will absorb methane, which has very high radiative force, and use the resulting gases as fuel. Another area that it is promoting is organic farming and the capacity-building of farmers in this domain, and helping them connect with high-value markets. The net effect of its efforts is that value-added jobs have been generated for local families. While earlier, few income-generating activities were available except during the three-month season of cultivating dates and olives, there is year-round income generation since the SSDI started its operations. Till date, UNDP reports, it has brought social and economic advantages to more than 600 families in the Siwa region. At the same time, it has preserved the ecology of the Oasis, leading to sustainable development.

A sustainable development model such as this has significant scope in desert regions where oasis-based PURAs can be established, which will protect the environment and the unique culture of the place. Eco-friendly income-generating activities can be extended to other areas as well. Take for example, the case of eco- and medical tourism. These combined with tourism promotion activities as a part of the PURA mission will have a three-fold impact. First, the enterprises will be created around the philosophy of protecting the environment and culture. Second, as a collateral benefit, the local areas will have access to quality health care.

Third, with the increase in enterprises, there will be quality jobs ranging from doctors and nurses to guides and hospitality, and jobs in other service sectors.[28]

BIODIVERSITY AS A GENERATOR OF WEALTH FOR THE NATION

India occupies only 2.4 per cent of the world's total land area, but its contribution to the world biodiversity is 8 per cent of the total number of species. India has ten distinct biodiversity zones with varying terrain, rainfall patterns and climatic conditions. Biogeographically, India is situated at the junction of three of the eight terrestrial eco-zones—the Afrotropic, the Indo-Malayan and the Palearctic. Hence, it has the characteristics of all of them. India is one of the twelve countries in the world with mega diversity. It has about 11.7 per cent of the world pisces (fish) and about 12.6 per cent of the world's bird species.[29]

India ranks seventh in the world as far as the number and variety of species in animal husbandry and agriculture are concerned. There are 166 types of crops and 320 types of wild and domesticated animals. More than 19 per cent of our land area is covered with forests, but the area of dense forests has to increase to 30 per cent.* This forest cover can be divided into sixteen major groups comprising 221 types. Our wetlands—while occupying only 3 per cent of the area—are home to about 320 species of birds and 150 species of amphibians. Similarly, we have a wide diversity of plants and animals in our mangroves, coral islands and islands. Indian deserts have more than 1,200 species of animals. The question we need to ask ourselves is, how can this biodiversity be preserved, enhanced and become a source of strength for the nation?

The biodiversity of the nation can be a core competency which can be used as the basis for undertaking a three-pronged mission of ecological conservation, societal empowerment and economic development.

Let us now analyse some of the areas where our biodiversity can help us attain this.

* 'Profile of Biodiversity in India', Bharatiar University

EXOTIC FOOD PRODUCTS

Mankind, during the long course of its history, has used approximately 80,000 edible plants, of which only about 150 have ever been cultivated on a large scale. Today, about ten to twenty species provide 80–90 per cent of the food requirements of the world. Most of the plants being used as a source of nutrition and food in the tribal areas of the nation are not known to the outside world. For example, such food varieties are *Ceropegia bulbosa* in central India; *Meliosma pinnata* in the northeast; *Cicer microphyllum* in Kashmir. Many of these may have special nutritional value or exotic flavours. Tapioca is a very important food item in the southern states. We should embark on a mission to collate and research the various forms of such traditional food varieties. This would help promote rural enterprises, which would be vertically integrated and could export processed and value-added traditional foods as exotic food products. This could be done through biodiversity-based PURAs.

One prominent initiative in this aspect was conducted by the Field Research Laboratory, Leh, of the Defence Research and Development Organization (DRDO). This laboratory experimented with a little-known Himalayan shrub, Seabuckthorn; botanical name, *Hippophae rhamnoides Linn.* The shrub bears berries only for around five weeks a year, which contain eight vitamins, twenty-four minerals and eighteen amino acids and antioxidants. The laboratory has made a pioneering contribution by converting them into packaged juice for commercial sales throughout the year. Thus, through the confluence of research, traditional national wealth and entrepreneurship, it is possible to create economic value based on biodiversity.

These examples can find replication in many regions of the nation.

TRADITIONAL MEDICINES

Today, as much as 70 per cent medicines are derived from natural products.[30] Around 20,000 plant species are believed to be used for medical purposes. In India too, 95 per cent of formulations in the traditional systems of Unani, Ayurveda and Siddha are plant-based.

India has 49,000 species of flowering and non-flowering plants, which represent 12 per cent of the world's flora.[31] There is a pressing need to carry out research to find the medicinal value of this wealth of biodiversity. I was reading about *Taxus baccata*, a sub-Himalayan tree which was once believed to be of no value. Recent research has proven it to be an effective medicine in certain types of cancer.

Similarly, when my team and I met with cancer researchers from the James Graham Brown Cancer Center of the University of Louisville, Kentucky, USA, in April 2010, we were pleasantly surprised to find that they are carrying out research on developing a low-cost vaccine for cervical cancer based on a protein obtained from tobacco leaves. The same tobacco—which is the commonest cause of cancer, especially of the lungs—can, through science, be a cure for another type of cancer. The traditional Indian *neem* tree has been used in various applications such as antiseptic, anti-fungal, anti-parasitic, anti-inflammatory, and even as an organic pesticide.

When I visited the Chitrakoot PURA in Madhya Pradesh in 2006, I saw a herbal garden with over 400 Ayurvedic herbs at its health centre called 'Arogyadham'. This herbal garden is vertically integrated with an Ayurvedic pharmacy laboratory called 'Rasshala'. The medicines formulated here are standardized and sold in the market and, at the same time, the local people are educated in the use of these medicines. Thus, biodiversity, when nurtured and researched, can be used simultaneously for economic advantage and societal welfare.

Through PURA's sustainable development systems we can consider establishing, across the nation, centres with global standards for researching and marketing biodiversity. These can capitalize on the floral wealth in the ten biodiversity zones of the nation and manage them in an efficient, entrepreneurial manner.

MEDICAL AND ECO-TOURISM

India's medical tourism sector is expected to experience an annual growth rate of 30 per cent, and the value of medical tourism in India, to go as high as $2 billion a year by 2012.[32] There are many advantages for medical tourists: reduced costs, availability of the latest medical technologies and a growing compliance with international quality standards.

With the tremendous medicinal wealth still untapped in our forests, the confluence of modern science and traditional methods, and the growing acceptance of alternative therapies, the mission can think of evolving eco-medico-centres which would give patients from all around the world a unique mixture of advanced Indian medicinal treatment in a green, clean environment and specially protected zones. These centres could be located in tribal areas and the tribal youths can be stakeholders in the mission, thereby offering them quality entrepreneurial opportunities that would not harm nature or the environment. Moreover, the availability of health-care facilities in remote regions would give social benefits to the local people and also spawn more green employment with the creation of markets for ecotourism and traditional forest products.

EVOLUTION OF ECO-FRIENDLY, ECONOMICALLY SOUND SYSTEMS

The Irula tribe is found in the states of south India, particularly the Kancheepuram district of Tamil Nadu. They used to live deep in the forests but deforestation has forced them to migrate to villages. These tribal people feed on forest products like fruits and tubers and also on small animals like lizards and jungle cats. For many generations, they have been traditionally engaged in catching and selling snakes and trading in skins and other parts of snakes. However, in 1976, the government banned snake skin trade, which put a stop to the primary economic activity of the Irula tribe.

However, the core skill of the Irulas—dexterity in catching snakes—could still be useful in an ecologically beneficial way. The Irulas, with the help of the leadership provided by Dr Romulus Whitaker—an American who has settled in India—went about setting up a cooperative society of their own. In 1978, two years after the ban was imposed on snake skin trade, they got approval to set up the Irula Snake Catchers' Industrial Cooperative Society with an initial membership of twenty-six participants.

The fundamental goal of this cooperative was to transform the traditional skill of the Irulas into an economically productive and environmentally sustainable activity, with the help of technology, investments and access to a new market. Thus the focus of the Irula Cooperative was on value addition to the skill of snake-catching by entering into the market of venom sales (primarily used for medicinal purposes), sale of live snakes, removal of rodents and gathering medicinal herbs and honey.

Every member of the cooperative society is provided with better and modern equipment for making snake-catching safer. Typically, each member can earn Rs 3,000 to Rs 4,000 per month by selling live snakes. To encourage environment-friendliness, the society pays Rs 100 to Rs 1,000 for different varieties of live snakes. Their venom is extracted, stored at $10\,^\circ$C, and then the snakes are let out again into the open forests. Thus, the process of snake-catching and venom extraction has been made sustainable.

With its profits, the cooperative society is able to pay a 14 per cent dividend to all its members against their share capital; make allowances

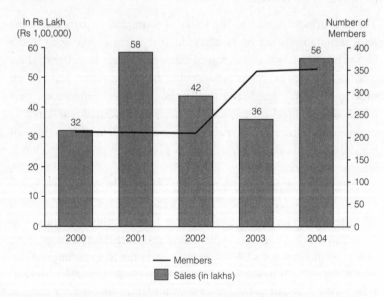

FIGURE **6.13**: Performance of the Irula Cooperative Society

Source: National Cooperative Union of India (NCUI) Publication

for education and medical expenses; give interest-free credit for housing; pay insurance against snake-biting incidents; and provide free transport for delivering live snakes.

By this innovative business technique, the Irulas have been able to continue using their traditional skills and, at the same time, earn greater economic profits and exercise ecological sustainability. In fact, since live snakes are a source of income, the members of the society have an incentive for protecting and preserving the dwindling snake population.

Although the Irula Snake Catchers' Industrial Cooperative Society is a small initiative, it sends out a great message for the building of ecologically sustainable development systems. Innovative thinking that adds fresh dimensions can be the meeting point of development, tradition and ecology.[33]

BUILDING VERTICALLY INTEGRATED ECO-PRENEURSHIP FOR CREATING VALUE

We have already stressed in the previous chapters the need to build vertical integration in development systems to make them robust and to augment the returns. It is equally applicable when we talk of the environmental sustainability of PURA's sustainable development models.

I have come to know about the United Nations Environment Programme's (UNEP) Rural Energy Enterprise Development (REED) Programme, which is offering incubation services to clean energy enterprises in Brazil, China and five African countries. Since its beginning in 2000, it has funded more than forty enterprises that are now returning capital to an investment fund, which is then reinvested in new enterprises. In addition to the returns on the investment, these enterprises have also led to economic and ecological development and the provision of environment-friendly activities to the poorest sections of society in the world. One such enterprise incubated and later analysed by REED was Tanzania's Biomass Energy Technology Limited (BETL), which works in collaboration with Tanga Cement Company Limited (TCCL).

BETL sources and supplies biomass and agricultural wastes which are used to provide heat for TCCL's cement kilns. This translates into a saving of 15 per cent on the 44,000 tons of heavy fuel oil that TCCL uses every year; a reduction in greenhouse emissions; and a generation of 42 per cent of profit margin for BETL, which delivers about 1,200 tons of biomass every month.

Lower down the sourcing chain, for sourcing its material, BETL employs women in urban areas who work individually and earn about US$60 (about Rs 3,000) per month by collecting forty bags of charcoal residue a day. Thus, the environment effort of these eco-preneurial women is aggregated by BETL, and by using technology is converted by TCCL into an economically feasible activity. Moreover, the benefits are flowing down to the bottom of the sourcing chain, which is an incentive. The investment is, of course, shared by TCCL and BETL, but most of the fixed equipment pre-existed in the form of cement kilns.[34] Let us further elaborate on linking environment and social assets.

LINKING ENVIRONMENT TO THE CREATION OF SOCIAL ASSETS

A unique biogas development model has emerged in Nepal out of its Biogas Support Programme, co-founded by the Government of Nepal, the Netherlands Development Organization (SNV), the German Development Bank (KfW), and financially assisted by the World Bank. It has installed over 120,000 biogas plants in Nepal that are providing 3 per cent of Nepal's households with low-pollution fuel for lighting and cooking. Moreover, since more than 70 per cent of these biogas plants are connected to human sanitation places, it has also led to improved hygiene conditions. This programme was the first of its kind to be set up under the Kyoto Protocol's clean development mechanism, and each of the biogas plants is equivalent to 4.6 tons of CO_2 per year, making it an economical and beneficial entity. This example was replicated in Vietnam for its animal husbandry section, where more than 25,000 biogas plants have been built, benefiting more than 100,000 people. The biogas is used as domestic fuel while the bio-slurry residue is useful as a crop fertilizer and fish food. Thus, innovative technology and aggregation of consumer demand have led to the development of a large-scale socio-eco enterprise model.[35]

India has more cattle than any other country, and these biogas models, which can directly yield benefits to local households, hold great potential

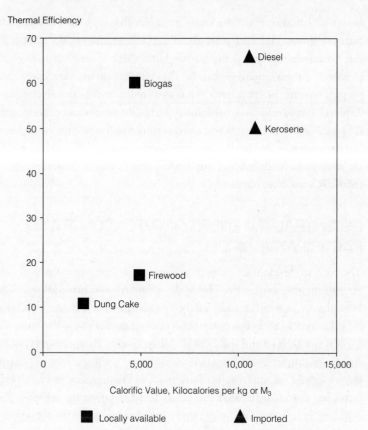

Thermal Efficiency

Calorific Value, Kilocalories per kg or M_3

■ Locally available   ▲ Imported

FIGURE 6.14: Thermal efficiency versus calorific value for different fuels

for implementation. Figure 6.14 shows different fuels with their relative qualities in the Indian context. It shows that biogas—which can be generated entirely domestically—is superior in its thermal efficiency* and also in its heat content (calorific value).[†]

Moreover, the biogas that is generated will be of great benefit for the women of the household. It will not only save them time—which they would have otherwise spent in collecting firewood—but also ensure them

---

* Thermal efficiency: Ratio of output work done or heat output to the input thermal energy.

[†] Calorific value: The calories or thermal units contained in one unit of a substance and released when the substance is burned.

better health as they will be saved from inhaling toxic fumes caused by burning firewood. Every year, about 200,000 women in the nation die due to respiratory problems arising largely out of unhealthy cooking practices. Biogas initiatives can be a saviour for them. Moreover, since biogas converts methane to CO_2 it is also environment-friendly, because, although both are GHGs, methane is thirty-one times more effective than CO_2 as a GHG. Let us now add another dimension where the community has been empowered in all aspects for energy independence. This will be the evolutionary, closed-loop sustainable system and an important lesson for PURA implementation.

DECENTRALIZED ENERGY INDEPENDENCE AND PARTICIPATIVE MODELS

The path to development can be realized as an integrated mission with environmental sustenance. In Mali, a remarkable innovation, using Jatropha to power the local energy needs, has been made by a local NGO called Mali-Folkecenter (MFC) Nyetaa, with support from the UNEP, the UNDP and the Global Village Energy Partnership (GVEP). An interesting idea was launched to convert the villages into an 'energy service centre' capitalizing on Jatropha oil. Planting unused land with Jatropha, the villagers used the oil as fuel for powering activities like grinding and battery-charging, and provided energy-intensive services to villages and even running motor cars. This successful idea is now implemented in the village of Garalo in southern Mali where 1,000 hectares of Jatropha plantation will run a 300 KW power plant that will provide 10,000 people with quality energy. The land for Jatropha cultivation is distributed across the fields of the villagers.[36] The project now aspires to provide clean, green, carbon-free electricity to 100,000 people in some of Mali's poorest and most isolated communities—across sixty-five villages in Sikasso and Koulikoro. The project will establish and maintain fifty Jatropha plantations and sixty-five energy service centres: fifteen solar-powered and fifty fuelled with Jatropha oil. To achieve this, 20 hectare plantations of Jatropha will be set up in each of the sixty-five villages and locals will be trained to work as technicians to manage the energy service centres. The Mali Folk Center project is an example of how clean green power can bring development to the remotest regions of the world. What is the cost of the project? About $2 million spread across five years, which is $4 per beneficiary per year.[37]

A similar initiative was carried out in the village of Ranidhera, Chhattisgarh, by a private company, Winrock International, in 2005. Ranidhera is a four-hour drive from Raipur, the capital of the state, and although high-tension wires run above the village, supplying power to the cities, Ranidhera itself was without power. It has a population of about

ENVIRONMENTAL MISSIONS IN PERIYAR PURA

Periyar PURA is operated by the Periyar Maniammai University, Thanjavur, in the state of Tamil Nadu. Large areas of the university campus itself have been planted with Jatropha trees, and the university is working on spreading the message of biodiesel and other green initiatives across the PURA region. The university operates many centres out of which three are directly linked with environment-friendly activity and research. They are:

1. Periyar Research Organization for Biotechnic and Ecosystem (PROBE)

This is an outreach wing started in the year 1996 with a prime focus on rural development through afforestation and biotechnology-based activities for the development of wastelands. PROBE has developed agro-modules in this locality for imparting hands-on training in various agro techniques in order to generate employment opportunities for the local people.

2. Periyar Centre for Environmental Energy Management (PCEM)

This centre was set up in collaboration with Cape Breton University (formerly, University College of Cape Breton), Nova Scotia, and the College of the North Atlantic (CNA), Newfoundland, Canada. It conducts training programmes in analysis and treatment of wastewater, remediation technologies and renewable energy technologies. The centre is currently involved in a project on the 'Generation of Power from Municipal Solid Waste in Thanjavur' in joint technical collaboration with RWTH University, Aachen, Germany.

3. Periyar Renewable Energy Training Institute (PRETI)

PRETI is a joint venture with the Ministry of Non-conventional Energy Sources (MNES), Government of India. It offers training courses in the use of renewable energy and energy conservation to suit the needs of various groups, for a duration of one day to one month. The courses are available to self-help women's groups, unemployed youths, panchayat presidents, council members, government officials, students, faculty members and others interested in using renewable energy.

600, largely tribal, people. The Ranidhera Jatropha mission began with garnering community participation in planting Jatropha on available barren land in the village and along the bunds between the fields. The village members planted and nurtured over 25,000 saplings. A unit of three special generators has been set up, which run on straight biodiesel (without processing) produced from the oil extracted from Jatropha seeds. This was established with the help of the British High Commission and the Indian government.

The idea behind this initiative was to create a local sustainable power project running on green fuel. A Village Energy Committee (VEC) consisting of the villagers was set up, and they were trained in basic operations for the running, accounting and administration of the power plant. Electricity is distributed using a wire network and street lights, too, have been installed. The VEC decides on the tariff and the timing for making the power available.

The villagers can deposit Jatropha seeds with the VEC and against it they can receive subsidies in the power tariffs. Under this small but interesting innovation, each of the 110 households has been given decentralized power points that supply four hours of power every evening, for two lights at about $1 per month. The VEC has managed to supply power without any unscheduled outages or breakdowns.[38]

The example of Ranidhera is being replicated across Chhattisgarh. Dr D.N. Tiwari, vice chairman of the State Planning Commission, told me that more than ninety villages were now green energy-independent, meaning that they are not only self-sufficient in their energy requirements, but that they are also green in the form of the energy they use. Biofuel has been a successful tool in achieving this ambition. In fact, there is an excess production of Jatropha seeds, which is sold in the external market and the benefits given back to the local people. Last year, 100,000 tons of Jatropha were sold as export, bringing in revenue for the rural population.

Thus, a local resource in the form of barren land has led to energy independence. The story of Garalo and Ranidhera highlights four key lessons. First, that technology can play a role in transforming barren land into a social asset in the form of power. Second, that a one-time initial investment—in this case, diesel generators properly constructed—can create self-sustaining systems. Third, that it is important to empower local people with skills and decision-making authority in order to ensure long-term usability, and to imbue them with a spirit of ownership in the asset being created. Fourth, that aggregation gives power to development systems, but it has to be linked to perceivable benefits. In the case of Ranidhera, the aggregation was done in the form of planting and cultivating Jatropha. Moreover, the benefit of participating in the cooperative venture is manifest in the form of four hours of power and subsidies in the power tariff for the seeds supplied.

THE KYOTO PROTOCOL AND CARBON CREDITS

The Kyoto Protocol, which came into force on 16 February 2005, was one of the first initiatives for following the course of eco-friendly development on a global scale. Under the Protocol, thirty-seven industrialized nations (called Annexure I countries) committed themselves to a reduction of the four greenhouse gases—carbon dioxide, methane, sulphur hexa-fluorides and nitrous oxide—and the two groups—hydrofluorocarbons and perfluorocarbons—produced. All the other member nations (including India) were to give a general commitment, though not as rigorous as the one given by the industrialized nations. The Annexure I countries agreed to reduce their collective emissions by 5.2 per cent from the 1990 level. The Kyoto Protocol was signed by 187 countries on November 2009. India is a member of the treaty while the United States has a status of 'signed but not intending to ratify' the treaty.

The Protocol allows for several 'flexible mechanisms', such as trading of emissions; the Clean Development Mechanism (CDM) and the Joint Implementation (JI), to allow Annexure I countries to meet with their GHG emission limitations by purchasing GHG emission reduction credits from elsewhere: through financial exchanges; projects that reduce emissions in non-Annexure I countries; from other Annexure I countries; or from Annexure I countries with excess allowance.

Under the International Emissions Trading (IET), countries were allowed to trade in the international carbon credit market to cover their shortfall in the stipulated amount of emission. Countries with surplus units were allowed to sell them to those which were exceeding their emission norms. This gave rise to a new 'carbon currency' called carbon credits. One carbon credit is equal to one ton (1,000 kg) of carbon dioxide or carbon dioxide-equivalent gases. While the concept of carbon credit trading is still nascent, even in a turbulent state, such platforms for the promotion of a clean environment are going to hold more significance with time.

Energy independence can be linked to economic and social goals and be driven in a decentralized manner by the community. This could be a model for national implementation. In fact, depending on local conditions, biofuels can be obtained from Jatropha, algae, sunflower and coconuts, which would help harness competency for energy-generation.

SIMPLIFIED ENVIRO-ECONOMIC MODELS

The Kyoto Protocol, which led to the introduction of carbon credits and carbon markets, was a remarkable initiative for incentivizing 'clean development' which is environmentally sustainable. It was the first time in a real sense that a benefit that could translate directly into monetary gain was associated with the effective implementation of initiatives for saving the planet and its environment.[39]

PURA's sustainable development system would have to draw on the emphasis laid by international initiatives on clean development, accept it readily and take it in a simpler form down to the rural level. For this, it is essential to develop derivative financial measures based on the carbon credit system. This will help in the promotion of environment-friendly initiatives and green enterprises to find space in the development profile of rural complexes. In a simple model, let us define the value of environmental contribution as a quantity P_E. This quantity can be directly associated to certain activities which lead to the emission or absorption of CO_2 and other GHGs emissions (weighted according to their heating power).

For example, let us suppose a tree that absorbs about 20 kg of CO_2 per year (net) is assigned a value of 1 P_E. In the same way, using the same measurement, different activities associated with an enterprise or initiative within the PURA complex can be assigned P_E equivalent values. Some of these are as depicted in Table 6.1. Hence, any initiative which saves 10 kg of coal from being burnt every day and replaces it with clean fuel is approximately worth +511 P_E annually. This value would be significant in deciding what kind of viability gap funding or priority lending should be given to a particular enterprise which is planned for setting up in the PURA complex.

TABLE **6.1**: Sample Tree Equivalent Table

Typical Activity	Approximate Absorption (+ive) or Emission (–ive)	Associated P_E Value
1 tree	+20 kg (annual)	+1 (annual)
Burning 10 litres of diesel	–27 kg	–1.35
Planting biofuel source equivalent to production of 10 litres of fuel supplement	+27 kg	+1.35
Burning 10 kg of coal	–28 kg	–1.40
Cultivating 1 hectare of Jatropha (average yield)	+20,000 kg (annual)	+1,000 (annual)

CONCLUSION

This chapter has highlighted how development and environment can move together and often in an interdependent way. We studied, through examples, how successfully environment-friendly initiatives have been carried out—often in conditions of poor access, low skills and low income—by activating the people and endowing them with knowledge and skill empowerment. These systems can lead to the creation of what is called the 'Rural Green-Collared Job' and a cadre of rural skilled and semi-skilled workers and entrepreneurs who use green practices to create wealth. The rural youths of the next generation in the PURA system will have to be trained to practise this green-collar outlook—with an amalgamation of technology, innovation, aggregation and resource management.

A COMMUNITY-DRIVEN SUSTAINABLE DEVELOPMENT SYSTEM

PURA AS A PRIVATE-PUBLIC-COMMUNITY PARTNERSHIP MODEL (PPCP)

Sustainable development systems for world prosperity and national development would have to be inherently community-centric. The community plays an important part in implementing a PURA initiative. PURA's vision is based on a public–private model with a crucial role for the community, which then evolves into a private–public–community partnership model.

The vital contribution of the community can be realized in many different areas. In fact, it would not be an overstatement to say that it is a necessary condition for the success of PURA at the ground level. The community's participation and ready acceptance of the transformation would lead to the application of knowledge; a bigger role for panchayati raj institutions; enterprise creation; cooperatives; collective environmental consciousness; and outcome-oriented approach to all the initiatives.

The economic, social and cultural transformation that PURA strives to bring about will be achieved only if an active part is taken at the household level, and the sharing of the benefits and the responsibilities is envisaged and implemented. The complete realization of a sustainable development model rests on the premise of empowering people and hence, the outcome of a development system—like PURA—would ultimately rest on the extent to which the system itself, in the long run, is managed by the community.

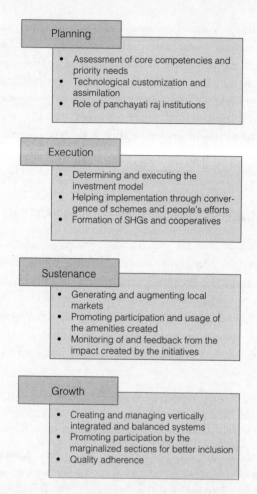

Planning
- Assessment of core competencies and priority needs
- Technological customization and assimilation
- Role of panchayati raj institutions

Execution
- Determining and executing the investment model
- Helping implementation through convergence of schemes and people's efforts
- Formation of SHGs and cooperatives

Sustenance
- Generating and augmenting local markets
- Promoting participation and usage of the amenities created
- Monitoring of and feedback from the impact created by the initiatives

Growth
- Creating and managing vertically integrated and balanced systems
- Promoting participation by the marginalized sections for better inclusion
- Quality adherence

FIGURE 7.1: Four-fold participation by the community

THE ROLE OF COMMUNITY ACTION

As already stated, the community has different roles to play which start from the planning stage itself, and keep increasing over time. Before implementing any development model, the community has to be made a partner in the process, beginning with an assessment of the strengths and weaknesses of the target area itself. This would generate the trust and the participation of the community members.

The community members would also play an important role in executing the initiatives and, through their empowerment, encourage local innovators and entrepreneurs. Similarly, the action of the community at large would activate markets, maintain quality standards, initiate social audits and promote vertically integrated and value-addition enterprises, which would help avoid inefficiency and losses.

The key to successful implementation is that the community has to be seen not just as mere consumers of the benefits realized, but also as knowledge-empowered implementers of the initiative itself.

WHAT MAKES COMMUNITY PARTICIPATION WORK?

One observation, commonly made across the world, is the lack of enthusiasm from the intended 'beneficiaries' of either a government scheme or a private initiative. Such apparent 'indifference' may exhibit itself through either a lack of interest or the total rejection of an initiative.

Such observations are counter-intuitive. It is difficult to find a reason why an impoverished person or group would not want to put in an

During my visit to Sandeshkhali in the Sunderban region of West Bengal, the village women described a problem occurring in multi-institution financing. Under a government-sponsored scheme for the development of rural enterprises, women entrepreneurs were to receive a 50 per cent seed fund through government grants and the rest through bank loans at subsidized rates. After their training, the women would eagerly apply for seed funds for starting their own business. The bank would sanction the loan almost immediately, thus starting an accumulation of the interest.

However, due to the lack of a single point for dispensing the funds, the other 50 per cent to be received through grants would take far more time—often years—stalling the entire enterprise. This was financially crippling for the aspiring entrepreneurs since they were being charged interest on the bank loan which, by itself, was insufficient to start the enterprise. By the time the grant fund arrived, the accumulated interest would make the enterprise unfeasible. Thus, due to unsynchronized efforts, lack of proper training and diffused investments, the community-enterprise creation model would end in failure and ruin the hopes of the women entrepreneurs.

effort to pull their family out of the vicious circle of poverty or the low-capacity trap.

In order to understand this social phenomenon, one needs to investigate more deeply into the main and common reasons that could make community participation work.

A NEED FOR PROPER INCENTIVES

One of the commonest reasons for a community not to participate is a lack of proper incentives, both long- and short-term. It is important to understand the need for both. The absence of clearly defined long-term incentives, that are sustainable, would eventually lead to an uncontrolled 'run' in the short term, ending in failure over a period of time or over a larger audience. At the same time, given the limited risk-taking ability—especially of the economically distressed—it is necessary for any initiative to yield gains in a short time frame. Hence, for any community to be truly motivated to participate, the incentive must be commensurate with the risks and the efforts.

MATCHING REWARD–NEED–EFFORT

Another crucial factor for ensuring participation is matching the real need with the stipulated reward, or the perceived effort with a surety of returns. At a time when most nations—especially India—are so disparate in economic and social conditions, it is important to develop a clear understanding of the needs of a local region before deciding on incentives and schemes.

ESTABLISHING PROPER COMMUNICATION

Even the best initiative may end up being rejected by the participants if there has been a lack of adequate communication with them. The dissonance between 'what was meant' and 'what was understood' may lead to an unintended, inaccurate

> 'The problem with communication . . . is the illusion that it has been accomplished.'
> —George Bernard Shaw

interpretation. Equally important is the credibility of the source from which the communication comes.

CREATING STREAMLINED AND SIMPLIFIED PROCEDURES

Even if the initiative is well understood and trusted, there can be a setback when it comes to taking the first step forward to participate. It has often been observed that processes are far too complicated and the overheads so taxing that it becomes impossible for a fresh rural entrepreneur or trainee to complete the necessary formalities. This problem has to be overcome by enlisting experienced and expert local development consultants who can absorb the non-essential 'process pains' and help the community members apply their efforts to the core activities.

OVERCOMING LACK OF TRUST

The initiatives are often met with doubt regarding the effectiveness and, sometimes, even the intention. The reason is largely the past history of performance and the perceptions which have been formed over the years. Thus, even a well-intentioned and meticulously planned initiative fails due to the lack of trust incurred by its predecessors. A feeling of trust needs to be carefully nurtured through continued communication and the proven examples of community-owned models.

~

BAREFOOT DOCTORS: THE COMMUNITY-OWNED NATIONAL HEALTH-CARE MOVEMENT IN CHINA

'Barefoot Doctors' is a part of the Chinese Rural Health Care Movement which began in the 1950s and gathered momentum after 1968. The barefoot doctors were essentially farmers who were given about six months of basic medical and paramedical training in a hospital and then sent back to their villages to farm and also to provide basic medical care to the people. Their training focused largely on preventive health care, prevention of epidemics and diseases specifically pertaining to their region.

Each barefoot doctor was provided with a set of forty to fifty Western and Chinese medicines for dispensing as required. They provided for immunizations, childbirth and improvement of sanitation. Each barefoot doctor had the option of training local youths as village health aides, who would work on a specific type of disease. Typically, a barefoot doctor would dedicate about half of his or her time to agriculture and the other half in providing health care.

The barefoot doctors were paid out of a collective welfare fund from the local farmers' contributions. They earned about half as much as a fully trained doctor. They provided health care to the people at the grass-roots level. They would attend to about fifteen patients a day, and make 150 home visits a month. In about 75–90 per cent of the cases, the problems would be solved locally, and for the remaining, the patients would be referred to a hospital.

This mission, under a rural cooperative medical system, at its peak, covered about 90 per cent of China's villages. The barefoot doctors were at the forefront of the Chinese rural health-care mission till the 1980s. The impact of this movement was reflected in the health-care system of the nation and set the foundation for a healthy and economically progressive society.

During the era of the barefoot doctors, the average life expectancy in China almost doubled, from 35 years in 1965 to 68.9 in the early 1980s. The IMR fell, from 200 at the start of 1950, to below 30 per 1,000 live births in the early 1980s.

The success of the barefoot doctors in the health-care system is attributed largely to the fact that the movement was essentially a community-owned, community-trained and community-benefiting model. The fact that they were essentially farmers made them more approachable and fostered a feeling of trust. Since they lived in the same village, they were also available for consultation 24x7 and, therefore, were further relied on by the people.

Post-1980s, the barefoot doctors were permitted to take a medical licensing examination and, subject to it, they were reorganized as village doctors, health-care workers and licensed assistant doctors. Today, China's villages have more than 880,000 rural doctors, about 110,000 licensed assistant doctors and 50,000 health workers.

~

CHILD JOURNALISTS: CREATING A VOICE FOR THE COMMUNITY

On the last Sunday of each month, an enthusiastic editorial team of twelve assembles in the Sohagpur Block of Hoshangabad district in central India to carefully select articles submitted by their journalists for their monthly newspaper which goes to five out of the total seven blocks in the district. The unique feature is that the editorial team and the journalists are all children, between the ages of eleven to fifteen, attending government schools in about twenty-five villages. The journalist team of 250 children—out of whom 130 are girls—publish a local newspaper, *Bacchon ki Pahel* (Children's Initiative), which caters to the local rural readers. It is an initiative started in 2006 and run by Dalit Sangh, an NGO, and UNICEF.

The child journalists of *Bacchon ki Pahel* raise issues of significance concerning the local and surrounding areas. They interview government officials and village council members, analyse local issues and put forth demands for better development.

Typical news articles include observations on the condition of schools and the Mid-day Meal Scheme; researched work on the potential dangers of chewing tobacco or smoking and other health issues; the preservation of local languages; and even analyses on modern issues of global significance, such as genetically modified foods and their impact. The newspaper is almost totally brought out by the children who have been trained in the skills of writing and journalism. Dr Gopal Narayan Aavte, editor of the newspaper, commented: '. . . children show immense enthusiasm in bringing out the truth for the community. Ninety-five per cent of the work is entirely managed by the children's group, most of them coming from underprivileged communities. They are sharp in their questions and accurate in their reporting.'

The newspaper acts as a local voice through the literary work of the children; it displays the visible and immediate impact of education especially on the girl child; and it is an effective tool for assessing the literary skills being developed in the government schools in rural areas. With limited investment, the number of journalists and the coverage have increased exponentially, and a wider array of topics is now being covered.

When I was in Bhopal, I met with some of the young reporters on 14 November 2010 at Raj Bhavan, where I interacted with them and listened to their ideas and issues. They showed me many different editions of the newspaper, which were all unique. In each edition, these young, dynamic and fearless reporters touch upon issues of local concern; the state of the schools and the village community areas; they highlight the latest trends in technology and science; and they interview local officials, including the district magistrate, about the progress on local developmental activities. One unique column that they carry in each edition is on the preservation of traditional tribal words. The October 2010 edition they brought with them had a list of words from vanishing tribal languages.

During my interaction with them, they asked me many questions, one of which I would like to share. One fourteen-year-old reporter, Gopal, asked me, 'Mr Kalam, you have told us about the right to free and compulsory education and how it would bring access to education to all the children. What I want to ask is, how can a child from a nomadic community, which keeps moving from one place to another, pursue education in a traditional school?' It was a brilliant question to which I replied that the need of the hour was to evolve mobile schools where education could follow the child. I would like all of you—IT experts and government officials—to evolve a strategy for addressing the problem highlighted by the young reporter Gopal.

This small but effective initiative is highly commendable and replicable, and it can generate a tremendous Knowledge Connectivity, using the local student strength. The model of *Bacchon ki Pahel* can go even beyond a printed newspaper. Once Electronic Connectivity reaches the villages, the same model can be extended over the Internet and community radios to reach a wider audience. It can also extend itself into a forum for ideas and information exchange across villages and regions.

> The ignited mind of the youth is the most powerful resource,
> On the Earth, above the Earth and under the Earth.

Based on interviews conducted with the young reporters and the publication team in Bhopal.

~

NURTURING LEADERSHIP

We have already discussed the role of a leader in PURA. In all the successful cases we have seen, there has been a clearly defined and accountable chain of command running through them.

NANAJI DESHMUKH
CHITRAKOOT PURA

Nanaji Deshmukh (1916–2010) was a social reformer who brought smiles on the faces of hundreds of thousands of people in Chitrakoot. He was deeply inspired by Lokmanya Tilak, the great freedom fighter, whose nationalist ideology fired Nanaji to take up social service in the rural sector as a lifetime mission. Nanaji's love of education and knowledge was reflected in his creation of India's first Shishu Mandir (Children's School) in 1950. After spending two months with Vinoba Bhave, a contemporary of Mahatma Gandhi's, Nanaji was inspired by the success and appeal of the agricultural land reform movement started by Vinoba Bhave, and he actively participated in it.

For Nanaji, the development of the people of the Chitrakoot villages was his aim and objective. In 1969, he established the Deendayal Research Institute for organized rural development in the region, and he devoted his entire time to it. He also set up Mahatma Gandhi Chitrakoot Gramoday Vishwavidyalaya, India's first rural university, and was its first chancellor.

Nanaji understood the importance of actively involving the community in order to achieve a successfully implemented development model. Hence, the Chitrakoot PURA evolved a number of unique models to encourage people's participation. These included 'Samaj Shilpi Dampati' (discussed later in this chapter), public participative appraisal in planning and execution, and an active attempt to build a society that is conflict-free and harmonious.

Without a person who is trusted by the community to champion its cause, it is difficult to find support over a sustained period of time. The need for guidance is felt most acutely when the target is to achieve a transformation, when it is a matter of not only managing success but also managing failures and facing difficult situations.

Nurturing creative leadership—on the principle of innovative management and a belief in working and succeeding with integrity—is essential for a thriving sustainable development system.

CREATING A SUPPORTING AND SUPPLEMENTARY ECOSYSTEM

True development can be achieved only when it is multi-pronged. In most cases, the problems are due to the confluence of multiple factors, some of which may be completely independent of each other. Alleviating a single factor would achieve little in solving the issues and hence the need for an integrated approach for solving the problem, where the outcome—rather than the outlay—is the goal.

The same would be the case in an incentive-based approach for engaging the local community. For example, creating a finance structure for an entrepreneurial activity—say, that of garment finishing—would be of little benefit unless accompanied by programmes for training and marketing the final product and vice versa. Such vertical integration at the micro level is an essential step towards the creation of a supporting ecosystem which would motivate community participation.

Third, ecosystems need to be designed according to the local demographics, culture, geography and economy. Every area has certain key stress points that demand priority and would be critical success issues when inviting large-scale participation.

~

MAGARPATTA: CREATING AN ECOSYSTEM FOR COMMUNITY-BASED ACTION

Magarpatta, a 430-acre area on the outskirts of Pune in the state of Maharashtra, is an example of how community-based action can achieve collective benefits and an advantageous situation for all. The Magarpatta land was owned by the Magar clan, a community of about

123 villagers, and came under the authority of the Pune Municipal Corporation. In the 1990s, seeing urbanization expanding and reaching their village, the Magars organized themselves and set up the Magarpatta Township Development and Construction Company, and prepared a city development plan for the area. The Magar farmers pooled their land and were made shareholders in the company in proportion to the value of their land. This plan was approved in 2000.

Today, the Magarpatta city is home to over 35,000 residents and a working population of 65,000. The city has developed a Cybercity Magarpatta IT Park which has attracted many multinational companies. Direct employment is being provided to over 60,000 professionals and indirect to an additional 20,000. The city of Magarpatta has been designed in an eco-friendly manner. About one-third of the area is reserved for parks, one of which is Aditi Park, the largest in Pune. The city is designed in such a way that residents can walk to their offices, schools or markets. The 170 tons of biodegradable waste from the city is used for vermiculture and compost. With about 7,000 solar energy collectors installed, there is a saving of about 15 million units of electricity every year. It is the first settlement in India to receive the ISO 9001 certification.

Magarpatta is the only such project in India where farmers have come together to convert their land into an enterprise and become shareholders in the company. They agreed to use a part of the value of their land to buy flats and shops in the township, thereby ensuring a fixed flow of income and enterprise opportunities. They are full partners in the success story of Magarpatta. Over 250 entrepreneurs have emerged from the Magar community in non-agricultural ventures due to the support of the community company, which has now evolved into a project execution company and is developing other similar projects.

This community-owned company is an excellent example of the need to involve the community as a shareholder and partner in development. As we realize sustainable development models and create economic entities in the rural region, there needs to be a mechanism which can ensure a win-win situation for both the entrepreneurs and the local community, which would, in turn, ensure smooth local cooperation in setting up the unit, avoiding delays. Magarpatta is a shining example of how such a model can be realized on the ground level.

This shareholding model can be adopted in various scenarios across a wide spectrum of initiatives. A hybrid ownership model based on enterprise creation, with inherent characteristics to convert stakeholders into shareholders, would be required. Three key stakeholders and contributors come in the form of labour, land and investment as shown in the table below.

TABLE 7.1: Stakeholders in a community-owned company

Stakeholder	Description	Focus
Labour	Knowledge, skilled and semi-skilled members from the community who can be involved in the setting up and operations.	This shareholder would work primarily towards protection of the interests of the local community and would also benefit from additional jobs locally via skill augmentation.
Land	This shareholder would be an individual or organization which could contribute in the form of land or other physical assets.	The inclusion of this shareholder would ensure market-linked returns to villagers who contribute their land and equity in profit-sharing. This would ensure added trust in the developmental process.
Investment	What is implied here is the role of the investor in the financial capital for good equipment and knowledge, for better processes and market linkages for profitable sales. This may come in the form of private-sector participants. The government can also be a significant enterprise-based investor among others.	The third leg of the enterprise would bring in better technology to assist the interests of the other two stakeholders and to maximize profits. It would also be the investor who brings in better equipment and opens up more markets, with the goal of improving the bottom line.

~

THE ROLE OF VISION IN GENERATING PARTICIPATION

For inviting community participation, it is important to have clearly set, objective goals for both the short and the long term. These should form the vision for a mission towards prosperity, welfare and inclusive empowerment through knowledge, employment and skill-building. The vision should have the power to spark off a dream in the community of a future with well-planned economic prosperity and of a congenial society with quality health care and education for all. The collective vision of the community should be translatable to the aspirations of the individual and the household.

ACHIEVING COMMUNITY PARTICIPATION

Getting the active involvement of the community is of paramount importance and often a key defining factor, which would be the dividing line between failure and success. As we have discussed earlier with examples, there can be numerous innovative models by which the community can be involved as an active participant in the realization of a sustainable development model. Let us further discuss two models—the Chitrakoot and the Loni PURA—which are comprehensive systems for 'people participation in development missions'.

SAMAJ SHILPI DAMPATI

Samaj Shilpi Dampati of the Chitrakoot PURA is a classic example of generating community partnership through persuasion and perseverance and in a bottom-up approach. This programme has been run by the Deendayal Research Institute (DRI) under the leadership of Nanaji Deshmukh. The DRI's vision statement observes:

> The commitment of the Deendayal Research Institute (DRI) to the implementation of the development process from the bottom to the top, formulated at the village level, necessitated sustained interaction with the villagers themselves to understand their problems and motivate them to change. However, after decades of exploitation, villagers are extremely wary of the intentions of outsiders who come to their villages claiming to want to help them.

In order to win the trust of the local people, to persuade them to take part in the process of planning and to accept the initiatives being undertaken, DRI started a unique brand of respected village-level community workers, called the Samaj Shilpi Dampati (SSDs).

An SSD is not an individual, but a couple, often newly married, their age ranging between twenty-five and thirty-five years. It is mandatory for both the spouses to be educated at least to the graduate level, and they should have a deep commitment towards community service. The duration of an SSD programme is five years, and each SSD couple works for a cluster of five villages.

The career of a typical Samaj Shilpi Dampati, or social sculptor couple, starts with a week-long orientation and training camp organized by the DRI. Here, the soon-to-be-deployed couples are exposed to a variety of the best practices relating to a wide range of issues such as technology, various procedures, value systems and motivation. The newly recruited SSDs are then shown around the Krishi Vigyan Kendras (KVKs) run by the DRI to let them have a first-hand experience of the impact of science on the agro sector. These camps also support horizontal learning between the SSDs, as well as between the older and experienced couples and the freshly recruited ones.

After the orientation and training camp, the SSDs are taken back to the villages where they normally reside. They live in the village primary school or with a family that is supportive to the cause of social development. Their work starts with a focus on the children, their health and education. This gradually generates good mutual trust between the SSDs and the local population. As the confidence builds up, the SSDs switch to a more diverse spectrum of activities involving greater community participation, and aimed towards achieving a common objective of a self-reliant village. This includes:

- Income-generating activities and promotion of enterprises
- Environmental consciousness and helping keep the village green and clean
- Improvement in farm practices and technologies
- Education for various age groups
- Increasing social consciousness and harmony through resolution of conflicts by mutual consent
- Acting as a nodal point for DRI interventions in the village group

SSDs are highly respected in the villages and many of their daily needs are taken care of collectively by the villagers. Besides that, each couple is paid about Rs 3,000–3,500 per month as a stipend. There are regular training camps held for the SSDs across the Chitrakoot region on various subjects of social relevance. Once the five-year period is

TABLE **7.2:** Samaj Shilpi Dampatis

Intervention	Effect
SSDs are graduates	They generally operate in remote areas with hardly any highly educated individual living in the village, and so, their education gets them the necessary initial acceptance and respect.
They are a couple	This is an important aspect from many angles. First, the role of the woman in an SSD is of paramount importance. She soon becomes an inspiration to the female population who learn from her the importance of educating girls. Seeing her active participation, they are motivated to do the same in their homes and activities. Second, the fact that both the spouses are recruited as one unit leads to stability in the SSD recruitment. A couple's consistency in service over a sustained period of time is important, as frequent changes would entail re-energizing the bonds already formed with the villagers.
They live in the village where they work	Since they live in the village, they are better aware of the potential and the problems of the village and its people. They are more trusted and their services are available to the villagers at all times. They also get to know the villagers individually, so they are able to spot the latent talent, which can benefit later from the other programmes (like enterprise development) conducted by the Chitrakoot PURA.
Post-SSD career path	The SSD couple, after completing their five-year tenure, are generally given the opportunity to join DRI as employees in its various initiatives. This acts as a motivation for them at the time of being recruited. The absorption also helps in facilitating transfer of knowledge as the older SSDs are able to train and share experiences with the fresh SSD couples.

over, the SSD couple are often absorbed as regular employees in the DRI operations.

DRI firmly believes that 'the success of the self-reliance campaign is directly linked to the success of the Samaj Shilpi Dampati'.

FEMALE HEALTH VOLUNTEERS AT LONI

In 2007, 235 female health volunteers (FHVs) of the Loni PURA, largely drawn from the local tribal community, were trained to operate as entrepreneurs in the health services extension.[1] Each of the FHVs, besides the customized training, is given a first-aid box, a disposable delivery kit and a water-testing (Othotone testing) kit. One of the primary functions of an FHV is to follow up cases in need of medical aid, especially those associated with childbirth. They coordinate the attendance of patients when the mobile clinics arrive in the village.

The FHVs are also involved in maintaining hygiene in their villages. The village-level FHVs are trained and equipped with an Othotone (OT) test for monitoring the purity of water from different sources every month. As many as 11,270 water samples have been tested by these trained women during 2007, only two-thirds of which were found to be fit for drinking.[2] The water-testing results are submitted to and endorsed by the local gram panchayats before presenting the project for water purification measures using a variety of locally available resources like drumsticks. Involving the FHVs in water-testing led to discussions between the village women and the gram sabhas regarding the merits and the effect of the system. The result is that many villages now respect the gram panchayat's directives to be more alert about the disinfection procedures for water sources.

With part-time employment and a well-paid job, the FHVs are able to conduct themselves as respected members of the family and society, and this has led to women's empowerment at all levels. With the added confidence, many of the FHVs are now involved in a host of entrepreneurial activities, thanks to the training and technology provided by the Loni PURA and, in particular, the Pravara Medical Trust. This includes a water purification system using drumstick seeds, harvesting Spirulina in small home reservoirs and vermicomposting, besides being absorbed in the Integrated Child Development Scheme (ICDS) and the National Rural Health Mission (NHRM) owing to their increased skill sets.

INVOLVING THE YOUTH FORCE

The Periyar PURA follows a participative model for generating community support and ownership for the initiatives being undertaken. Periyar Maniammai University runs many programmes pertaining to the development domain including masters in social work (MSW), MPhil and PhD in social work and certificate courses in organic farming, landscaping, herbal physiotherapy and agricultural marketing. These certificate programmes are providing technological leaders to the local community to become a part of the PURA mission.

Students of MSW and volunteers for the National Service Scheme (NSS) are given the responsibility of mentoring the rural families in the PURA region. Five families are allotted to each student and, throughout their academic tenure, as part of their curricular or co-curricular activities, they are required to guide the families and track their progress.[3] This includes imparting to them knowledge of the technological processes available, training options, basic knowledge about education and health care and ridding their minds of superstitions. The students track their allotted families and document their progress, thereby helping to create an unbiased evaluation and monitoring system for the Periyar PURA. This programme of interaction fosters a sense of mutual respect and understanding and gives the students a hands-on, grass-roots level understanding of rural life, which is useful for expanding their vision of life. It also helps in their future professional life in the field of their choice.

About 40 per cent colleges imparting higher education are based in rural regions,[4] and many in urban areas, too, are located on the outskirts of cities. It would be advantageous for all these colleges to follow this student-to-community model of participative learning and mentoring. With more than 2,300,000 college students graduating every year,[5] and with more than 13,000 colleges,[6] there would be about 15–20 million higher education students who are pursuing education in different courses across the nation. There is an opportunity for knowledge empowerment, technology support and mentoring over 50 million families through these graduates.

THE COMMUNITY AS AN ECONOMIC ENGINE— COOPERATIVES

Amul,* Mother Dairy† and Lijjat Papad# are national brands well known to almost every Indian household for decades. They all share a unique business model—that of cooperatives. Cooperatives are defined[7] 'as autonomous associations of persons united voluntarily to meet their common economic, social and cultural needs and aspirations, through jointly owned and democratically controlled enterprises'.

FACTS ABOUT COOPERATIVES IN INDIA

- 97 per cent villages are covered by cooperatives.
- Rs 3,485 billion deposits in cooperatives (2007–08)
- 54 per cent is the share of cooperatives in the handloom industry.
- 46.6 per cent of the total production of sugar is through cooperative models.
- 45 per cent is the share of cooperatives in ice-cream manufacture.
- 33.5 per cent of wheat procurement is managed by cooperatives.
- 20.3 per cent of all retail fair price shops (rural and urban) are managed by cooperatives, often by women.
- 1.22 million is the number of people directly employed, generated by cooperatives.
- 15.47 million is the number of people with self-employment generated by cooperatives.

* Amul is managed by the Gujarat Cooperative Milk Marketing Federation Limited (GCMMF) and was formed in 1946. It is the world's largest pouched milk brand with revenues over $1.7 billion (2009–10).

† Mother Dairy was formed in 1974 and includes the brands Mother Dairy, Safal and Dhara. It has about two-thirds market share in the National Capital Region of India.

It is a women's cooperative whose full name is Shri Mahila Griha Udyog Lijjat Papad. It was started in 1959, when six women got together to make papad (papadum) on the terrace of their homes, with an initial capital of merely Rs 80 (less than $2). The cooperative today employs over 40,000 women and has a turnover of over Rs 650 crore and about 5 per cent of that from exports.

In a rural context, it is an organization, generally for profit, owned and managed by a group of farmers or villagers, working towards mutual benefit in both the economic and social development sense.

The first successful cooperative was founded in 1844 as the Rochdale Society of Equitable Pioneers by a group of twenty-eight weavers and artisans in Rochdale, England.[8] They formed the society to open their own store, selling food items they could not afford to buy. The cooperative movement in India was formally introduced with the promulgation of the first Cooperative Societies Act in 1904.*

The cooperative movement in India has met with mixed success. In the more successful cases, with the proper technological know-how and leadership, they have expanded well beyond their core economic activity and diversified organically into a variety of need-based initiatives including health care, banking and education. For example, both the Warana PURA and the Loni PURA originated in a cooperative movement by sugar farmers in the 1950s. They then evolved into creating many other socio-economic assets to reach their current form.

The cooperatives are an excellent mechanism for community-owned and community-oriented action at the grass-roots level. They have the inherent characteristic of generating support from the local area, largely due to their ownership pattern. However, even with more than 549,000[9] cooperatives, the successful ones—howsoever extraordinary their stories— are few in number. The challenge lies in finding ways of implementing the lessons of success across cooperatives and expanding their entrepreneurial reach in terms of the economic and social transformation that they are capable of bringing about in the rural regions.

---

* This was enacted to enable the formation of 'agricultural credit cooperatives'. It was later repealed by the 1912 Cooperative Societies Act, which provided for the formation of cooperative societies other than for credit.

8

ENTERPRISE CREATION LEADING TO EMPOWERMENT

PURA AS AN ENTERPRISE MODEL

Building avenues for quality employment for people in the PURA complex is one of the fundamental pillars of the PURA vision. The most effective path towards this goal is the creation of 'job generators' or entrepreneurs who are sustainable and societally beneficial. For the realization of a global sustainable system, the solution is to focus on empowerment through entrepreneurship.

It must be understood that sustained development can be realized only through empowerment and employment generation. While subsidies and 'freebies' of all kinds—from food and shelter to even television sets—can generate temporary relief and a sense of opulence, real national growth and people empowerment require efforts which are more deeply thought out and with far-reaching consequences. The PURA system strives for a long-term and permanent solution to perennial problems, and one of the best ways to achieve this is by generating enterprises at the local level, both in products and services.

Creating entrepreneurs has a multiplier effect on the economy and employment in the rural complex. For example, the creation of every one micro entrepreneur would typically lead to the opening up of about five wage employments, with around 20–30 per cent returns on a well-planned business. Similarly, a well-planned small enterprise may lead to forty to fifty wage employments of different kinds.

Each PURA, on an average, is a business proposition of about Rs 1 billion with public, private and community partnerships over a project period of about five years. Already, the Central government and certain states like Chhattisgarh, Karnataka and Kerala have taken up PURA as a programme for implementation. The government and a few private initiatives have established working PURAs in Tamil Nadu, Maharashtra, Madhya Pradesh and Andhra Pradesh, which we have studied in the previous chapters. PURA offers an entrepreneurial opportunity which generates social transformation and is financially feasible. Entrepreneurs have to link together all the angles—financing, introducing innovation and technology, establishing brands and marketing, employing the best operational practices and developing local competencies. By achieving this, they will not only establish a social enterprise of excellence and impact but also change the way thousands of people live their lives.

The Ministry of Micro, Small and Medium Enterprises (MSME) has reported 26 million enterprises which employ close to 5.9 million people. This means that, on an average, the MSME enterprises are employing only 2.2 persons per enterprise.[1] This scenario highlights the need for better planning and the creation of an environment which is enterprise-friendly and cooperative. Let us explore how to realize this scenario.

UNIQUE OPPORTUNITIES AND CHALLENGES FOR CREATING RURAL ENTERPRISES

With more than 45 per cent of the total MSME sector concentrated in the countryside,[2] the scope for enterprises is bright and needs to be systematically approached. The Indian hinterland is rightly placed as regards time and opportunity for attracting entrepreneurs from both within and outside the country. The cost of setting up a business is far lower in rural areas—the cost of land compared to a metro city would be in the ratio of 1:200, rail and power lines to the grid, and they have a pool of young workers. Information and communication technology (ICT) in the form of mobiles and the Internet is now reaching them with a concentration of 21 per cent of mobile connections, with the government targeting more than 200 million mobile phones in the rural and interior regions of the nation.

The government and the banks are also supportive with priority lending to certain provincial ventures especially those in the domain of agro-processing and clean energy. Rural India offers a clean, green environment devoid of the regular traffic delays of the cities. Moreover, an immense amount of potential, natural talent, human skills and local competencies lies untapped while the primary urban areas are getting too saturated.

TAPPING HORIZONTAL MARKETS

The enterprise networks of the PURA complex have to look at two kinds of markets when positioning their products or services. Of course, it is essential to tap the high-value export and urban markets that fetch higher prices but, at the same time, it is equally essential to concentrate on satisfying the local demand, which has to be met in terms of services, knowledge or products. Horizontal markets may also exist in close proximity within the PURA complexes where they can share the benefits of each other's competencies.

The right blend would be a mixture of both markets, and sometimes it is possible to use the same fixed assets and position them for different customer groups.

Let us take the case of Arogyadham (place of health) in the Chitrakoot PURA. Arogyadham is a health-care centre based on Ayurveda, yoga and traditional healing sciences. It is a place of lush greenery and beautiful

TABLE 8.1: Export/urban vis-à-vis horizontal/domestic markets

Export/Urban	Horizontal/Domestic
Higher value per unit	Cost-effective in transporting
Common branding helps tap the market	Sense of ownership and pride in PURA
Help available for building the brand in the outside markets	Societal and human development
Standardized production possible	Customization possible according to local needs
	Additional enterprises for sales and marketing

ambience spread over an area of 43 acres situated on the banks of the river Mandakini. It is also a research and production centre for herbal, Ayurvedic and traditional medicines.

As a health centre, it operates an outpatient department (OPD) and a 100-bed inpatient department (IPD). It is a medical tourism spot where patients suffering from chronic diseases come from various parts of the nation and the world to receive well-researched traditional Indian treatment from experts. Using the same infrastructure, Arogyadham provides health care to the local people from about 500 villages, even for chronic diseases. It is able to extend health-care services with its unique first-aid kit of thirty-five herbal medicines called 'Dadima ka Batua' (grandmother's purse), which is given to its village representatives.

Besides this, Arogyadham also runs a cow shelter (go-sadan),* which is a state-of-the-art research and production facility for producing cow's milk and milk products, linking it to traditional health care. It has a garden with over 400 herbs and a research laboratory for the production and processing of Indian herbs. Arogyadham also operates an Ayurvedic research centre called Ayurveda Sadan, which acts as an interface between traditional knowledge and modern research. It consists of five modern laboratories, with the latest scientific equipment for standardizing and validating Ayurvedic herbs and for isolating the 'active ingredient' so that the preparation can be marketed globally as a recognized medicine.

All the research and production carried out in Arogyadham caters to the wide export market, which is seeing an exponential demand growth. Moreover, through its fixed cost and infrastructure sharing, the Chitrakoot PURA is able to provide quality health care through this facility to the horizontal markets across 500 villages as well.

INTEGRATION AND A VERTICALLY BALANCED ENTERPRISE NETWORK

Earlier we had stated that one of the fundamental challenges of rural enterprise is the fact that its output would require significantly more time

* Sadan (Hindi) = house or building.

and would cover a longer distance to reach the urban or the export markets. Thus, it is important for the products and services that come out of rural enterprises for export outside the complex to be as high on the value chain as possible—this processing and value addition would reduce the size of the product and increase its net value.

The rural entrepreneur or producer faces another problem—their scale is

> **THE LABORATORIES IN AYURVEDA SADAN INCLUDE:**
>
> 1. Pharmacognosy Laboratory for studying the toxicity of herbal medicine
> 2. Bio-molecular Laboratory for studying the effect of herbal medicines at the molecular and gene levels
> 3. Tissue Culture Lab
> 4. Core Instrumentation Facility

usually very low and the process mostly manual and hence more time-consuming and economically inefficient. In contrast, a mechanized unit with a larger investment and focused production would be able to share the fixed cost over a larger production volume and thereby cut

TABLE **8.2:** The effect and the benefits of localized vertical integration

Effect of Localized Vertical Integration	Benefits
Enhanced value at localized enterprise network	More revenue for the producer, more employment opportunities; localized vertical integration helps cut cost on movement of goods.
Reduced size	Transportation cost reduced and wastage minimized.
Longevity increased	Product can be exported over greater distances and access better markets. Also, the bargaining power of the producer is increased.
Waste minimization	Enhances profitability and controls environmental impact.
Inclusive integrated value: chain from raw material to final high-value goods	Economies of scale would occur even in the case of small producers.
Pooling of resources	Better access to credit and ability to absorb entrepreneurial shocks.

down on the cost. Fixed costs such as land, building, equipment and technology could be better utilized. This is called 'economies of scale' and it makes the cost of individual smaller enterprises uncompetitive. Let us take an example.

Typically, the cost of a product per unit is inversely linked to the volume of production and this is the total production cost (TPC). The marginal production cost (MPC) implies the additional cost of producing each extra unit over the previous state. Let us suppose there are five enterprises, each producing 100 units of a product per day. Each of these units would operate at a level of the TPC corresponding to the production value of 100 units—thus the net cost of production would be 5 × Cost of 100 units. Now, if these enterprises were vertically integrated and shared some fixed infrastructure and costs, it would give them a higher bargaining power in the market and with the suppliers. As a result, they would collectively operate at an even lower level of the TPC. Thus, the cost of 500 units would be less than 5 × Cost of 100 units due to the economies of scale.

This is where our next focus area for the creation of a successful rural enterprise under PURA would be: vertical integration of the production cycle so that value addition can be achieved within the local PURA complex.

The principle of vertical integration in the PURA complexes

TRIPLE BOTTOM-LINE APPROACH TO ENTERPRISE VALUE

Enterprise value generated in a sustainable development system like PURA would not be judged merely on the basis of the profits. Each PURA complex will evaluate its enterprises based on the sum total of three contributions: People (P1), Planet (P2) and Profits (P3).

People (P1) would refer to the direct (P1D) or indirect (P1N) returns achieved on the basis of the social development radar as explained in Chapter 5. The equitable distribution of profits is also an ingredient of this component.

Planet (P2) refers to the impact on the natural resources, tree cover, soil condition, landscape, water and air of the PURA complex area as explained in Chapter 6. This value would be proportional to the positive impact on these components.

Profits (P3) is a mixture of the traditional balance-sheet understanding of monetary income and of how sustainable the income levels are over a period of time.

would be based on the lines of maximizing the triple bottom line of People (P1), Planet (P2) and Profits (P3). The equivalent values of P2 and P3 can be evaluated along the lines of Social Capital (C_s) and Environmental Capital (C_E), which will be discussed in later chapters.

Vertical integration would have to consider the impact on all these parameters and also account for the cultural aspects and the stability of the model.

BUILDING AN ENVIRONMENT THROUGH AN ENTERPRISE NETWORK

We have discussed the various elements necessary for starting a successful, enterprise-driven model for a PURA complex at the village level. Now we shall construct a model for an enterprise network which is vertically balanced and integrated, taps into various markets, is technologically flavoured, and has investment and incubation potential. This would be a carefully crafted and customized way of creating enterprises based on local competencies and external and internal markets, in such a way as to maximize the yield and minimize the risks.

The necessary condition is the building of a robust network where every stakeholder would have the incentive and intent to assist in the creation of enterprises, which would lead to income generation and societal transformation. A block diagram for the different components of such an enterprise network is shown in Figure 8.1.

Essentially, an enterprise network is composed of three distinct categories, each of which can be an entrepreneurial avenue or be managed by a dedicated stakeholder:

THE PRIMARY BUSINESS (PROCESSING AND MARKETING) CHAIN

Every competency in the village complex—whether in the form of a natural product or skill—can be nurtured and have value added to it. An entrepreneurial approach should be employed to move up the value chain, adding quality to the product or service, thereby enabling it to obtain bigger income yields. On the procurement side, there can be

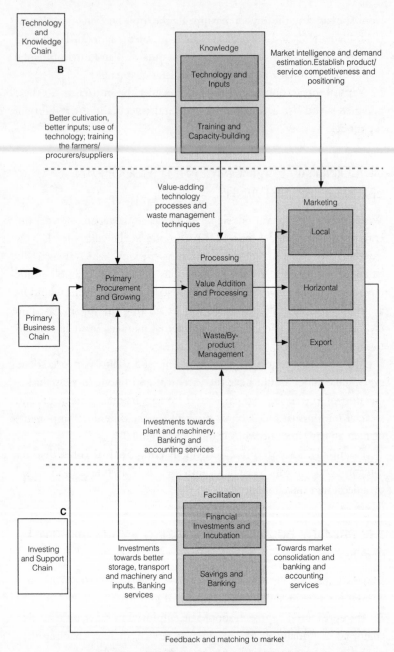

FIGURE 8.1: A PURA enterprise network model

value-adding enterprises which help get higher returns and better storage facilities to minimize waste. At the processing stage, the most cost-efficient and quality measures need to be employed to optimize the value. At the same time, the waste, the by-products and other collateral benefits need to be harnessed and converted into socio-economic gains.

Finally, the marketing side, too, can be enterprise-driven—it needs to find the optimal mix of serving the domestic, the export and the horizontal markets in order to enhance incomes and also serve the local population. This would affect the kind of final storage mechanisms required; the advertising that needs to be conducted; and the logistical arrangements that need to be drawn up. Of course, the market also needs to have a mechanism for feedback which can help match the product to the demand.

The entire chain—from procurement to the market—can generate a number of jobs for different skills sets with capacity-building. It may be managed jointly under a cooperative of producers and marketeers, or segmented into different, but balanced parts, each of which can be under smaller entities like NGOs, SHGs and small-scale industries.

THE TECHNOLOGY AND KNOWLEDGE CHAIN

Building on Electronic Connectivity and Knowledge Connectivity, knowledge support systems would help in integration. This can be a part of the PURA Complexes Cooperative or be managed by local experts, local academic institutions, NGOs or corporate bodies as a social responsibility with government support. Typical examples of this would include Village Knowledge Centres (VKCs) of the Indian Space Research Organization (ISRO), e-Choupal of ITC and the Krishi Vigyan Kendras (KVKs) of the Indian Council of Applied Economic Research (ICAER).*

This support system of enterprises would help gather optimal technologies for value addition; evolve methodologies for waste and by-product management; strategize vertical integration; and help gather market intelligence. It would be the technological partner of the processing and marketing value chain. It would help apply technology

* We have already discussed the concept of KVKs in Chapter 3. We have also discussed the typical working of KVKs in the case of the Loni and the Chitrakoot PURAs.

in procurement and harvesting to improve yields, and reduce the risk of weather changes by the information management system. In order to be successful, it would have to adapt knowledge to local conditions, and evolve models where the end-user of the technology—the rural population—has an active stake.

The knowledge support enterprises may be linked via Electronic Connectivity to the expert centres of technology and management across the world. They would facilitate electronic input and output markets. They could also act as providers of education—conventional as well as vocational education.

THE FACILITATION AND INVESTMENT CHAIN

No enterprise can be realized unless adequate arrangements for providing the necessary credit are made in a time-bound manner. This would require a customized micro credit linkage policy and one-stop integrated financial services. The need for this service itself will create an enterprise network of financing and incubation.

Moreover, as entrepreneurs and employees grow in number, they would need access to better financial services for their personal and business needs. This would include savings, investments, consultation, financial management and insurance services.

For an equitable and balanced development it is important to cultivate and nurture—especially among the rural youths—entrepreneurship which, at the grass-roots level, has far-reaching benefits and which, if successful, would help local competency develop and thrive. An entrepreneur can potentially generate at least four to five additional jobs, can also serve the local markets and bring amenities to the people in the PURA region and thereby build up their standard of living. Above all, it is the natural way to achieve value addition for the products and services coming out of a rural complex.

We have given many examples of local entrepreneurship and ideas about generating it, and the opportunities for outsiders to be a part of the sustainable development mission of PURA. Building an entrepreneurial culture would make it flourish, but it would require a multi-pronged focus which envisages the creation of the following direct enablers:

- Skill-building opportunities (S)
- Access to inputs and quality equipment (I)
- Process technology with adaptability and upgrading (T)
- Timely access to credit (C)
- Vertical integration management (V)
- Aggregation and access to markets (M)

$$\text{Strength of Entrepreneurial Culture} = S \times I \times T \times C \times V \times M$$

To promote an entrepreneurial culture, all these enablers would have to be activated through a combination of private, public and community initiatives. It is important to understand that all the six enablers are interdependent. Skill-building with access to equipment

EMPOWERMENT OF RURAL EASTERN UTTAR PRADESH THROUGH ENTERPRISE CREATION

In February 2011, we visited the district of Basti in eastern Uttar Pradesh where we met a number of village entrepreneurs who, through their innovative business models, are carrying out economic development of the region and its people. One of them was Jitendra Singh who used to work as a corporate lawyer for reputed firms. He resigned from the post of associate vice-president of a company to come back to his village. The ground water of his ancestral land was locally considered as having health benefits, probably due to its mineral content. He capitalized on this village resource to build an enterprise model. He got international certification for the water of his own tube well as authentic mineral water and then started running his own bottling and filling plant in Marwatia Babu, a remote village in Basti district. At present, he has a testing laboratory, employs three managers and twenty-five skilled workers on a regular basis, and fills 200,000 bottles per month. Marketing, packaging and retailing this natural resource have generated employment and self-respect for many villagers in the area. He markets his product under the brand name of Lumbini, after the birthplace of Gautam Buddha, and has created an identity for Basti.

This example of harnessing local resources and inherent strengths to achieve larger economic benefits needs replication across the nation and the developing world. Of course, while doing so, sustainability in terms of ecology also needs to be factored in.

would not yield any results unless coupled with well-timed access to credit in order to start an enterprise. Similarly, even if an enterprise were created it would be unsustainable unless there was access to market and market intelligence. The creation of an enterprise environment requires a focused approach through the four-fold connectivity of PURA. Let us discuss some examples which highlight the nurturing of such an environment.

UDYAMITA VIDYAPEETH AT THE CHITRAKOOT PURA

Udyamita Vidyapeeth at Chitrakoot is a novel step towards the achievement of the self-reliance objective of the Chitrakoot PURA. Deendayal Research Institute (DRI), the initiator of this PURA, realized that the there was a need to create non-farm income-generating activities in the area, which would ease the pressure on farmlands, and prevent them from being divided into smaller and less economical holdings. This led to the birth of the enterprise-creating mission for enabling local youths to emerge as village-based entrepreneurs.

Udyamita Vidyapeeth is described as a production-cum-training centre to emphasize that it is essentially a hands-on industrial training centre with emphasis on building a financially sustainable enterprise system, rather than just a skill-development workshop.

Sheds have been erected in Udyamita Vidyapeeth—each for a particular area of specialization—where the local youths can come for hands-on industrial training in their field of interest. They are also given a live demonstration of how economic returns can be gained using their skill, and are encouraged to go back to their villages, start their own enterprise and emerge as employment generators.

ENTERPRISE TRAINING COURSES AT UDYAMITA VIDYAPEETH

- Radio Electronics
- Fabrication
- Screen and Offset Printing
- Cane and Bamboo Crafts
- Soap- and Detergent-making
- Bakery
- Computer Application
- Fruit and Vegetable Processing
- Oil Expeller Unit
- Readymade Garments
- Processing of Cereals and Pulses Industry (PCPI)
- Garments and Textiles

The contribution of Udyamita Vidyapeeth does not end with mere training. Its organizers realized that unless the youths were backed by credit facility it would be impossible for them to actually start any enterprise which involved advanced processing. While it does help out by arranging for loans from banks, in some cases that is not sufficient as the novice entrepreneur youths are either unable to fulfil the bank's requirements or are not in a position to take the additional burden of payment of interest.

However, Udyamita Vidyapeeth was determined to create as many entrepreneurs as possible, and hence, devised a unique financial tool for addressing the credit needs of these trained youths. With the various funds received by DRI—the principal institute behind the Chitrakoot PURA—it opened a bank account called 'Swavalamban' (self-reliance), to give interest-free micro loans to the talented and reliable but needy

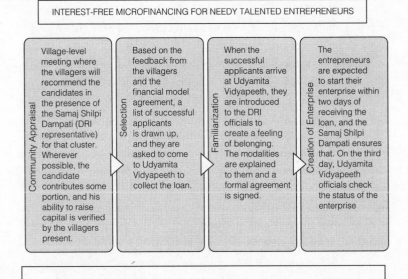

INTEREST-FREE MICROFINANCING FOR NEEDY TALENTED ENTREPRENEURS

Community Appraisal: Village-level meeting where the villagers will recommend the candidates in the presence of the Samaj Shilpi Dampati (DRI representative) for that cluster. Wherever possible, the candidate contributes some portion, and his ability to raise capital is verified by the villagers present.

Selection: Based on the feedback from the villagers and the financial model agreement, a list of successful applicants is drawn up, and they are asked to come to Udyamita Vidyapeeth to collect the loan.

Familiarization: When the successful applicants arrive at Udyamita Vidyapeeth, they are introduced to the DRI officials to create a feeling of belonging. The modalities are explained to them and a formal agreement is signed.

Creation of Enterprise: The entrepreneurs are expected to start their enterprise within two days of receiving the loan, and the Samaj Shilpi Dampati ensures that. On the third day, Udyamita Vidyapeeth officials check the status of the enterprise

More than 200 beneficiaries have benefited under this zero-interest microfinance scheme. The loan recovery in all Samaj Shilpi Dampati clusters has been 100 per cent.

FIGURE **8.2:** The microfinance model of Chitrakoot PURA

entrepreneurs in the rural areas. The process for deciding the loan is very participative, in which even the local villagers and the Samaj Shilpi Dampati* are involved. This is shown in Figure 8.2.

Udyamita Vidyapeeth also guides farmers by providing market intelligence from the urban areas so that demand–supply matching can be optimally utilized. One of the improvements it has carried out is in the packaging of high-value agricultural products so that they can be supplied to urban demand centres and farmers can get a fair price for their products. Udyamita Vidyapeeth and the Chitrakoot PURA mission are encouraging the farmers to switch to high-value and healthy organic food which can generate better returns.

The Chitrakoot PURA region is rich in forests, which are sources of biodiversity strength and numerous forest products that can generate economic returns for the local tribal population; and, if done in a scientific way, this would also lead to the preservation of the ecosystem. Till recently, the tribal people were largely engaged in the low-income business of selecting and picking fresh herbs to be later processed in factories. In this process, the returns to the tribal people were very low, partly due to a lack of knowledge of the true value of the product, and more significantly because, being ill-equipped to process the forest products, they did not have any bargaining power. Chitrakoot Udyamita Vidyapeeth took up the challenge of taking the profits back to the tribal people by empowering them entrepreneurially. The tribal youths were taught the benefits of the herbal plants and the method of processing them to an intermediate state. Using this knowledge and training, many of them were able to partake in the value addition and could thereby increase their income significantly, which further translated into better living standards. They were in a better bargaining position vis-à-vis the companies, and were able to get a higher price for their effort.

A part of this enterprise creation was done through the SHGs initiated by Udyamita Vidyapeeth in partnership with the KVKs. It undertook the responsibility for training the SHG members, and their initial inputs

---

* Samaj Shilpi Dampati (SSD) are graduate couples who are representatives of the DRI's Chitrakoot PURA mission in the local village cluster. We have explained about SSDs in detail in Chapter 7.

were often subsidized by DRI to overcome the usual stumbling blocks in starting an enterprise.

JUST-IN-TIME MANAGEMENT EXPERIENCE: LESSONS FROM TOYOTA

In April 2010, we visited the Toyota Engineering and Manufacturing Plant in Georgetown, Kentucky, USA. The plant has two parallel lines operating in two shifts and cumulatively producing 2,000 cars a day. This makes it the largest automobile manufacturing plant in North America and Toyota's second largest manufacturing plant. But even more significant was seeing the management principles of a successful enterprise translated into human and machine action. Toyota has given the world the principle of just-in-time (JIT) production on which their Georgetown plant operates. JIT is an example of how to achieve vertical integration of dissimilar production units—often with different production cycles—towards the common top of the value chain. JIT follows the principle of elimination and minimization of three key points of wastage:

- Time: Minimizing the time taken for converting the raw material into the final product or service. This can be done by using optimal technology and balancing the different segments of processing.
- Scrap: Elimination of wastage in the process caused by poor technology, lack of skill or uncoordinated operations.
- Inventory: Ensuring that there is a minimum amount of work in progress between the first and the last stage.

This management fundamental of modern times is of tremendous significance for the PURA enterprise network, in which the production units are represented by individual micro or small enterprises. Starting with the core competency of the local region, the network operates in unison to create high-value products and services. The realization of a competitive advantage would be complete only when sound management is carried out in an entrepreneurial fashion like Toyota. This visionary management of a process can be a potent tool for converting core competency into income generation and societal benefit. Let us take an example of a rural enterprise.

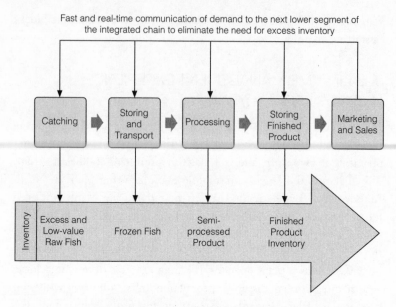

Fast and real-time communication of demand to the next lower segment of the integrated chain to eliminate the need for excess inventory

FIGURE **8.3:** JIT in a fishing PURA context

Let us imagine that there is a rural, vertically integrated, coastal PURA fishing enterprise network linking the raw fish from the sea to some form of processed seafood sold in an urban or export market. A rough idea of the stages involved and the inventories produced with communication as needed in the process is shown in Figure 8.3.

Note that this is where the Physical, the Electronic and the Knowledge Connectivity converge towards a common Economic Connectivity goal. Table 8.3 shows the role played by each of them and the effect.

ENTERPRISE INCUBATION BY AN ACADEMIC INSTITUTION: PERIYAR PURA

The Periyar PURA, initiated by the Periyar Maniammai University (PMU), Vallam, in south India, has a unique and multi-pronged focus on generating entrepreneurs in various disciplines and social groups. The Periyar PURA covers sixty-five villages and benefits a population of about 100,000 people.

TABLE 8.3: Convergence of Physical, Electronic and Knowledge Connectivity

Connectivity	Effect on Realizing Economic Connectivity
Physical Connectivity (roads and waterways with landing facilities)	Would ensure that the time taken from the raw state to processing to marketing is minimized. Faster transport can be used between the different elements of the chain, minimizing wastage and giving better bargaining power in the market.
Electronic Connectivity (real time and high devices integrated with weather forecast, information on location of fish and connectivity to market)	Can help the fishermen get weather forecasts and information on the best locations for catching fish. Also, the back-and-forth communication of requirements and tunings can move across the chain. This would ensure speedy response and eliminate the need to keep a large inventory.
Knowledge Connectivity (network with various expert agencies and technologies)	Would ensure that the best output, both in terms of quality and quantity, is harnessed with the minimum input. Moreover, it would help towards value addition for better revenues and less scrap.

The Periyar PURA has followed the one-village one-product model, which means that each village (or a small group of villages) within its purview focuses on achieving excellence of quality and maximization of returns for a particular product or service. This was implemented in 2007 through a strategic partnership with the Japan External Trade Organization (JETRO). The people of the Periyar PURA villages, technologically supported by PMU, worked with experts from JETRO on various products for which core competency and raw material were available in Thanjavur district. The PMU students and experts were instrumental in identifying the core competency and facilitating the training. They developed prototypes for 123 products such as bed sheets, table runners, cushion covers, brass drums, curtains and bread baskets. Interaction with the JETRO specialists included comparison with Japanese products, discussion on selection of raw material, technical advice on product development and final quality inspection. Based on this intensive interaction, the people of Vallam produced 123 products from which JETRO selected forty for the international market. These finalized products were displayed in exhibitions in New Delhi and Tokyo. The feedback from each exhibition was used for improving the product so as to enhance customer acceptability of the product. The local technical consultancy support for improving the product was provided by PMU. This cooperative venture has boosted the innovative ability of the village people and transformed it into developing and producing internationally acceptable products.

Besides the partnership with JETRO, the Periyar PURA is organized into different blocks of villages, each charged with developing a specific core competency based on the local agro-climate and availability of native skills. Some of these are coconut-based activity, bamboo-related enterprises, herb cultivation, dairy integration and biofuel and alternative energy sources.

The Periyar PURA has initiated or promoted a number of enterprise activities through many of its specialized centres or social organizations. It has the following organizations and initiatives for carrying out its work in the villages:

- Periyar Organization for Women's Emancipation and Renaissance (POWER)
- Periyar Business Processing Outsourcing (PBPO)
- Periyar Technology Business Incubator (TBI)
- A centre for rural development (CRD)
- Periyar Research Organization for Biotechnology and Ecosystem (PROBE)
- Periyar Centre for Environment and Energy Management (PCEM)
- Periyar Renewable Energy Training Institute (PRETI)
- KVIC Regional Extension Centre (biomanure programme)

All these centres work in close synergy and share knowledge to attain the common goal of transforming the villages.

PERIYAR ORGANIZATION FOR WOMEN'S EMANCIPATION AND RENAISSANCE (POWER)

POWER is an NGO for the transfer of technology and assistance in enterprise formation to the beneficiaries of the Periyar PURA villages, especially the women. It identifies the potential aspirants in the locality,

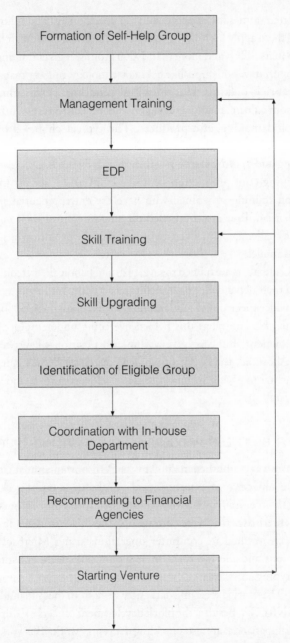

FIGURE **8.4:** Stepwise implementation under POWER

offers programmes for entrepreneurship development and follows up by helping them apply for funding schemes to start their venture. It has 8,000 women in its SHGs and more than 1,000 groups. It gives training courses and support in various areas like baking technology, nursery management, hollow brick-making, mat weaving, retailing, vermicomposting, mushroom culture, manufacturing fibreboard, cultivation of ornamental plants and making jute products. The typical chain—from SHG formation and the Enterprise Development Programme (EDP) to the financing and venture start-up—is shown in Figure 8.4.

Training-cum-production centres (TCPCs) are set up for giving hands-on training to women who have the entrepreneurial spirit and the potential. They are counselled on how to control their enterprises and face challenges, and given an insight into the evolution of successful business models.

SHG members are trained to save, plan and handle their credit. This has reduced their dependence on agricultural activities for income and given them a wider spectrum of jobs and non-farm employment opportunities to pursue. Not only has this helped overcome underemployment and unemployment, but also given women a position of respect in the family. Above all, the SHGs of women created by POWER have been instrumental in giving women a sense of self-recognition and wings to their aspirations.

PERIYAR BUSINESS PROCESSING OUTSOURCING (PBPO)

This centre was established in 2009 by the Periyar Maniammai University, with the objective of training local youths in computer skills and making them employment-worthy for the business process outsourcing (BPO) enterprises that were coming up. The thirty students in the first batch were trained in computer operations using Microsoft Office applications and the Internet. Their typing skills were enhanced with special typing software.

PBPO has started receiving data entry work from the Budalur block for the MGNREGA. Besides, the block development officers of Thiruvonam and Thiruppanandal are also providing data entry work. The work is being done in the PBPO centre and the data are sent online to the concerned blocks. This has led to the creation of a previously unknown knowledge-based industry in the form of BPO in Periyar PURA.

PERIYAR TECHNOLOGY BUSINESS INCUBATOR (PERIYAR TBI)

Periyar TBI is a grant-in-aid project aided by the Department of Science and Technology, Government of India, through the National Science and Technology Entrepreneurship Development Board (NSTEBD). It has the broad objective of promoting knowledge-based and innovation-driven enterprises in the region under the Periyar PURA. Periyar TBI was established in the year 2006 to promote enterprises based on herb processing with small-scale manufacturing facilities for herbal products and tissue culture, and for testing them. It is also involved in activities such as enterprise promotion in phytopharmaceuticals and nutraceuticals.

Periyar TBI is a well-equipped facility with conference rooms, classrooms, space for display and sales, a library and facilities for applying for patents. It conducts workshops in awareness, process improvements and skill development. TBI's Entrepreneurship Development Programme benefits aspiring entrepreneurs who may be students, pharmaceutical industries, farmers, women or small institutions.

Periyar TBI has features like:

- An embedded-system development centre, with certificate courses in embedded systems and commercial design development for engineering students
- A bio-fertilizer/bio-pesticide production centre: training is given on scientific methods of production and market support is provided through the Rural Business Hub
- Food Products Order (FPO) licensed production facilities: products like fruit jams, squashes and tomato ketchups available for sale
- Rural BPO service

IMPACT OF PERIYAR PURA'S ENTREPRENEURSHIP MISSION

The entrepreneurship and employment promotion missions carried out by the Periyar PURA mission have had a significant impact. In the non-farming sector, more than 2,000 skilled jobs have been created in the field of welding, fitting, carpentry, electrical and plumbing services, CAD/CAM and CNC. This has greatly arrested migration to the cities and reduced the unemployment problem among the youths who are now fruitfully employed.

Also, more than 5,000 SHGs have enrolled 30,000 rural women who are engaged in many income-generating activities and small enterprises. Empowered by the training they have received, and supported by access to credit facility and market linkages, they have become entrepreneurs in areas such as vermicompost production and plant nurseries; tailoring, embroidery and bakery; coir and fibre-reinforced products; hollow brick-making; and carpentry. The impact of the effort in enterprise creation is visible in the Periyar Maniammai University campus itself where most of the services like catering, provision stores, cafeterias, laundry, printing, tailoring and student amenities are run as small enterprises by these trained women's groups.

~

BRINGING SUSTAINABLE ENERGY TO BRAZILIAN VILLAGES THROUGH ENTREPRENEURSHIP: FABIO ROSA

If we look around us, our industries, commerce, amenities, heating and cooling systems, entertainment and home lighting, even our water purification systems are dependent on one form of energy—electricity. And yet, even in this era when our most basic amenities depend on electrical power, as of today, nearly 30 per cent of the world's population—mostly living in rural areas—does not have any access to it. Electricity is both a challenge to development and an opportunity to make a difference in villages across the globe. Of course, governments around the world are making this a priority issue, but the question remains: how can this be achieved sustainably through social entrepreneurship at local levels?

One entrepreneur who has accepted this challenge is Fábio Luiz de Oliveira Rosa of Brazil. His career as a social entrepreneur in energy started in the early 1980s, at the age of twenty-two, when he visited a rural municipality in the Palmares area of Rio Grande do Sul, Brazil's southernmost state. He came in contact with the local mayor who was impressed by him and appointed him secretary of agriculture. At that time, the area of Palmares was lagging behind in all dimensions—economy and social statistics. Over 70 per cent of the population did not have access to electricity and the lack of this one amenity had a significant cascading impact on almost all other areas.

This being a region where the primary occupation was rice cultivation, the biggest problem was the lack of availability of water for irrigation. Most of the channels and dams were owned by rich landlords who charged a very high price for the water. In fact, the smaller farmers were paying more than thrice the world average for their water needs, and about a quarter of the net input cost was solely on water.

Rosa believed that it was water alone that could give a major boost to the agricultural income of the farmers, and concluded that the area needed many artesian wells. However, the biggest obstacle to that was the fact that the area generally lacked access to electricity, which was vital for drawing water out of the ground. The lack of electricity also meant that the rural population did not have access to lighting, refrigeration, entertainment, information and computers. Thus, 70 per cent of the population of Palmares—about 9,000 people—had no future to speak of. All the electric companies found it an expensive exercise to extend the grid to the rural areas and, under the current excess capacity installation, the cost of bringing electricity to each household would have been about $7,000, roughly equivalent to five years of its annual income.

That is when innovation came to the rescue. Rosa and his team noticed that the three-phase bulky lines in use were not needed for rural application. Instead, by replacing them with a mono-phase current system with a single wire and grounding into the earth, the cost of installation could be brought down to $400 per family. This access to electric power opened the floodgates to multiple agricultural and household applications. One of the first was the availability of water for irrigation, with 75 per cent of the farmers investing in water pumps and refrigeration sets. The combined effect of water and better agriculture methods was reflected in the income levels, which jumped from $65 to about $250 per month. One result of the electrification was the return of the local population that had migrated to urban areas for better incomes and amenities. One man with one idea had addressed the real underlying problem and changed an entire rural district.

But Fabio Rosa did not stop there. He understood that rural electrification had to be made as independent of the government as possible. He saw an opportunity in solar photovoltaic cells, which were portable and easy to use, but very costly. He realized that the technology had to be repackaged and delivered in a different form with higher yields. One of the problems of rural Brazil was inadequate fencing that failed to control animal grazing and which, in turn, destroyed crops and lowered yields. Rosa packaged electric fencing and solar energy together and concluded that, by this method, the cost of fencing could be reduced by 85 per cent. Additionally, farmers would gain from the excess electricity available and thus improve their productivity. Rosa further noticed that many of the families were spending up to $25 per month on energy items like candles, kerosene, batteries and diesel. So he repackaged their solar device as a solar home system consisting of a solar battery, panels, lighting fixtures and other electrical items with 12V electricity supply. This system, customized for rural households, was able to provide adequate power for lighting, TV, water pump, radio, refrigerator and water heater against an installation cost of $150 to be paid off in twelve months.

Fabio Rosa and his team demonstrated how closely societal amenities like electricity are interlinked with income-generating activities and productivity. Better amenities reversed the trend of urban migration. Best of all, this was achieved not through subsidies but through the way of entrepreneurship with community participation. What may appear to be economically unfeasible technology—like solar power and mono-phase lines—can be made economically vibrant when coupled with core issues like irrigation, home lighting and fencing. To be successful, technology has to assume the shape of an enterprise, and enterprises have to delve into the depths of societal needs.[3]

GOVERNMENT OF INDIA-SUPPORTED MICRO ENTERPRISE CREATION SCHEMES

Swarnajayanti Gram Swarozgar Yojana (SGSY)

The government, both Central and state, runs many schemes that promote enterprise creation at the rural levels. One of the most prominent of them is the Swarnajayanti Gram Swarozgar Yojana (SGSY) which was launched in April 1999 after the restructuring of the Integrated Rural Development Programme (IRDP) and other programmes. It is basically a self-employment and micro enterprise creation scheme that targets the economic empowerment of the impoverished. The objective is to bring the assisted swarozgaris (self-employed) above the poverty line through the creation of income-generating assets through bank credit and government subsidy. The Central and the state governments implement this scheme on a cost-sharing basis in the ratio of 75:25 (Centre:state). By 2009, there were 3.6 million SHGs with more than 13 million self-employed people with an investment of Rs 308.96 billion.

Such schemes can be dovetailed as part of entrepreneurship promotion to realize the sustainable development model of PURA.

Rural Business Hub (RHB)

The Rural Business Hub, promoted by the Ministry of Panchayati Raj and the Confederation of Indian Industry, is a public–private–panchayat partnership model to address the gaps in the market structure by establishing a direct linkage between rural economy and industry.

The thrust of the RHB is to improve locally available resources and produce goods of international standards. The industry is supposed to assist in terms of technology, good farming practices and inputs; value addition, standardization and quality enhancement measures; branding and marketing; and training and skill development.

This intervention is expected to lead to higher yields and higher returns. The RHB is designed to address a wide spectrum of activities including handicrafts, handlooms, poultry, aquaculture, food processing, biofuels and herbal plantation.

With such value addition and advanced processes, the RHB aims to create a linkage whereby industries can directly source from the rural hubs, which have been standardized and are equipped to produce goods of international standard. In 2010, the Ministry of Panchayati Raj identified thirty-five districts for establishing Rural Business Hubs.

This partnership scheme can be useful for creating economic activity and linking products to markets. Models like the RHB can be a part of designing and implementing sustainable development systems, especially those being created by industries and small-scale industries.

9

REALIZING A PURA

IMPLEMENTING PURA

PURA is a socio-economic developmental tool that aims at the economic and social empowerment of people, rather than confining itself merely to the alleviation of poverty. Only empowerment is the sustainable solution to the problem of the urban–rural divide, societal bias and poverty.

But empowerment of the people is a complex and challenging process, and covers many dimensions of the economic, social and cultural domains. It requires a careful and customized analysis of a particular area and the development of an action plan which is sustainable and implementable. It takes time for empowerment to be complete and hence, a long-term commitment is required, with a high initial investment.

As discussed earlier in the book, India requires about 7,000 PURAs of different kinds. We have calculated that, for the entire global rural community, about 30,000 PURA complexes would be required. Each PURA would be a centre for vibrant economic activity and human development. The entire implementation of this sustainable development scheme would require a variety of contributors and initiators. We have already seen that with the Union and the state governments of India, organizations, universities, cooperatives and companies who are all engaged in the PURA mission. A mission of such a scale can indeed be accomplished only with the participation and partnership of multiple entities, including academic institutions, the private sector, non-government sectors, entrepreneurs, financial institutions and, of course, the government at both the Centre and the state levels. All these partners will have to work together, often sharing core competencies, to achieve a profile of vibrant development starting at the Indian villages, with a socio-economic focus and environmental concern.

REALIZATION OF A PURA

PURA is a model of customized connectivity with integrated action leading to sustainable development of the rural complex. PURAs can be realized in different sizes, covering various competencies and across different areas, under a range of individuals and institutions. It would require a sound focus on evolving four forms of connectivity along with action on the core competencies of the rural village complex for the attainment of sustainable development goals as depicted in Figure 9.1.

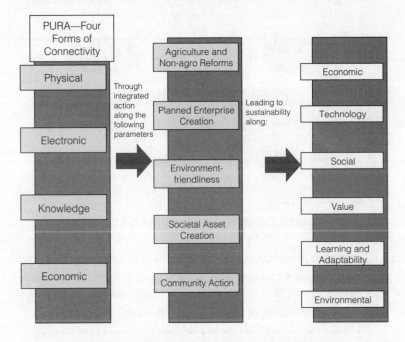

FIGURE **9.1:** PURA, its four forms of connectivity, action
and sustainability

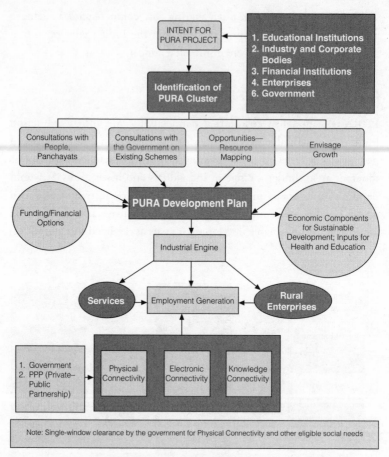

FIGURE **9.2:** Flow diagram for realizing a PURA

The generic flow sequence for the realization of a PURA as shown in Figure 9.2 describes a comprehensive list of actions to be taken towards the creation of a PURA. However, there is always a scope and need for customization according to the local needs and challenges.

We will now discuss the typical processes involved in the realization of a sustainable development system in the form of PURA, and how such a sustainable development system can be realized by different stakeholders.

There is a variety of institutions and individuals who can set up a PURA (Figure 9.3), and the steps involved in creating and maintaining it are as follows:

1. An educational or financial institution, industry, societal transformers (NGOs), small-scale enterprise, corporate bodies, an individual or the government who intend to create a PURA cluster. We have already seen that different stakeholders are capable of creating PURAs using their core competencies. This can also be done by a consortium which would bring in the core competencies of the different institutions—academic, NGOs, banks, cooperatives and industry. For example, a prominent academic institution may take the responsibility for building knowledge networks and imparting skills to the people by using their existing infrastructure. A bank may participate by providing easy loans to the PURA missionaries who are being trained. Then another

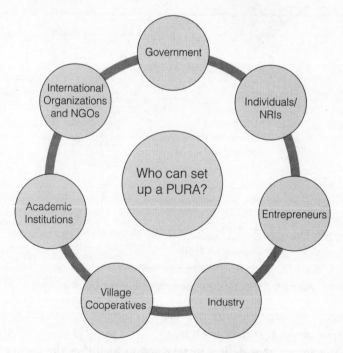

FIGURE **9.3:** Who can set up a PURA?

Many of the PURAs which have been already realized or are in the process of realization across the nation have different initiators:
- Loni PURA has been initiated by a medical university.
- Warana PURA is run by a chain of cooperative societies.
- Chitrakoot PURA was started by an NGO under the leadership of a visionary leader.
- Periyar PURA is run by an educational institution.
- Bakhtara PURA was initiated by the state government of Jharkhand.
- Madurai PURA is being initiated by an alliance between a hospital, social organizations and corporate bodies.
- The Government of India's PURA mission is being pursued under a public–private–panchayat partnership.

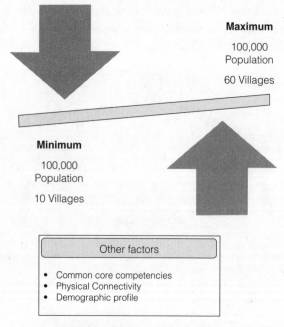

Maximum

100,000 Population

60 Villages

Minimum

100,000 Population

10 Villages

Other factors

- Common core competencies
- Physical Connectivity
- Demographic profile

FIGURE **9.4:** Factors that determine the choice of villages

partner—an industry—may take the responsibility for connecting the villages' products with the markets.

2. The agency that desires to take action identifies the groups of villages in the chosen district, which are suitable for the creation of an economically empowered PURA cluster.

The selection of villages is an important step and has to be carefully conducted as it will determine the economic backbone of PURA. There must be a population of between 10,000 and 100,000 within a single PURA complex, and each complex would cover from about 10 to 100 villages depending on the size of the villages.

The guiding principle here is that each PURA has to operate as a fairly independent economic entity and hence would need to have a basic minimum of workforce, space and resources. This would determine the minimum number of people and villages. But a PURA complex has to be internally well networked for speedy movement of people, and this fixes the upper limit for the number of villages (or the maximum time required for movement from end-to-end in the complex), which a PURA complex can cover.

Besides the population and the number of villages, it is also important to select the villages so that they share a few core competencies on which economic assets can be built up, leading to economies of scale. We have already talked about the pressing need to evolve vertically integrated systems, and this would be possible only if the core economic potential were uniform.

3. Depending on the size and scale of the PURA, it would be necessary to establish a local PURA Complex Development and Facilitation

CREATING A PURA: LEADERSHIP AT THE PANCHAYAT LEVEL

PURAs, at the lower end of the scale, can be started at the level of one or two panchayats (covering about ten villages) and expanded later. Many of the schemes under panchayats can be directly integrated with the PURA vision implementation.

Let us understand this with a case study of an innovative panchayat leader, Rangaswamy Elango, an engineer by education, who developed and implemented a model of village trade zones in the state of Tamil Nadu in south India.

Rangaswamy Elango is an example of how a successful and visionary panchayat leadership can lead to prosperity and development for a village. He is an engineer for whom the whole wide world was open. As the first technical graduate from Kuthambakkam, he was selected from the campus in 1982 by Oil India and posted on an exploration site in Orissa, but he chose to return to his village. (*Contd*)

CREATING A PURA: LEADERSHIP AT THE PANCHAYAT LEVEL (CONTD)

Kuthambakkam village is about 30 km from Chennai on the road to Tirupati. The panchayat covers a 36 sq km area and has a population of 5,000 people belonging to 1,040 households spread over seventy hamlets. Kuthambakkam is a delightful village with numerous ancient small temples.

In 1994, Elango contested the post of president of the village panchayat and won. He carried out a thorough study of the Tamil Nadu Panchayat Act (TNPA) and availed of all the possible schemes for his village. His thrust area was the empowerment of the village by creating employment through innovative ideas. In most cases, he ensured that local development was carried out by the local people and that contractors were avoided.

The panchayat asserted itself in the design and execution of the housing scheme of the Tamil Nadu government. It got the Housing and Urban Development Corporation (HUDCO) to design better houses, while the villagers pressed local soil into mud bricks to build their homes. The end result was—more wages for the local people, better and bigger construction because they constructed their own houses and cost-saving on the overall project.

Elango got a door-to-door survey done in the village and found that it consumed Rs 60 lakh worth of goods and services per month. He was amazed to find that nearly Rs 50 lakh of that could be produced at the village level. Since then, he has been evolving an economic theory of village clusters and gradually expanding the impact zone.

In simple terms, seven or eight villages form a free trade zone. They identify and produce goods and services without overlap and they consume each other's produce. The money stays back and gets invested in human development. In this way, the message and mission of Kuthambakkam is spreading to cover other villages around it. Village federations are being formed leading to economic clusters, each with a budget of about Rs 5–6 crore.

Rangaswamy Elango has proved that by innovative leadership, socio-economic development along the PURA model can be started on a smaller scale with a plan to integrate and expand with time. Visionary leadership at the local panchayat level is a crucial ingredient for the evolution of such models. The youths of the nation can look up to Elango as a model case of entrepreneurial leadership based on development of the villages.

Committee in a participative manner. It would also act as a local PURA champion.

Once the primary core competencies and societal goals have been decided, the next step is the development of a PURA facilitation committee. It has been stated earlier that PURA complexes have to act as vibrant investment-friendly economies which promote an entrepreneur-friendly environment. One of the primary goals of this committee would be to facilitate an environment where any new initiative that is proposed (based on the Triple Bottom-Line Assessment), and which matches local needs, is given full assistance and is integrated into the PURA mission. This committee may be evolved on the lines of a private–public–community partnership model, where each side brings in its own competencies and, according to them, shares clearly demarcated responsibilities.

One structure of the PURA Development and Facilitation Committee is suggested in Figure 9.5.

It is important to ensure that the responsibilities of all the different stakeholders in the committee are clearly defined based on their respective authority, capital investment and location. Moreover, the facilitation committee would have to be customized according to the PURA implementation plan. In those cases where the PURA model is being implemented completely under private initiative, the role of the district administration would be primarily to assist the procedural issues and integration of schemes as object-oriented packages. Where the implementer is the government itself, the role of the district administration would be significantly towards implementation and delivery.

The PURA Development and Facilitation Committee would keep a track of the local competency and the societal indicator alterations resulting from the combined PURA initiatives in the locality, of whose progress they would keep a macroscopic track, and then devise further strategies for the respective areas. The PURA Committee would also determine the local PURA champion/s who could be individuals of reputation, primary sponsors and initiators of the PURA mission, or a locally respected institution or organization. They would be proactive facilitators of the PURA mission and ensure the day-to-day implementation of the PURA mission, empowered by the different authorities.

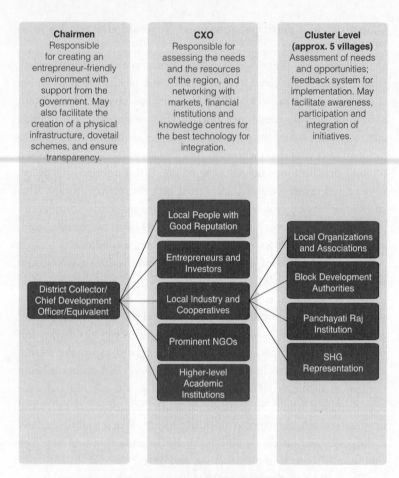

FIGURE **9.5:** The PURA Complex Development and
Facilitation Committee

The PURA champion would coordinate with the different authorities present on the committee or otherwise, on behalf of the intended entrepreneurs, the implementer of the societal mission, the environmental missions, SHGs, or cooperatives looking to generate jobs or assist human development. It is necessary to have locally based PURA champions who would be a one-stop shop for the implementation of PURA, since they would act as a pivot for generating community ownership and support for sustainable development.

4. The initiating institution identifies the core competency of the region and its current status of connectivity. At the same time, a human development plan is drawn up, based on the social needs of the local region.

The core competencies can be identified along the various dimensions as shown in Figure 9.6. Some of these dimensions are:

- Natural—rainfall, geological formation, insolation, wind, climate
- Traditional—crafts, arts, cultural heritage
- Skills and innovations
- Proximity-based—opportunities to be an ancillary supplier to a larger nearby industry

In a similar manner, an analysis of social requirements has to be done, based on the development radar model (we have discussed this in detail in Chapter 5). Key problems and issues need to be identified along the parameters defined on the development radar map (Figure 9.7), and these should be urgently addressed to reach the targeted development profile.

A synergized plan has to be developed, based on the above competencies and the identified societal needs, with a focus on harnessing specific competencies, and on the targeted processes to meet with the socio-economic development objectives. This is depicted in the sustainability-potential matrix in Figure 9.8.

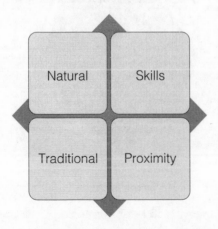

FIGURE **9.6:** Competency mapping

FACILITATION OF THE WARANA PURA MISSION

As discussed earlier, the Warana PURA has been initiated and is managed by a cooperative set-up, largely emanating from the sugar cooperative which has about 20,000 members. The Sugar Parliament—as it is called in Warana Valley—is a collective meeting point for all the stakeholders (farmers) and the officials who have initiated the PURA mission. Here, the farmers and other cooperative members can openly discuss plans and put forth their suggestions and needs. This group of cooperative farmers, officials of the Warana project, local leaders and experts acts as the chief facilitators of the PURA mission, and it is in the Sugar Parliament that important decisions are taken on how to extend it.

The group acts as the central point for the facilitation of the PURA mission and reverberates with faith in democratic, economic, social and educational empowerment of the grass-roots level of the rural population. This is vital for the long-term sustainability and growth of the twenty-first-century socio-economic mission of PURA with enhanced enterprise value.

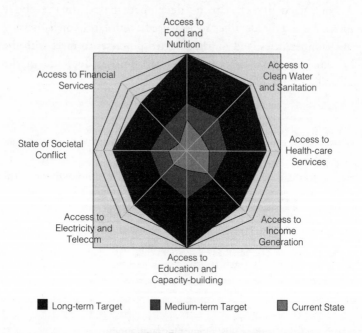

FIGURE 9.7: Development radar

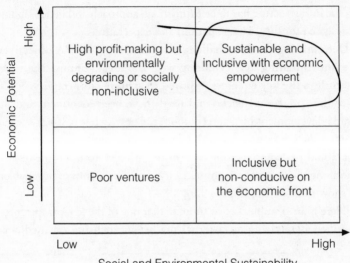

FIGURE 9.8: Sustainability potential matrix

Each competency and the value-added socio-economic entity around it can be analysed on two parameters:

1. Its economic potential, which means its financial impact and employment opportunity; and
2. Its social inclusion and environmental sustainability. This means the overall benefits of the economic growth are able to reach the bottom of the pyramid in ways of participation and at the same time they preserve, if not enhance, the ecosystem of the region and its surroundings.

In fact, each PURA complex would comprise a set of three to four core competencies which will provide a spectrum of employment to the local population, present investment opportunities to the institutions and, at the same time, be sustainable from the environmental perspective and inclusive for creating an atmosphere of growth for all.

The next step would be a detailed and timeline programme which would act as a blueprint for the development of the region. This has to be according to PURA's initial objectives. The goals should be organized time-wise, while the complete vision for development may be broken into modules, and phase-wise implementation may then be carried out, leaving adequate leeway for future expansion.

The infrastructure has to be futuristic in approach and hence, should be designed for future usage pattern and expectations.

5. Determining the key challenges for achieving PURA objectives. The implementing agency, along with the local support channels, determines the key enablers required to achieve connectivity.

Once the core competencies and needs have been identified, and the desired development plan agreed upon, the next step is to assess the gap between the current state and the desired vision, and the interventions that would be required along each of the enablers to reach the desired state along the lines of each connectivity. The dimensions of the enablers are shown in a matrix (Figure 9.9).

Here is an example. Let us suppose that one of the key competencies identified is servicing an external market by focusing on medicinal

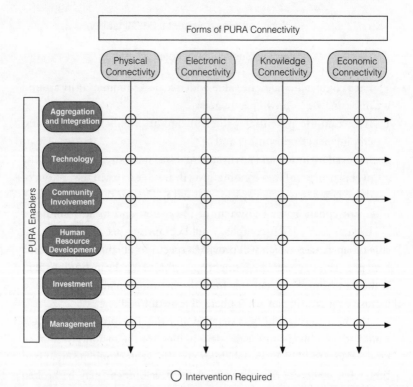

○ Intervention Required

FIGURE **9.9:** Enablers and forms of connectivity

TABLE 9.1: Enablers required to achieve connectivity

ENABLER/ CONNECTIVITY	Physical	Electronic	Knowledge	Economic
Technology	Identifying cost-reducing technologies for storage and transport		Finding the most suitable processes given local conditions	Identifying the optimal technology based on market needs
Fixed Investments	Building for processing and storing the inventory and material	Additional Electronic Connectivity which needs to be established for facilitating business	Initial investment in training, market intelligence and quality control	Establishing connectivity with the market
Human Resource Development	Finding space for training the local people in the new business model	Enabling people to use the electronic interface for better productivity	Setting up the training facility for the local population	Enabling vertical integration through people empowerment
Community	Setting up the mechanism for the movement of people for training, sales and processing	Using Electronic Connectivity as a tool to connect inclusively, empower women in their homes and use e-connectivity for knowledge	Training some innovators first and enabling them to impart knowledge through community-initiated learning	Financial services which need to be extended for supporting local micro enterprises
Aggregation	Optimal connectivity needed to facilitate faster transport of raw material and storage	Formulating ways for Electronic Connectivity to help reduce transport cost and waste		Ensuring that the benefits flow back to the planter and first member of the value chain
Management	Managing the logistics and support infrastructure		Knowledge empowerment for enterprise creation	Finding the best value-market

plantation. The next question would be, which interventions have to be enabled to lead to a vibrant medicinal plantation in the PURA complex?

The value chain would flow from planting to processing and packaging and ultimately, sales, and the interventions would have to account for all these segments. We can see some of the enablers required in Table 9.1.

6. The PURA initiator plans the services and the rural enterprises, and determines the total potential for generating employment and the expected societal change of the PURA complex, both during commissioning and subsequently, during its operation.

Since the fundamental principle behind the creation of PURA is income-generating activities for all, it is important to determine what the employment potential of the complex would be. In this context, it is necessary to look at a wide variety of support and service industries which would be additional employment-generators besides playing the role of capacity-builders. These would include technology, marketing, branding, quality control, financing and human resource development services as shown in Figure 9.10. It also shows how the harnessing of core competencies for economic goals needs to be managed synchronously with capacity-building to provide better skill sets to the employees and the entrepreneurs in the PURA design.

A detailed listing of employment potential along these lines would need to be conducted and documented. This would help find the right balance between industry and services and facilitate their timely initiation.

7. The initiating institution would simultaneously work out the funding requirement, including those funds which have been allotted for the government's development schemes in the area.

PURA is an empowerment programme that targets permanent, self-sustaining solutions. The focus on employment-generation and capacity-building translates into significant investment requirements at the start. Of course, later on, the capital investments will yield returns and make the model sustainable.

The capital cost may be met by the creation of a PURA Fund (Figure 9.11), which would be a union of different kinds of financial assets—equity (investment), debt (loan) and development grants. To cut down on costs, government schemes may be dovetailed into PURA goals, and the

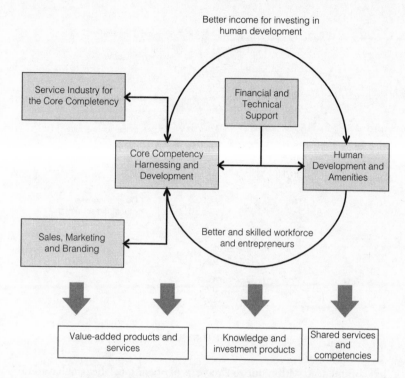

FIGURE **9.10:** Industrial model of PURA implementation

panchayati raj institutions may step in to attract investment through the PURA mission by identifying land for the socio-economic development of their villages.

Typically, every average-sized PURA, with twenty-five to thirty villages, would require about Rs 100 crore ($20 million) of capital funding, which would be used to spawn a number of initiatives, which works out to about Rs 15,000–25,000 of investment per person in the complex. These investments would be spread over a period of time (about four to five years) and be dependent on the scale of operation.

Also, for non-government initiators, a significant portion of this funding can come by dovetailing with existing government schemes. Investments may also come from community ownership models like cooperatives and self-help groups, especially if economic empowerment

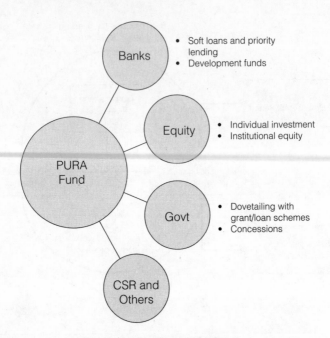

FIGURE 9.11: The PURA Fund

has commenced within one to two years of operation. The panchayati raj institutions can also be a significant partner in the implementation, and help in channelizing government schemes towards the creation of assets for a PURA creation. The panchayati raj institutions can also actively partner PURA by helping with a grant of land for the establishment of centres to facilitate the Physical, Electronic, Knowledge and Economic Connectivity for the creation of PURA.

Since PURA is a tool focused on empowerment and economic development, after a while, the investment requirements would be met with from the profits generated. Figure 9.12 shows how a typical PURA investment flow would look, but the investment plan and the returns would be customized according to local conditions and needs.

The initial investment requirement would be quite high as the bulk of it would go into setting up the 'enablers'*; on which the 'growth engines'

* See Chapters 2 and 3 for details on the sustainable development tool methodologies.

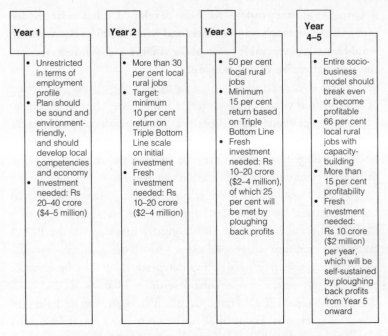

Year 1	Year 2	Year 3	Year 4–5
• Unrestricted in terms of employment profile • Plan should be sound and environment-friendly, and should develop local competencies and economy • Investment needed: Rs 20–40 crore ($4–5 million)	• More than 30 per cent local rural jobs • Target: minimum 10 per cent return on Triple Bottom Line scale on initial investment • Fresh investment needed: Rs 10–20 crore ($2–4 million)	• 50 per cent local rural jobs • Minimum 15 per cent return based on Triple Bottom Line • Fresh investment needed: Rs 10–20 crore ($2–4 million), of which 25 per cent will be met by ploughing back profits	• Entire socio-business model should break even or become profitable • 66 per cent local rural jobs with capacity-building • More than 15 per cent profitability • Fresh investment needed: Rs 10 crore ($2 million) per year, which will be self-sustained by ploughing back profits from Year 5 onward

FIGURE **9.12:** Typical investment and return targets on a PURA

can later be created. Thus, the initial investment would largely be in the form of long-term loans and equity-holding, and grants. After one to two years of creating a sustainable network of enablers, there would be an influx of growth engines which would start yielding economic benefits and employment for the local people. At this stage, an increasing fraction of the investment would be in the form of putting back the profits into further development. From this point, the financial portfolio would change to shorter-term loans and institutional investing.

Towards the later phase of the implementation, the focus would gradually shift to the creation of 'sustainers' which would include the service sector, where the additional disposable income can be exchanged for improved living standards, and for developing ecological sustainability and a technologically advanced PURA framework. After four to five years, the PURA complex should be able to start working as an economically independent entity with little or no need for any external financial aid other than in the form of equity capital.

8. Once the master proposal has been developed, it has to be divided into a village or panchayat (or other local governance) level plan which would act as a blueprint for each of the villages and be integrated into the comprehensive PURA mission.

The village-level development plan for each of the villages (or a group of three to four villages representing a mini cluster) in that particular PURA complex would include specifications for residential, commercial and recreational areas; institutional areas (hospitals, schools, offices, KVKs or Village Knowledge Centres); rural industrial areas; and parks, through the community mobilization procedures.

The plan would also make it possible to approach the PURA implementation by a modular approach. The investment cost of a PURA can go as high as Rs 100 crore. By breaking up the PURA implementation into village-level plans—which can gradually integrate into a comprehensive PURA implementation—it can be a viable option to start with a smaller total investment of about Rs 2–3 crore ($4–6 million) per village, a large part of which, again, can be dovetailed into existing schemes. This method can be an attractive option for smaller investors, small-scale industries and interested individuals who can get together and pool their efforts for developing individual modular villages which fit into the main PURA objectives.

The block diagram in Figure 9.13 shows how the integrated objectives of a PURA complex can be applied to individual villages. At each stage of implementation of the individual village layout, the overall PURA objective has to be kept in mind; the economic and social assets being created at the village level must meet the criteria of the PURA plan and suit the local competencies. The layout must determine the finer aspects of Physical and Electronic Connectivity, and the layout for them which best suits the intra-village connectivity. It must also serve the external market and connect with the knowledge resources outside the village. The Knowledge Connectivity—in the form of training, information and technology—must be futuristic in planning, and be capable of emerging as a shared mutual resource across multiple villages (or panchayats), since the PURA implementation will expand to cover more villages. In this way, a self-sustained village, which would also fit the overall PURA framework, will be realized.

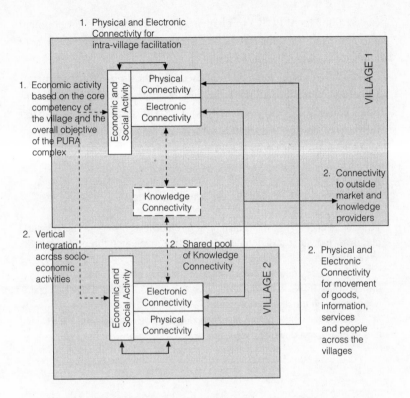

FIGURE **9.13:** Village-level planning for PURA and integration across the different villages

As the PURA implementation occurs, expanding into many villages and panchayats, the same architecture can be employed with a provision for integration and sharing of resources and knowledge across the various villages.

9. A) Deciding on objectively measurable and accountable indices

B) Sensitivity analysis of the action plan

In the preceding chapters, we have continuously stressed the need to have objectively measurable parameters which can be used to assess the impact of any development initiative. In Chapter 8 we evolved a new Triple Bottom Line measure of performance which can be used to judge the projected impact of PURA implementation. Similarly, the development radar approach (Chapter 5) can be instrumental in judging the effect of the initiative over a period of time.

The PURA vision must be translated into these objective parameters and communicated to all the stakeholders—investors, the government, PRIs (panchayati raj institutions) and the community. A brief summary of certain parameters which can be employed is shown in Figure 9.14.

VILLAGE-LEVEL IMPLEMENTATION

The Chitrakoot PURA, while setting overall objectives, distributes the master plan over individual villages and delivers and evaluates the performance using the Samaj Shilp Dampatis.

It also clearly defines deliverables at the level of each village. All these deliverables have to be fulfilled covering various dimensions—social, economic, cultural and environmental.

This is an example of how planning, delivery and evaluation of the PURA has to be broken down at the village level.

Economic and Growth Indicator	Societal Change Indicator
• Change in the GDP within the cluster of PURA implementation vis-à-vis the average • Augmentation of the core competencies of the region in terms of quality and adherence to standards • Access to financial institutions and technology • Outside investments attracted • Collateral benefits from generating connectivity with the public and the private sectors • Inflow of people into the region • Entrepreneurs created or attracted both from within and outside the region	• Inclusion parameters: contribution to the GDP by marginalized social groups like women, and the impact on the bottom 25 per cent of the region • Human development from the income: impact on health and education parameters—IMR, MMR, malnutrition, school dropouts, access to clean drinking water, and proper sanitation as compared to the average • Cultural impact: child marriages, widow remarriages, disputes and litigation, child labour

FIGURE **9.14:** Setting the parameters for evaluating performance

Next, the PURA implementation agency, with the help of the local PURA champion, should conduct a sensitivity analysis of the PURA plan. This may be based on:

- Sensitivity and inherent risks within the markets
- Dependencies on the input side—bargaining power of the supplier and the buyer
- Risk of substitutes
- Risk of technology obsolescence
- Weather-related risk
- Political risk

This analysis of sensitivity to dynamic situations will help establish guidelines for mitigating the vulnerability associated with external factors.

10. Implementation phase: key challenges and how to overcome them. Even though the PURA plan may be described as robust with optimal technology and investment, when the actual implementation of the project begins in a village cluster, many unforeseen challenges may crop up and need to be addressed.

These would have to be dealt with largely on an individual basis, but some broad precautions can be taken which would make it easier to overcome the operation-phase challenges.

First, PURAs should focus on developing self-sustainable models to the extent possible, with the maximum room for local entrepreneurship. The existing local entrepreneurs can be trained further to enhance their output. Moreover, the local youths would be a potent pool for developing into a world-class, skilled cadre. The empowered entrepreneurs would generate many independent jobs, which would lend stability to the system.

Second, it is of paramount importance to involve the community and to constantly interact with it. We have discussed various ideas and innovative examples of community-owned models which can be customized according to the needs of the local region. Once the community becomes the owner of the implementation, the socio-political stability will be enhanced and the needs, too, would be better matched.

Third, the creation of social and economic assets should be carefully implemented so that the needs of one are matched with the supply from the other. As the economic assets become more complex and demand better skills, the social assets should be able to fill the gap. This can be either in the form of capacity-building avenues or as better amenities that can attract and retain a better and more skilled workforce which may come from outside.

THE GOVERNMENT OF INDIA'S NATIONAL PURA PLAN

In May 2010, the Ministry of Rural Development, Government of India, launched a national PURA plan under a public–private partnership with an active role for the panchayati raj institutions. The scope of the scheme 'would be to develop livelihood opportunities, urban amenities and infrastructure facilities of the prescribed service standards and to be responsible for maintenance of the same for a period of ten years'. Under the private–public partnership mode, the selected private partner would have the choice of selecting the PURA project area and a revenue-generating project thereon. This has to be done in consultation with and with the approval of the local panchayati raj body. The cost of each project is estimated to be about Rs 110–120 crore and the government would be offering a capital grant of about 35 per cent of the total project cost for meeting the viability gap. The PURA area would have the following parameters:

- Areas of about 25 sq km
- Population of about 25,000
- Three to four adjoining panchayats (each panchayat usually has about five to six villages)

The selected private partner would be required to provide amenities like water supply and sewerage, village streets, drainage, solid waste management, street lighting, telecom, electricity generation, development of economic activity and skill development as part of the PURA project.

The private partner, in consultation with the local panchayati raj institution, may also provide additional revenue-earning facilities such as village-linked tourism, integrated rural hub, rural market, agro-common services centre and warehousing, and any other rural-economy based projects.

The key features under the scheme would be:

- 100 litres of water availability daily
- 16.75 km of roads and drainage
- Five pits for solid waste management (one for every 5,000 people)
- Skill development for 5,000 people
- Primary economic activity for 1,000 people
- 840 street lights
- Five Internet kiosks
- 1 MW biomass-based plant

The private implementer will enter into a tri-party concession agreement with the state government and the panchayati raj, which will commit to necessary approvals required for covering the construction risks, trunk connectivity of utilities like water, telecom and electricity. The private player would have to complete all the construction activities within the first three years of operation and thereafter it will be responsible for the operation and maintenance of all the amenities and services for a period

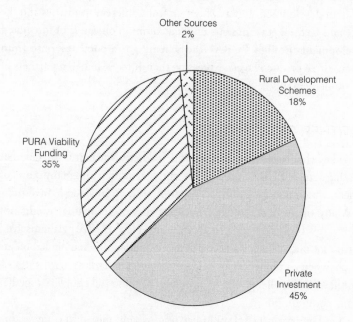

FIGURE 9.15: Sources of funding for PURA

of ten years. There would be a concession period agreement with the private party, covering all these terms and commitments from all the stakeholders, for a period of thirteen years (three years for construction and ten years for operation and maintenance). After the termination of the concession agreement, all the urban amenities and add-on facilities created, for which the land was provided by the gram panchayat, will be transferred to the respective gram panchayat, hence the ownership will pass on to the community.

The monitoring of the project will be done by independent engineers who will supervise and monitor activities during the life cycle of the project and check for compliance under the standards laid out in the concession agreement. Moreover, the gram sabha will also monitor performance of the development activities during the concession period.

The essential thrust of this PURA scheme lies in its inherent nature to make it a financially sustainable model of development and facilitating the implementation by the private player in partnership with the government and the panchayat. The scheme also aims at finding a confluence of different development initiatives, often from different ministries and the state and Central governments under a common objective of integrated development through PURA. The scheme got a good response from ninety-three private players expressing their interest in being partners of the implementation.

FURTHER CHALLENGES

Some key challenges have to be considered here. The first is the fact that creating a single PURA means an investment running into many crores of rupees, which may be a difficult proposition for a small-scale investor.

Many of the stakeholders, entrepreneurs or companies might not be in a position to be able to create a complete PURA by themselves. But, there might be certain competencies across different stakeholders which, when combined, may yield a well-integrated solution for a PURA complex. The challenge lies in bringing all these stakeholders together at one common point.

I have met many people of Indian origin living abroad who are seeking an opportunity to contribute to the nation. In the case of the PURA mission, there are also stakeholders and individuals who are unable to engage in ground-level implementation but can certainly contribute by equity investments, access to markets and sharing knowledge. This is our second challenge.

Our third challenge would be how to integrate them in the mission of sustainable development by the creation of investment, marketing and knowledge networking.

PURAs would be established across regions that differ in terrain, rainfall, people and language. The final output coming out of PURA complexes would be a wide spectrum of products and services, each carrying the uniqueness of an Indian village. Thus, there would be diversity in both the inputs as well as the output from the PURA complexes. The opportunity would lie in identifying and applying the optimal technology with customization. On the output side, it would be a significant advantage if PURA were integrated as a national brand while the processes may still be decentralized. This aggregation of technology, investment and skills on the input side, and aggregation as a common brand on the output side would be our fourth challenge.

We will now discuss a sample PURA implementation plan that can act as a specimen of how PURAs need to be planned and the action flow to be developed.

~

THE SANDESHKHALI PURA

Sandeshkhali-II is a part of the 24 North Pargana district in the Sunderban region of West Bengal in the eastern part of India. Sandeshkhali is marked by underdevelopment, poverty and poor human development indices. More than 80 per cent of the population is living below the poverty line according to the 2001 national census of India. The situation worsened after disaster stuck in 2009, with the cyclonic storm of Aila destroying flora and fauna and affecting the livelihood of the local people.

Sandeshkhali-II block consists of five islands with a huge number of water bodies. In fact, for the 27,000 families living there, the number of water bodies exceeds 60,000. With such a background, let us now discuss a potential PURA plan for the area.

1. Potential PURA initiator

Here we will consider that the initiation agency is a group of entrepreneurs who will draw support from the local self-help groups and panchayats.

2. Group of villages and size of PURA

The total population under the area is about 130,000 across five islands. Hence, we would break the Sandeshkhali PURA into five smaller PURAs, each with a population of about 25,000 and belonging to one particular island. Many of the resources would, however, have to be shared across all these five PURAs.

3. PURA Facilitation Committee and PURA champions

Each of the sub-PURAs will have one or more entrepreneur champions who will coordinate the economic activity and social asset creation with the help of the local panchayat and the people. These would be the CEOs of the PURA complexes. The chairman of the facilitation committee can be the development officer or the district collector of the 24 North Pargana district. At the cluster level, local village representatives and SHG champions will lead PURA in the individual villages.

For example, let us take the primary economic activity—marine products. It would entail the balancing of enterprises and SHGs along

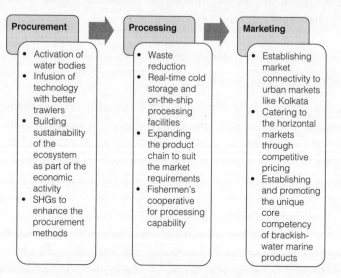

Procurement

- Activation of water bodies
- Infusion of technology with better trawlers
- Building sustainability of the ecosystem as part of the economic activity
- SHGs to enhance the procurement methods

Processing

- Waste reduction
- Real-time cold storage and on-the-ship processing facilities
- Expanding the product chain to suit the market requirements
- Fishermen's cooperative for processing capability

Marketing

- Establishing market connectivity to urban markets like Kolkata
- Catering to the horizontal markets through competitive pricing
- Establishing and promoting the unique core competency of brackish-water marine products

FIGURE **9.16:** Flow of production chain for marine products

the primary procurement to the marketing chain in an integrated and balanced manner as depicted in Figure 9.16.

Moreover, the primary economic engine of fishing would also have to be evolved as a knowledge-based industry where the best practices of fishing, ecology protection, management of markets and processing are shared in a practically useful format with the fishermen groups. This can be done in the format of a KVK in collaboration with the Central Inland Fisheries Research Institute (Barrackpore) which is about 100 km from Sandeshkhali.

The economic activity needs to be diversified to include other activities core to the area like bamboo crafts, animal husbandry, apiculture, sericulture, etc. Many of these can be done at the SHG level, dovetailing existing schemes and forward linking with markets.

Another economy booster would be the provision of a better credit extension facility in the form of banking and microfinance. The PURA entrepreneurs would have to find customized schemes for the requirements of the local people—much of the credit requirements, given the nature of the primary activities, would be very short-term loans of smaller sizes. This can be facilitated through the creation of multiple SHGs (and leveraging on the already existing SHG network in the area).

We also need to analyse the societal improvements needed to ensure that the added income levels do translate into a better life for the local people. This would include better health-care facilities customized for the local needs. Innovative ideas like the water ambulances and mobile dispensaries would be of great usage in the areas and service multiple islands. Another health-related requirement is that of the provision of safe drinking water for all. This can be achieved by using dedicated SHGs equipped with medium-scale equipment based on solar or biomass-based power, which can manage the provision of drinking water. One such equipment, which I analysed with my students at the Gatton College of Business and Economics at the University of Kentucky (USA), is called the 'Slingshot' water purifier invented by Dean Kamen, an American innovator, which runs on biomass fuel and can even purify sewage water. I am sure many such inventions can find use in the Sandeshkhali PURA. Similar innovations are needed in the construction of houses and the provision of sanitation facilities.

4. Identify core competencies and human development plan

The core competencies of the PURA complexes are:

- Richness in natural beauty with unique flora and fauna
- Presence of over 1,300 SHGs with almost 50 per cent of the families participating in them
- More than 60,000 water bodies, many of which have brackish water with unique varieties of fish, prawns and marine life
- Availability of workforce largely comprising the youth
- Large areas of cultivable wasteland, which can be used for a variety of purposes (more than 50 per cent of the cultivated area)
- Proximity to Kolkata, which is one of the metropolitan cities of India and the capital of the state of West Bengal

The key human development needs, which are largely derivatives of extreme poverty, can be enlisted as:

- Literacy levels and vocation training
- Lack of access to financial services, with only three commercial bank offices present in the area
- Lack of health-care facilities (there are no hospitals in the block and only three health centres) propels the demand for innovatively laid out health-care services

Based on these competencies, a range of product and service industries will find relevance in the area, which will be closely interlinked and vertically integrated.

Given the core competencies of the area, the primary activity for the PURA enterprises would be fish and marine products and marketing. However, we also need to diversify the portfolio of economic activities and hence improved agriculture, apiculture, sericulture and bamboo-based craft products would be of significance as well. For each of these products, procurement to processing to marketing chains will have to be established using the best available technology.

5. Total employment generation and targets for societal change

For each of the economic activities, the employment-generation potential and the skill requirement map would have to be estimated. In a phase-wise manner, within five years, the Sandeshkhali PURA should be able to generate about 8,000–10,000 jobs in fishing and fish processing and marketing alone. Additional 3,000 jobs would potentially be generated in other industries of sericulture, apiculture and other agricultural activities. The service industry, in the form of boat kiosks, boat maintenance, shopping centres, mobile health care and education would have a potential for the generation of about 3,000 additional jobs. Finally, the infrastructure industry, like solar plants and water body maintenance would have a potential of about 2,000 jobs. Besides this, many other small-scale industries based on the SHG model would spawn with time, bringing additional employment for the people. All of these workers would have to be knowledge empowered with globally competitive skills. This would need an additional focus on facilities for skill enhancement and upgrading.

The targets for societal development should closely map the income generation in the Sandeshkhali PURA. The first target should be to treble the nominal income of the individual household within the next five years. This should be accompanied with the target to bring every citizen above the poverty line in the area. Similarly, the IMR and MMR should be brought down to less than half of the present figure within four years. The nutrition levels, especially in children and women should see significant improvements and reflected objectively. Communicable diseases and those related to unclean drinking water should see at least a 50 per cent drop in incidence rate, with 100 per cent coverage of clean drinking water, using a variety of purification techniques and mobile boat-based health-care centres. Similarly, education with value-based learning should encompass all the youth and reflect objectively in not just the enrolment rate but also retention and quality of education. This should also include access to global standards of vocational training and a linked employment facility for the local youth, especially the women.

These and other objectively defined socio-economic goals should be mapped on to the developmental radar of the area with clearly defined annual targets and action plans.

Further, the PURA also needs to set clear environmental goals, which would include activation of water bodies and moving along the goals of energy independence through a mix of solar power and biofuel in its wastelands and wastewaters.

6. Key challenges and enablers needed to achieve the connectivity

The economic and societal plans mentioned earlier can be enabled only when the necessary connectivity is enabled. For that the PURA initiators would need to analyse the existing challenges and opportunities according to each necessary connectivity for PURA. Let us briefly evaluate them.

- **Physical Connectivity**: The main island of Sandeshkhali, called Dhamakhali, is well connected with Kolkata through road but the condition of the road is not good. This serves as the primary connectivity to the urban market and hence needs improvement. Inter-island connectivity is by boats, most of which are small. Intra-island connectivity is probably the poorest of all, by ad-hoc vehicles called 'Jugaad' which are somewhat like motorcycle-powered carts. Till today, all the villages have not been provided with electricity and even in cases where there is power, the availability is erratic, making it useless for business purposes. This situation needs significant improvement.

  Once the islands become vibrant socio-economic entities, with significant sharing of facilities and resources, the demand for transport across the islands would significantly escalate and hence transport based on boats would emerge as a significant enterprise with value-added facilities of boat medical centres and even mobile centres of knowledge dissemination and water-based communication access facilities (like a boat-based cyber café). This would also require activating the various water bodies. Within the island, better roads, maintained by the local population, need attention and it can be done through government schemes like the MGNREGA and other panchayat empowered schemes.

  The problem of power needs special attention as it would be the backbone of the value-adding industry in the area. The solution for this is two-pronged—solar and biomass-based power. Out of the 102 islands in Sunderbans, forty-eight are uninhabited and can be used as solar power centres. Typically, for each megawatt of power about 5–10 acres of land would be required and roughly 5–6 MW would be sufficient to power the Sandeshkhali PURA. This can be managed as an enterprise or through a cooperative. Many of the schemes of the

Ministry of New and Renewable Energy Sources can be employed for acquiring the required capital and technology.

- **Electronic Connectivity**: While private mobile phone operators are already connected to most of the area, for enabling market connectivity and e-health and tele-education, high-speed Internet is a necessity. In this context, cabling would be a difficult proposition given the geography of the area and its size. Hence, WiMAX connectivity can be established across the islands. Similarly, mobile boat-based e-kiosks can be shared across the islands. Community radio across each of the islands can also be enabled.

- **Knowledge Connectivity**: Once the Electronic Connectivity is enabled in the area, facilities like tele-based education can be put to service. There is a specific need for improvement of higher education, especially for women, which has to be addressed. Vocational skills and enterprise development training needs to be enabled, and premier institutions like the Indian Institute of Management, Kolkata, can be instrumental in content development for the youth of the area in basic enterprise skills. There is a need for at least one vocation training institute for each of the five islands based on local competencies. Knowledge Connectivity also needs to handle the problem of a fragile ecosystem and its implications. People need to be knowledge empowered in fishing and agricultural practices that are eco-friendly and sustainable. Significant awareness and usage of metrological data needs to be used as a tool to empower the people. Knowledge networks also need to expand in enabling a service industry for the economic assets created—like boat servicing and solar power servicing.

Once these three connectivity forms are enabled, the Economic Connectivity based on the core activity of marine product processing and marketing, and other industries as discussed can be facilitated.

7. Funding and investment plan

The total funding, spread out over a period of two to three years would be about Rs 150 crore for the entire PURA structure. This would include the creation of economic assets, social assets and connectivity. Besides these, additional investments are needed for activation of the river bodies. Since the vision of any PURA is to be financially sustainable with balanced social and economic activities, the Sandeshkhali PURA would emerge as a financially feasible investment with returns on investments made being in excess of 12 per cent.

The investments can be made through a spectrum of sources that would include:

- Private investment from leading industries and people (15 per cent)
- Bank loans (25 per cent)
- Community investments and re-investment of profits (15 per cent)
- Dovetailing of existing schemes with the help of local panchayats and local government agencies (25 per cent)
- Social equity share investments (as explained under PURA Corporation) (20 per cent)

A clear and transparent mechanism needs to be established to ensure that investments lead to the asset creation with quality and relevance and this must be reported to the concerned shareholders.

8. Breaking down into village-level plans

The plan of the PURA needs to be broken down into an integrated island-and-village-level plan. Each island needs to contribute a unique product or value addition and the individual villages within the island need to focus on one or two core processes that evolve into the island-level mission. The processes at the village level can be handled by SHGs and those at the island level can be undertaken under an enterprise or cooperative set-up.

A typical figurative representation is shown in Figure 9.17.

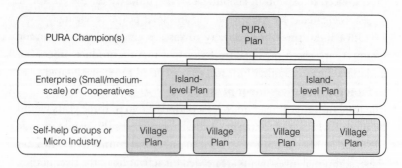

FIGURE 9.17: Village-level plans

9. Setting performance measures

The Sandeshkhali PURA would have to set comprehensive and objective targets for its performance evaluation on economic, social and environmental fronts and transparently report them over the community radio and the Internet.

It may include:

- **Economic**: Gross production of the PURA, people below the poverty line, value addition to the primary product, access to financial services, vocational skill levels, service industry quality and access, employment profile and employment levels of the local youth
- **Social**: IMR and MMR, enrolment and dropout ratio, societal conflict and court cases within the PURA complexes, access to health care and education, access to clean water and sanitation coverage, banking and telecom service penetration levels
- **Environmental**: Active water bodies, solar power resources, biofuel generated and usage, employment of wasteland and wastewater resources

Thus, we believe, that the Sandeshkhali PURA would be a vibrant zone of economy which generates income for the local people and all the stakeholders, and also improves the standard of living. It would thereby create disincentives for rural to urban migration, and lead to the creation of an urban quality lifestyle and income at the local rural levels. It would be an asset to the state and the nation. Furthermore, it would carefully balance growth with the environment, thereby bringing sustainable prosperity to all.

The authors would like to acknowledge the work of Mr Amlan Das, who prepared a detailed study on the Sandeshkhali PURA, which is one of the sources for drawing this PURA plan.

10

PURA CORPORATION

In the previous chapter we discussed the stepwise implementation model for realizing sustainable development. We also saw that the Central and the state governments are engaged in PURA implementation.

Earlier in the book we had also stressed that approximately 7,000 PURAs would be required to cover India's 600,000 villages and about 30,000 PURA complexes across the world to transform rural areas into vibrant economic and socially advanced entities that would propel growth in the coming decade. Such large-scale implementation would, beyond doubt, require unparalleled collaborative effort from many stakeholders, both private and public.

To ensure the success of such a multi-pronged effort, it is essential to create a framework through which different initiatives towards PURA can be promoted, synergized and economized. Towards the end of the previous chapter, we discussed key challenges which need to be overcome in order to make the PURA mission a truly participative process for all the stakeholders who wish to engage in the mission of sustainable development. In this chapter we will discuss the creation of this platform and how it can act as a flexible creator of enterprises and an integrated developer and pool of technology and investment for rural India.

FROM 'WHEN CAN I SING THE SONG OF INDIA?' TO 'INDIA CAN DO IT!'

During the last few years, and especially in this decade, I have seen how India Vision 2020 has inspired people, particularly the youth of

India, and has resulted in many taking up missions directed towards it. The youths of today's India and of different nations of the world, filled with self-confidence, are prepared to take up the challenge through entrepreneurship, hard work and technological leadership.

I recall a situation at the beginning of 1990 when I was interacting with the youths of Ahmedabad in the state of Gujarat. One lively girl asked me: 'Mr Kalam, can you please tell me when I can sing a song of India?' I tried to find the reason for her question and came to know that at that time her elder brother was in the United States and he was always talking about what was good there and how that country had assumed leadership in development, prosperity and technology amongst all the nations of the world. This little girl, sitting in India, was fed up with her brother's stories and had posed the question to me in her quest to find an answer.

How did I reply? I explained the developed India Vision 2020 to her and told her to be confident and that she could certainly sing the song of India by 2020. The same spirit—of when and how India would emerge as a nation with global prominence—echoed everywhere at that time.

But, during the last few years, while interacting with young people, I have seen a remarkable change in their thinking. Long gone are the doubts about the 'song of the nation'. Today, the young at heart ask me, 'What can I give to the nation?' That means they are prepared to contribute to national development. And recently, in the last three years, I have seen a further change: they tell me, 'I can do it,' 'We can do it,' and 'The nation will do it.' This spirit and urge to contribute is found in almost all walks of society regardless of whom I meet—students, professionals, homemakers, people of Indian origin living abroad, industrialists and social workers. This means the nation and its citizens are ready to undertake, relentlessly and untiringly, the challenge of developing the nation. And this development has to start in a sustainable manner at the grass-roots and the rural levels. The task before us is to create a platform where the energy, talent, commitment and knowledge of all Indians can find a confluence and emerge into a well-directed resplendent growth.

PURA CORPORATION: A SUSTAINABLE DEVELOPMENT PLATFORM

In 2008, I conducted a course on 'Globalizing Resurgent India through Innovative Transformation (GRIIT)' at the Indian Institute of Management in Ahmedabad, where my co-faculty and I worked with students towards objective missions for attaining Vision 2020 and sustainable development systems. My students evolved a unique enterprise-driven model of a sustainable welfare model through the idea of a PURA Corporation.

PURA Corporation is a virtual and physical platform which aims at the facilitation of ideas into investment and of investments into results. It envisions being a one-stop repository for all stakeholders who are working, or desire to work, for implementing sustainable development across the nation. The fundamental principle behind PURA Corporation is to establish feasible sustainable development models along the lines of economics, societal structure, environment, technology and stability, through a chain of entrepreneurial ventures. This would be achieved by

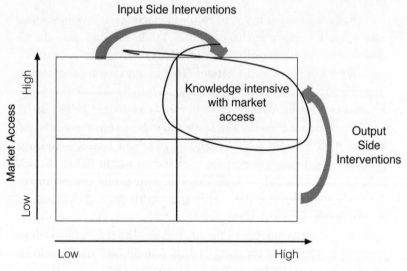

FIGURE 10.1: The input–output matrix

interventions on the input and the output (sales or delivery) side of the system. This is depicted in Figure 10.1.

KNOWLEDGE REPOSITORY

PURA Corporation will act first and foremost as a repository of knowledge, an open source for technologies and innovation, which can be of practical use in the rural context. A contributor to the repository can be an individual or an institution who can either generate the idea or report an existing significant implementation from across the globe. The knowledge repository would be translatable into various media and languages. This would also enable village-to-village learning across the nation, where a village in Gujarat can learn and replicate, in its own context, a venture that has been started in Assam. If all the 600,000 villages could present one unique workable idea each, then through village-to-village learning itself, the knowledge repository would be enriched by more than half a million practical solutions.

To connect the different stakeholders that would lead to the evolution of PURA plans, multiple communication media would be employed to network with each other. For a start, a web-based platform would be created to facilitate the inflow of knowledge from all around the globe. This would open up fresh knowledge and technology resources, introduce new market opportunities and help form a network of interested entrepreneurs and investors. Concurrently, alternative channels for establishing a knowledge network would have to be worked on, which would reach remote villages and bring out the best inputs through media in the form of community radio that could be customized according to the local language and context.

Academic institutions can play a significant role in acting as source points of knowledge and students can be encouraged to conduct projects on development plans for the villages near their institutions.

MAPPING OF CORE COMPETENCIES AND NEEDS

PURA Corporation and its partners would also conduct comprehensive resource-mapping and profiling of the intended PURA complex. To

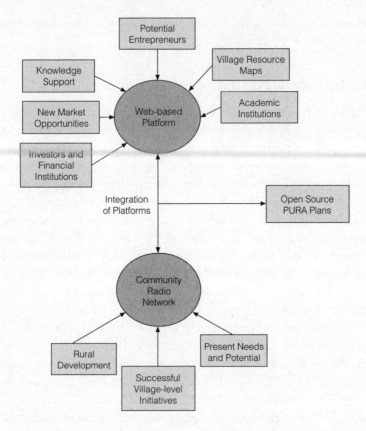

FIGURE 10.2: PURA Corporation: Knowledge-system architecture

accomplish this, the respective panchayats need to be included and the views of the local community taken into consideration.

INTEGRATION

PURA Corporation would also act as a knowledge-provider in terms of integration of ideas and innovations. Technologies—to grasp the practical implication at the ground level—need sustainable enterprise models that can ensure their delivery. This requires an integration of multiple ideas and solutions for a common problem with customization at the local level.

CREATION OF LOCAL PURA CHAMPIONS

Each PURA complex would be endorsed by a regionally acclaimed champion—it may be an institute or an individual—who will do the handholding for the PURA entrepreneur in his journey to realize the PURA mission and help him with local support from the community. PURA Corporation will facilitate the creation of such local PURA champion agencies for each PURA.

PROMOTING ENTREPRENEURSHIP

The essence of PURA Corporation is to generate jobs through the determined creation of enterprises at the micro level. These would not be merely enterprises that are based on core competencies, but also enterprises based on servicing the primary economic activity; enterprises involving capacity-building and providing amenities, as was discussed in Chapter 9. Through its network of industries, academic institutions and youths, PURA Corporation will encourage the spawning of such enterprises at the local level through its incubation channel.

PURA Corporation will nurture two kinds of entrepreneurs:

1. Resource Entrepreneurs: With the help of customized technology and modern management techniques for enhancing the income level for every household, they will focus on an economic realization of natural, traditional and human resources. They will play the critical role of moving resources up the value chain by applying the best practices and by matching product to market. This will generate wealth for the community and augment the purchasing power of the people. Their performance will reflect in the overall growth of the GDP of the rural complex.

2. Social Entrepreneurs: This second category will work closely with the resource entrepreneurs. They will focus on improving the human development index (HDI) in terms of education, health care and the standard of living by providing amenities and equity across diverse areas. These entrepreneurs will, therefore, promote the translation of the purchasing power into a better life and, in turn, introduce a more skilled workforce into the area. Their performance will reflect

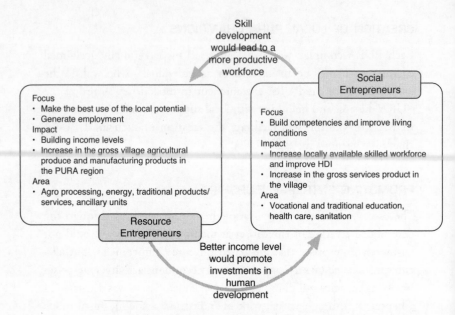

Skill
development
would lead to a
more productive
workforce

Social
Entrepreneurs

Focus
• Make the best use of the local potential
• Generate employment
Impact
• Building income levels
• Increase in the gross village agricultural
produce and manufacturing products in
the PURA region
Area
• Agro processing, energy, traditional products/
services, ancillary units

Focus
• Build competencies and improve living
conditions
Impact
• Increase locally available skilled workforce
and improve HDI
• Increase in the gross services product in
the village
Area
• Vocational and traditional education,
health care, sanitation

Resource
Entrepreneurs

Better income level
would promote
investments in
human
development

FIGURE **10.3:** PURA Corporation: Enterprise network

objectively in enhanced literacy levels; reduced IMR, MMR and
sickness; enhanced nutrition; access to good habitation, sanitation
and clean drinking water; and quality energy. It will also lead to
environmental consciousness and a reduction in societal conflicts.

The entrepreneurs of PURA Corporation would work in close
synchronization and integration with the help of local PURA champions.
They would be partners with the government, the local administration and
the panchayati raj institutions. The enterprise network of PURA Corporation
has to evolve with technical collaboration from a multidimensional
array of technological and managerial institutions (Figure 10.3).

INCUBATION AND INVESTMENT MECHANISM

One of the most significant factors that inhibits the creation of enterprises
is the lack of timely financial investment which, at rural micro levels,

is even more critical. On the other hand, the financial market in the nation has been vibrant with significant investors, even in the time of global recession.

We have seen how rural enterprises that are managed well have been consistently yielding returns upwards of 20 per cent over the decades. Besides being social missions, they are thus also excellent investment opportunities which can be mutually beneficial to the enterprise creator, the rural population and also the financers.

PURA Corporation, through its management team, would act as a business forecasting engine and present each venture as a unique investment opportunity, with provision for vertical integration for enhanced returns. Thereby it would accept responsibility for attracting equity investment for the creation of rural enterprise. The primary shareholding in this case would be based on monetary transaction.

Moreover, there are numerous corporate social responsibility initiatives which can be channelized into objective and integrated development systems of PURA creation, especially on the side of capacity-building. With PURA emerging as a national brand, the CSR investments would lead to public participation on a large scale. Similarly, many individuals and institutions may like to work on a specific sector of rural transformation within the PURA framework. All these non-profit-oriented investors can also be given equity, which would be notional and would correspond to a particular form of capacity-creation. For example, a particular investor who wished to invest in improving the primary education centre could be presented with a series of options to invest, based on the existing proposed sustainable models generated and, against the investment, given a shareholding in the initiatives which would correspond to the education capacity created. This is shown diagrammatically in Figure 10.4.

Another method of attracting investment is in the form of local cooperatives which would lead to community ownership. PURA Corporation, with the help of local PURA champions, would work towards creating such cooperatives to implement PURA by lending them technological, marketing and managerial support.

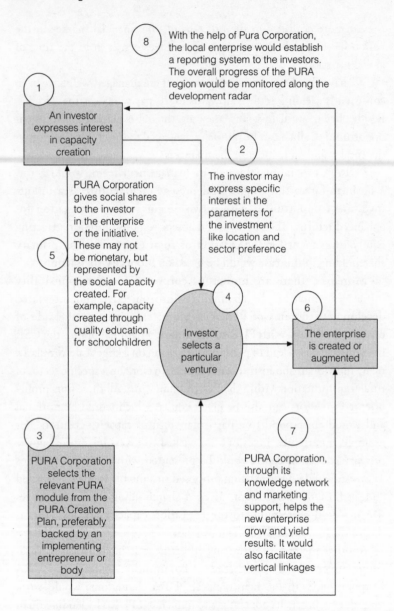

8 With the help of Pura Corporation, the local enterprise would establish a reporting system to the investors. The overall progress of the PURA region would be monitored along the development radar

1 An investor expresses interest in capacity creation

2 The investor may express specific interest in the parameters for the investment like location and sector preference

5 PURA Corporation gives social shares to the investor in the enterprise or the initiative. These may not be monetary, but represented by the social capacity created. For example, capacity created through quality education for schoolchildren

4 Investor selects a particular venture

6 The enterprise is created or augmented

3 PURA Corporation selects the relevant PURA module from the PURA Creation Plan, preferably backed by an implementing entrepreneur or body

7 PURA Corporation, through its knowledge network and marketing support, helps the new enterprise grow and yield results. It would also facilitate vertical linkages

FIGURE **10.4:** Stakeholder investment model

SHARING FIXED COSTS

Since PURA Corporation would be engaged in the creation of a sustainable development system, many of the fixed costs—based on both equipment and knowledge—can be shared across the ventures, making each of them more feasible and stable.

TYPICAL COST SHARING

- Equipment
- Marketing and advertising
- Technology identification
- Administrative support
- Monitoring tools
- Human development
- Financial tools and capital-raising costs
- Integration

ASSESSMENT AND MONITORING

PURA Corporation would set up a mechanism for objectively monitoring performance, based on the initial conditions of the rural region, the connectivity and the basic model of the initiatives. The assessment would be based on the 'real impact' created from the perspective of the end user, and not merely focused on the outlay. The quality of the product or service would also be a criterion for monitoring. The audited report of the individual PURA initiatives and the overall PURA status in all the complexes would be worked out as a performance benchmark for the purpose of establishing accountability to the investors and the knowledge-providers. In the monitoring and assessment realization, local academic institutions can play a significant role by designing effective tools; by ensuring student participation for in-depth impact assessment at the household level; and by suggesting strategies for improvement in performance.

MARKET INTERFACE, BRANDING AND QUALITY CONTROL

One of the foremost contributions of PURA Corporation would be through the evolution of common brands which can establish market positioning through a shared brand-building exercise. It would be difficult for rural brands to establish themselves individually in export and city markets but, aggregated under the common umbrella body of PURA Corporation, and backed by well-directed promotion, small and micro enterprises at the rural level can be popularized as significant market brands. Moreover, large industries can partner with PURA Corporation and source their inputs from PURA enterprises.

PURA Corporation, through its knowledge channels, can also set up a mechanism for providing market intelligence to support PURA enterprises, and thereby ensure that the products and services being created are matched to the market needs in order to lead to better yields.

Of course, access to a high-value market would also imply standardization and quality control techniques. This would be collectively formulated by the market demand and the rural enterprise specifications, and quality control would be enforced by PURA Corporation.

FUTURISTIC GROWTH

The PURAs being created by PURA Corporation have to have a stable and feasible system over the long run. In view of continually changing technology, research, market demands and the emergence of competition, they have to be tuned in to the changing times. To achieve this, a constant evaluation of the PURAs has to be conducted, and fresh ideas and markets have to be regularly explored. This would lead to the process of an unrelenting evolution of the sustainable development system.

DIFFERENT STAKEHOLDERS AND ROLES IN PURA CORPORATION

PURA Corporation strives to bring a wide range of people and experts towards the common integrated mission of realizing PURA. Essentially, it would be composed of the following stakeholders in the system:

VILLAGE PROPOSERS

The stakeholders would aggregate and analyse the needs of a particular cluster of villages where PURA could be implemented and also lead to the creation of open-source PURA designs. They can be local community members or government officials, panchayats, academic institutions through their projects, or entrepreneurs. The overall PURA plan would also have to be broken down into village-level layout plans pertaining to specific initiatives, like a primary health centre for a particular village.

KNOWLEDGE-PROVIDERS

The knowledge-providers would be students, researchers, technologists, social workers and professionals from a global audience who would contribute the best ideas, technologies and innovations to transform the rural enterprise models. Another part of the knowledge-providing exercise would be scouting around for existing village solutions which are impactful, in order to facilitate village-to-village learning.

INVESTORS

Investors can be interested parties who wish to invest in resource-harnessing or creating a particular social asset class. They may be individuals, industries, CSR implementers, development funds or financial institutions. Investments can also be put into local cooperatives where the community itself would be a collective stakeholder. (Cooperatives have been explained in Chapter 9.)

LOCAL CHAMPIONS

Local champions would act as the empowered one-stop solution point for the creation of PURA. They would facilitate linkages with the government, ensure quality, manage integration and guide the entrepreneurs at the beginning. They would also mobilize community participation. They can be local institutions, local industries or trusted individuals of high repute.

ENTREPRENEURS

The entrepreneurs would be the backbone of the implementation under PURA Corporation. They would take up specific roles within its master plan and be supported by the local champion. They would be provided incubation support and technology know-how by PURA Corporation. They will be expected to objectively set a target, after giving due consideration to community needs and local conditions, against which their performance will be assessed and monitored.

COMMUNITY

The community members would be a crucial element of the PURA implementation, ensuring that the benefits expected from PURA are realized on the ground level. For this, community opinion has to be considered at all stages, and the members from the community empowered and encouraged to be PURA activators. This also envisions a significant role for the panchayati raj institutions, which can play a most significant role in granting land for the development projects under PURA.

MARKET LINKERS

Stakeholders can also be in the form of active marketeers for PURA products and brand, both within the nation and for export. For this, individuals in their geographic location can take up the task of creating a market for the products and services coming out of the PURA complexes. Similarly, industries can help in quality-building in the PURA complexes and create permanent sourcing from them, thereby helping them reach markets where the best value can be realized.

GOVERNMENT AGENCIES

The government bodies, through their various officials and departments, will have to play a significant role in the PURA implementation by helping dovetail the existing schemes and initiatives with those of the PURA complex project. They can also empower the local champion and be an active partner in the championing body at the local level. The government officials can help in encouraging community orientation towards PURA.

EVALUATORS

PURA Corporation would set up objective goals for each of the entrepreneurs and the initiatives, and also the overall vision for the PURA complex. Local institutions, through their students and faculty can take up projects to monitor the progress and to find ways to accelerate the transformation of the rural complex.

GROWTH PROPELLERS

Even after PURA has been set up, it needs to undergo a constant process of evolution. This would require critical inputs based on the external environment changes with time and the internal performance of the PURA complexes.

Thus, PURA Corporation is an attempt to bring together multiple stakeholders in the fold of PURA implementation, depending on their individual ability and competency. In many cases, these roles will definitely overlap, and a single entity would be in a position to take up multiple roles in the life cycle of the PURA implementation.

CONCLUSION

PURA Corporation is an ambitious yet practical solution, unique in its approach to provide everyone with space to contribute and be a stakeholder in the process of the development of the nation, beginning from its roots. It is based on integration, sustainability and enterprise creation. Such a system can be a cornerstone for achieving vibrant socio-economic entities in the villages which would bring empowerment and growth to the 700 million people in India's villages and also across the developing world. Such an empowered society would be the foundation of a nation which is inclusively prosperous, universally empowered and a true symbol of a dynamic knowledge society, where none lives in poverty and where a lack of fundamental amenities is not a hindrance to one's pursuit of missions.

11

THE FACE OF TWENTY-FIRST-CENTURY DEVELOPMENT

GLOBAL CHALLENGES AND THEIR DYNAMICS

Today, the challenges that the world faces are poverty, illiteracy, lack of safe drinking water, supply of clean and green energy, equitable distribution of resources, quality education with values for all, societal imbalances, diseases, quality health care for all and good living conditions. Various nations are working to find solutions to these challenges, which take on different manifestations based on local dynamics that are interconnected on various issues.

VISUALIZATION FOR PURA

Throughout this book, we have emphasized the need for a new-generation approach towards development. The most pressing problem in the world today is not that of pressure on resources, but the need for applying them for the collective development of mankind. As we find ourselves in a precarious position at this point in history, the key to a bright future appears to be sustainable and inclusive development. Sustainability does not mean hindered development; it is an agenda for growth rather than a roadblock to it. Similarly, inclusive does not mean disbursing charity to the underprivileged but the empowerment of the deprived to unleash their potential. Individual empowerment will lead to happy homes; happy homes will make developed villages and towns; developed villages and towns will lead to prosperous nations; prosperous nations will be generators of enlightenment and, finally, it will be this enlightened society which will not merely coexist but also collaborate in creating a peaceful world with sustainable growth. The road to magnificent global goals begins at the atomic level of the empowered individual, and we believe PURA is an excellent tool to realize it.

We have examined and studied various development initiatives from many different parts of the world, with a special focus on India as a case study. All these initiatives—different in scope and scale—fundamentally carry a few common threads: knowledge-empowered individuals; community ownership; democratic control; market connectivity; and above all, customization according to the needs and the potential of a place and society. We have seen how PURA complexes in India are integrating all these factors into one common effort which can be a model for the entire developing world and even some underdeveloped parts of advanced nations.

These PURA complexes would be transformed into dynamic rural complexes with a focus on employment potential for all the families in a PURA cluster. They will have an umbilical connectivity with the nearest university, research facility or hospital. Let us now present the portrait of a PURA cluster based on the already operational PURAs and other ideas for empowerment discussed in the book:

1. Dwelling units for all the village citizens with sanitation facilities and a supply of clean water available 24 hours a day, 7 days a week.

2. The village complexes will have 100 per cent literacy, with significant efforts to build on a minimum level of literacy and move towards a knowledge-empowered society.

3. Besides upgrading the existing schools, the complex will have a few colleges, world-class vocational training institutes in various areas such as construction, carpentry, welding, and natural art; computer maintenance and services; IT-enabled services, business process outsourcing (BPO) and a call centre.

4. People in the PURA complex will be brought under a corporate health-care scheme. They will get quality medical care through tele-medicine and mobile clinics via the primary health-care centres.

5. Each PURA village complex will be free of diseases like polio, TB, leprosy, malaria and other waterborne diseases. The infant mortality rate will be lower than ten.

6. The PURA complex will promote horticulture, floriculture and agricultural products in collaboration with nearby agricultural universities and research institutes.

7. It will have agro-processing industries for value addition to these products for the realization of the goals of the farmers.

8. Setting up dairies and fish farms for providing additional non-farm revenue to farmers who can produce various dairy products.

9. Revival of all existing water bodies in the PURA cluster.

10. Provision of employment to all employable people in the village through additional jobs in dairy farming, agro-processing, construction, handicraft and tourism enterprises.

11. There may be many villages with important tourist spots. It would be financially advantageous to impart training in tourism for managers and operators, and to set up facilities for tourists, including accommodation, in a private enterprise partnership.

12. Overall, the per capita income of the PURA cluster should increase by three times and the number of people living below the poverty line should come down to zero in six years from the beginning of the initiative.

13. The PURA complexes are evolved as value-based societies with compassion and absence of internal conflicts.

Of course, to achieve the above goal, it is vital to have a dynamic, empowered PURA management board structure. This has to be set up with the active participation of state governments, district authorities, societal transformers, educational institutes and small-scale industries or enterprises, in association with leadership and governance at the village level. Finally, it will be managed as a viable and sustainable business proposition through local entrepreneurship. Every individual and organization has a role to play in the realization of such a global, sustainable development system. Let us briefly explain some basic roles.

WHAT CAN I DO TO EMPOWER 3 BILLION?

CITIZENS

Each one of you, in your respective organization, can act as a champion of PURA empowerment missions and contribute according to your own expertise and organizational capabilities. Form a small group of interested people and visit a nearby target site, where you can study the local strengths, weaknesses and opportunities which can be the 'game changers' for the place. Find ways of synergizing your strengths with the needed action. Publish your results and findings for action at the organizational level. If, from within your organization, you can support the task of creating or augmenting a PURA nearby, that will be a worthy contribution to the mission of empowering 3 billion.

STUDENTS

You are both architects and stakeholders of the future. Focus on being a job generator rather than merely a job seeker. There is no better opportunity to give wings to your entrepreneurial spirit than in the untapped rural regions of the nation and the world.

Even while pursuing your studies, you can choose to contribute to the mission of empowering the people of your country. Choose five families from rural or suburban areas near your home or institute and instruct them in getting better education for their children and better health care for the family. Tell them about their rights as a citizen and help them explore new options of socio-economic transformation which technology and market access have now opened up. You can support the PURA mission in your own way.

RETIRED AND SENIOR CITIZENS

You represent the key knowledge strength of the nation. With your vast experience in dealing with the public and the private sectors, and your knowledge of the social and geographical dynamics, you can take on the role of mentor in the development initiatives and help structure them for better results.

ACADEMIC INSTITUTIONS AND UNIVERSITIES

Knowledge is power. Academic institutions, as the intellectual resource of every nation and as the collection point of thousands of students and youths, can play a vital role in PURA-based empowerment.

Select a group of five to ten villages and deploy a team of faculty and students to work for the development of these villages, by mapping the local competencies and identifying the best technology for value addition to them. You can also scout for grass-roots innovations and help the local population plan improved products and services around them. We have already shown that many universities and academic institutions across the world have pioneered empowerment missions; they can serve as examples for similar missions.

PRIVATE SECTOR: LARGE INDUSTRIES

You can execute one PURA mission in each of the major operating regions. With your improved access to markets around the world, you can provide new export markets where the local products can find space, especially with the help of your distribution channels. The PURAs established by you can be based on the matching of your core business theme with the local competencies.

Contributions can also be made on the consumption side. Mainstream products and services need to reach the PURA-empowered villages. Besides these, advanced knowledge too has to reach the local population. Ask yourselves whether you can provide for such dissemination of Knowledge Connectivity to the rural regions.

SMALL-SCALE INDUSTRIES

Identify local competencies and lead an enterprise-driven movement for development at the rural level. Train local youths for various industries and thus emerge as a job generator. You can provide the last mile of connectivity of technology to the rural regions and, with localized operations, give grass-roots-level value addition to products and services.

PUBLIC SECTOR UNITS

You can take up one PURA mission for implementation in each of the regions where you operate. Bring in different stakeholders and lead an integrated development mission of PURA.

Public sector banking units can act as financers of the PURA mission, and developmental impact along socio-economic lines should become a benchmark for assessment.

LARGE HOSPITALS AND SPECIALTY HEALTH-CARE CENTRES

Health care is a major issue in both social uplifting as well as in ensuring economic growth. Health-care centres can act as leaders of the PURA mission in rural regions.

Send your doctors and medical teams to rural regions on health-care missions; it will be a great learning experience for them and also contribute to better health for the nation. If you are located in urban areas then, using technology, your specialist doctors can give some time to treating rural patients, and you can lead in preventive health care through e-health missions.

NON-GOVERNMENT ORGANIZATIONS

You can start a PURA mission in specific regions of the country, especially those which are remote and affected by poverty and unrest. You can play a vital role in assessing the impact of empowerment missions. You can work with local governance institutions (like the panchayati raj) and give them knowledge support on how to be a part of the PURA empowerment missions, and how they can plan better with the existing schemes available to them through the government and other agencies.

NON-RESIDENT NATIONALS

Many developing nations, including India, have non-resident nationals living and prospering across the world. In this capacity, you can choose to contribute to the place of your origin, or any other place nearby. The most important resource you can give back is knowledge. Tell the people of your native place about your success, and the reasons behind it. Bring access to international markets and cutting-edge technology to help the home population create and obtain better products and better value. This will, indeed, be a great contribution to the economic growth of the rural regions through PURA.

MEDIA

Be the lighthouse which spreads great ideas and innovations across the length and breadth of your country. Focus on highlighting at least ten previously unheard stories of successful rural enterprises in your particular media format. These success stories will inspire others and create hope and admiration for the existing empowerment models. Half of the world population lives in rural areas and we need to give their stories a rightful share in the popular media.

GOVERNMENT MINISTRIES AND DEPARTMENTS

An organized and integrated effort by the Central government is needed to transcend the boundaries of departments and ministries, and create an integrated development system with adequate private and community participation for empowering the rural region. The focus should be on creating an outcome that empowers the people rather than merely spending on freebies and unplanned assets which do not converge towards the common, desired goals.

The Government of India has already started the PURA mission on a pilot basis, but, of course, much more needs to be done and on a much larger scale.

ELECTED REPRESENTATIVES IN THE STATE ASSEMBLIES AND THE PARLIAMENT

Besides advocating and practising sustainable development as your agenda, you can undertake the task of championing developmental politics by advocating the PURA mission in your constituency. Investments in PURA can be made through the Local Area Development Fund which would ensure unhindered implementation of a sustainable development model.

DISTRICT COLLECTOR AND OTHER ADMINISTRATIVE ENTITIES AT THE DISTRICT LEVEL

As local officials, you can help by dovetailing different schemes in the areas towards the integrated purpose of PURA. You can also act as the synchronizing force for bringing the private and the public sectors together, and help them plan a PURA-based development model that could be launched in partnership with the local administration.

PANCHAYAT BOARD OR OTHER VILLAGE-LEVEL ADMINISTRATION

Panchayats can also help by allocating land for the developmental activities through PURA. They can organize community awareness, participate and contribute to the mission. As the ground-level body, they can play a major role in identifying the competency and the needs of a particular place where PURA has to be developed.

The future progress of any nation, society or region will henceforth be based on how innovatively and efficiently they are able to execute such sustainable missions with broad objectives across multiple dimensions. The leaders will be tested on the implementation of such a futuristic vision; the companies will be judged on how well they are able to develop and serve these new markets; and all our health-care and education systems will have to be geared towards inclusive growth for all.

This is the future we see towards which we need to channelize our efforts.

PURA is indeed the model for a sustainable development system that will generate 3 billion smiles, 3 billion empowered citizens, 3 billion healthy family members, 3 billion human beings who will aggressively contribute to human growth; and thus PURA will be the tool that will lead to the evolution of a happy, peaceful and prosperous world.

NOTES

CHAPTER 1

1. P. Kotler, K. Keller, A. Koshy and M. Jha, *Marketing Management: A South Asian Perspective* (Prentice-Hall of India, 13th edition).
2. 'Iceland volcano: Airlines "to lose $200m a day"', *BBC News*, 16 April 2010.
3. Andrew Cliff and Peter Haggett, 'Time, travel and infection', *British Medical Bulletin* 2004.
4. Muhammad Yunus, *Banker to the Poor: Micro-Lending and the Battle Against World Poverty* (New York: Public Affairs, 2003).
5. 'Human Development Report 1998: Consumption for Human Development', United Nations Development Programme (UNDP), New York, 1998.
6. 'Human Development Report 1999: Globalization with a Human Face', UNDP, 1999.
7. W. Lambers, '25,000 Die from Hunger Every Day', History News Network, 2006. Accessed at http://hnn.us/articles/27396.html.
8. David Woodward and Andrew Simms, 'Growth is Failing the Poor: The Unbalanced Distribution of the Benefits and Costs of Global Economic Growth', United Nations, Department of Economics and Social Affairs, Working Papers, March 2006.
9. Craig Simmons, 'Can the Earth keep up with human consumption?', *The Guardian*, 22 February 2001, accessed from http://www.guardian.co.uk/greenliving/story/0,,441590,00.html.
10. Data from Union Budget of India, 2009–10.
11. 'The State of the World's Children 2005: Children under Threat', United Nations Children's Fund (UNICEF), 2005.

12. Drawn from data in the *World Development Indicators* 2006, World Bank, p. 73. Available at http://siteresources.worldbank.org/DATASTATISTICS/ Resources/table2-7.pdf.

13. Ibid.

14. David Woodward and Andrew Simms, 'Growth Isn't Working', New Economics Foundation, London, 2006.

15. C.K. Prahalad, *The Fortune at the Bottom of the Pyramid: Eradicating Poverty through Profits* (Wharton School Publishing, 2006).

CHAPTER 2

1. A.P.J. Abdul Kalam and Y.S. Rajan, *Indian 2020: A Vision for the New Millennium* (New Delhi: Penguin Books India, 1998).

2. Nicholas Ionides, India's airports finally being expanded, dated 16 November 2007. Accessed from http://www.flightglobal.com/ articles/2007/11/16/219611/indias-airports-finally-being-expanded.html. The figure stated is the sum of domestic and international passenger figures as given in the article.

3. 'Farm Suicides: 12-year saga', *The Hindu*, 25 January 2010.

4. Economic Survey of India, 2009–10.

5. The Millennium Development Goals Report 2007, United Nations.

6. 'Slum Dwellers to double by 2030: Millennium Development Goal Could Fall Short', UN-HABITAT, 21st Session of the Governing Council Report, April 2007.

7. 'Mumbai tops in accidental deaths', *DNA* (Daily News & Analysis), 24 February 2010.

8. 'Delhi: 1,200 deaths in road accidents so far', reported on NDTV, 17 August 2010.

9. C.K. Prahalad, *The Fortune at the Bottom of the Pyramid: Eradicating Poverty through Profits* (Wharton School Publishing, 2006), pp. 10–12.

10. 'The Himalayas of hiring', *The Economist*, 5 August 2010.

11. ASSOCHAM's Report, 'The Rise of Rural India', 2010.

12. Reserve Bank of India Guidelines on Priority Sector Lending, available at www.rbi.org.in.

13. ASSOCHAM's Report, 'The Rise of Rural India', 2010.

14. Bharat Nirman Report, available at http://bharatnirman.gov.in/road .html.

15. 'India: Reducing Poverty in India: Options for More Effective Public Services', documents of the World Bank, 1998.
16. ASSOCHAM's Report, 'The Rise of Rural India', 2010.
17. Ibid.
18. S. Gangopadhyay and W. Wadhwa, National Sample Survey (NSS), 2004.

CHAPTER 3

1. Keynote address on 'Educating Earth-literate leaders', given by Stephen Martins, from the Open University, United Kingdom, and Rolf Jucker, University of Wales Swansea, United Kingdom.
2. 'The Naxalite Challenge', *Frontline*, 8–21 October 2005; Ashok Handoo, 'Naxalite Problem Needs a Holistic Approach', Press Information Bureau, 22 July 2009.
3. 'Naxal Violence: 10,000 People Killed in Past 5 Years', Outlookindia.com, 25 June 2010.
4. Ajai Sahni, 'Naxalism: the retreat of civil governance', *Faultlines: Writings on Conflict and Resolution*, New Delhi, Vol. 5, May 2000. Available at http://satp.org/satporgtp/publication/faultlines/volume5/Fault5-7asahni.htm.
5. R.P. Cincotta, R. Engelman and D. Anastasion, *The Security Demographic: Population and Civil Conflict after the Cold War* (Washington DC: Population Action International, 2003).
6. Ibid.
7. United Nations Statistics Division, Millennium Development Goals Indicators: Carbon dioxide emissions (CO_2), thousand metric tons of CO_2 (collected by CDIAC).
8. Randolph E Schmid, '2000–'09 Warmest Decade on Record, U.S. Reports', *The Seattle Times*, 19 January 2010.
9. United Nations Statistics Division, Millennium Development Goals Indicators: Carbon dioxide emissions (CO_2), thousand metric tons of CO_2 (collected by CDIAC).
10. Calculated from data available in the Economic Survey of India, 2009–10.

CHAPTER 4

1. 'India: Reducing Poverty in India: Options for More Effective Public Services', documents of the World Bank, 1998.

2. The International Fund for Agricultural Development (IFAD) Report on Rural Poverty, 2001.

3. A.P.J. Abdul Kalam and Y.S. Rajan, *Indian 2020: A Vision for the New Millennium* (New Delhi: Penguin Books India, 1998).

4. Himanshu Thakkar, 'Assessment of Irrigation in India', World Commission on Dams, 1999. The gross irrigated area of India is about 61.78 million hectares.

5. Economic Survey of India, 2010–11, Statistical Appendix.

6. Ibid.

7. 'Food Supply, Food Shortages', in *Encyclopedia of Food and Culture*, ed. Solomon H. Katz, Vol. 2 (Gale Cengage, 2003), eNotes.com. Accessed on 1 March 2011, http://www.enotes.com/food-encyclopedia/food-supply -food-shortages.

8. Ibid.

9. Ravindra H. Dholakia, 'Has Agriculture in Gujarat Shifted to High Growth Path?', in Dholakia (ed.), *Frontiers of Agricultural Development in Gujarat* (Ahmedabad: Centre for Management in Agriculture, Indian Institute of Management, 2010).

10. Calculated from data given in the Economic Survey of India, 2009–10.

11. Dholakia, 'Has Agriculture in Gujarat Shifted to High Growth Path?'.

12. Mahesh Pathak and V.D. Shah, 'Five Decades of Gujarat Agriculture: Some Reflections', in Ravindra H. Dholakia and Samar K. Datta (eds), *High Growth Trajectory and Structural Changes in Gujarat Agriculture* (Ahmedabad: Centre for Management in Agriculture, Indian Institute of Management, 2010).

13. B.R. Shah, 'Gujarat Agriculture: Prospects and Problems', in Dholakia (ed.), *Frontiers of Agricultural Development in Gujarat*.

14. K.P. Prabhakaran Nair, *Issues in National and International Agriculture* (Hyderabad: ICFAI University Press, 2008).

15. This section is derived from the convocation address at National Dairy Research Institute, Karnal, 2010.

16. Derived using data from Food and Agriculture Organization (FAO).

17. Ibid.

18. Ibid.

19. Data from Government of India figures available at the portal http://india .gov.in/sectors/agriculture/fisheries.php.

20. Samar K. Datta, Srijan Pal Singh, Milindo Chakrabarti, Subho Biswas and Sah Bittu, 'A Perspective on Fisheries Sector Interventions for Livelihood

Promotion' (Ahmedabad: Research and Publications Department, IIM, 2010).

21. Calculated using data from World Bank database.

22. Ibid.

CHAPTER 5

1. Bryan Haig, 'Review of *The World Economy: Historical Statistics* by Angus Maddison', *Economic Record*, Vol. 81, 2005.

2. Economic Survey of India 2009–10. The figures are calculated at 1999–2000 price levels.

3. Calculated using data from the International Monetary Fund (2010 figures).

4. Percentage and Number of Poor in India (1973–74 to 2004–05) and by Experts Group 1993 and Expert Group 2009 (Tendulkar methodology), available at http://planningcommission.nic.in/data/datatable/0211/Databook_comp.pdf.

5. State-wise Literacy Rates (1951 to 2001), Planning Commission of India.

6. India at a Glance: Census 2011, available at http://www.censusindia.gov.in/2011-prov-results/indiaatglance.html.

7. David Crystal, 'Subcontinent raises its voice', *The Guardian*, 19 November 2004, accessed from http://www.guardian.co.uk/education/2004/nov/19/tefl.

8. 'Performance of States in India (Rural)—ACER Report (% of Children who can Read, Read English & Do Arithmetic)', available at the Planning Commission of India portal.

9. Arunjana Das, 'An Incubator in Every Campus', *DARE*, 1 October 2007.

10. ASSOCHAM Report on Rural Development 2010.

11. Zeenat Nazir, 'Just what the hospital ordered: Global accreditations', *The Indian Express*, 18 September 2006.

12. Derived using data available at the World Bank database.

13. Based on personal interactions with Dr Raju and various visits to his health-care and development centres.

14. Based on the visit to Teach for India Centre in Pune and the material available on their portal www.teachforindia.org.

15. Based on meetings and interviews with Dr Sudarshan.

16. Sample Registration System, Registrar General of India, October 2008. Figures are for the year 2007. Loni figures are derived from an independent baseline survey for all the categories.

17. India and Maharashtra figures from the Economy Survey of India 2007. For Ahmednagar, the National Family Health Survey-II (NFHSII) figures have been used.
18. For India, UNICEF 2005 figure have been used, available at its portal. For Maharashtra and Ahmednagar, the NFHSII figures have been used.
19. First three figure are from the NFHSII.

CHAPTER 6

1. Fourth Assessment, AR4 SYR 2007—Appendix Glossary (Geneva, Switzerland: Intergovernmental Panel on Climate Change [IPCC]).
2. Figures are for 2008. United Nations Statistics Division, Millennium Development Goals Indicators: Carbon dioxide emissions (CO_2), thousand metric tons of CO_2 (collected by CDIAC).
3. Figures are for 2005. 'Greenhouse gas emissions growing faster since 2000: new data on worldwide emissions 1970-2005', JRC European Commission News Release, 25 May 2009.
4. IPCC 2007: Climate Change 2007: Synthesis Report. Contribution of Working Groups I, II and III to the Fourth Assessment. IPCC Report, core writing team (eds), R.K. Pachauri and A. Reisinger.
5. Jerry Hannan, 'Your Role in the "Greenhouse Effect"', Institute for Theological Encounter with Science and Technology—Bulletin, 1997.
6. Data for 2007 retrieved from *World Development Indicators*, World Bank.
7. Andrew Cliff and Peter Haggett, 'Time, travel and infection', *British Medical Bulletin* 2004.
8. Srijan Pal Singh, 'The Balanced Carbon Equation', *Economic Times*, 2010.
9. IPCC 2007: Climate Change 2007: Synthesis Report. Contribution of Working Groups I, II and III to the Fourth Assessment. IPCC Report, core writing team (eds), Pachauri and Reisinger.
10. Ibid.
11. Ibid.
12. Ibid.
13. Ibid.
14. *Forests and Climate Change: A Convenient Truth*, video produced by FAO and the Forestry Commission, UK.
15. A. Voiland, '2009: Second Warmest Year on Record; End of Warmest Decade', NASA Goddard Institute for Space Studies, 21 January 2010.
16. *A Convenient Truth*.

17. 'Deforestation continues at an alarming rate', FAO Newsroom, November 2005.

18. Ibid.

19. Derived using data from *The World Factbook*, CIA (Central Intelligence Agency, USA).

20. Data from the web-portal of the Ministry of Power, Government of India.

21. Basic Statistics on Indian Petroleum and Natural Gas (2009–10), Ministry Of Petroleum and Natural Gas, Government of India.

22. Ibid.

23. Johnzactruba (edited by Rebecca Scudder), 'Compare the Efficiency of Different Power Plants', Bright Hub, 27 May 2010. Accessed from http://www.brighthub.com/engineering/mechanical/articles/72369.aspx.

24. S. Kristoff, 'What Is the Availability of Solar Energy?', available at http://www.ehow.com/about_5518265_availability-solar-energy.html.

25. 'India's wind power potential more than 45,000 megawatts', *Energy & Enviro Finland*, May 2008.

26. 'First flights worldwide with pure biofuel from algae', EADS, 2010.

27. Ibid.

28. Caroline Ashley, Peter De Brine, Amy Lehr and Hannah Wilde, 'The Role of the Tourism Sector in Expanding Economic Opportunity' (Harvard University: John F. Kennedy School of Governance, 2007).

29. Dr S.K. Puri, 'Biodiversity Profile of India' (Bangalore: Centre for Ecological Sciences, Indian Institute of Science).

30. 'New treaty on search for life-saving medicines in remote areas', ScienceBlog, 2 March 2011. Available at http://scienceblog.com/43294/new-treaty-on-search-for-life-saving-medicines-in-remote-areas/.

31. Sharad K. Jain, Pushpendra K. Agarwal and Vijay P. Singh, *Hydrology and Water Resources of India*, Water Science and Technology Series, Vol. 57 (Springer: 2007).

32. Zeenat Nazir, 'Just what the hospital ordered: Global accreditations', *The Indian Express*, 18 September 2006.

33. 'Cooperative Societies in India', NCUI [National Cooperative Union of India] Publication, 2007; and 'The Irula tribal snake venom extraction cooperative', UNDP Report, available at http://ssc.undp.org/uploads/media/Snake_Venom.pdf.

34. 'REED Returns More Than Money', REED Report, October 2005, available at http://www.unep.fr/energy/finance/documents/pdf/REEDreport05.pdf; and the Rural Energy Enterprise Development (REED), UNEP, available at http://www.unep.fr/energy/activities/reed/.

35. Sundar Bajgain and Indira Shakya, edited by Matthew Mendis, 'The Nepal Biogas Support Program: A Successful Model of Public Private Partnership for Rural Household Energy Supply', World Bank, 2005. Available at http://siteresources.worldbank.org/INTENERGY/Publications/20918309/ NepalBiogasSupportProgram.pdf.

36. Compiled from the following sources: Mali-Folkecenter website, at http:// www.malifolkecenter.org/; and a presentation on the Jatropha project available at http://www.unido.org/fileadmin/import/70747_Mali__Case _Study__I._Togola.ppt.

37. Report on 'Mali Folk Centre: Investment Opportunity in Mali', available at http://www.gaia-energy.co.uk/index.php?option=com _content&view=article&id=52.

38. Information compiled from the following sources: Lit by Bio Fuel, India Environment Portal, at http://www.indiaenvironmentportal.org. in/node/266960?quicktabs_2=0; and a video on the Ranidhera Project, available at http://wn.com/jatropha_plant_winrock_succes_story_self _supporting_village_ranidhera_india_posted_by_gino_smit__youmanitas _energy_farms_foundation.

39. 'An Introduction to the Kyoto Protocol Compliance Mechanism', United Nations Framework Convention on Climate Change (UNFCCC), available at http://unfccc.int/kyoto_protocol/compliance/items/3024.php.

CHAPTER 7

1. Based on the Annual Report of the Pravara Medical University, 2007–08.

2. Ibid.

3. Based on interviews with the students of the university.

4. ASSOCHAM Report on Rural Development 2010.

5. 'India has more science graduates than in US, EU, or China', d-sector .org, 11 November 2009, available at http://www.d-sector.org/article-det .asp?id=564.

6. Arunjana Das, 'An Incubator in Every Campus', *DARE*, 1 October 2007.

7. International Co-operative Alliance, Statement on the Cooperative Identity, available at http://www.ica.coop/coop/principles.html.

8. David Thompson, 'Co-op Principles Then and Now', *Cooperative Grocer*, No. 53, July–August 1994.

9. 'Selected Case Studies and Successful Stories of Cooperatives', NCUI, 2007.

CHAPTER 8

1. Annual Report 2009–10, the Ministry Of Micro, Small and Medium Enterprises, Government of India.

2. Ibid.

3. Derived from the following: David Bornstein, *How to Change the World: Social Entrepreneurs and the Power of New Ideas* (New York: Oxford University Press, 2007); 'Fabio Rosa', Schwab Foundation for Social Entrepreneurship (2004); and 'Fabio Rosa—Making the Sun Shine for All', global envision, 7 February 2006, accessed from http://www.globalenvision.org/library/10/954.

BIBLIOGRAPHY

'A Model of Modern Development'. *The TMTC Journal of Management*. December 2003.

Achten, W.M.J., E. Mathijs, L. Verchot, V.P. Singh, R. Aerts and B. Muys. 'Jatropha biodiesel fuelling sustainability?' *Biofuels, Bioproducts and Biorefining* 1(4), 283–291. 2007.

'Agrarian Reform in Brazil'. FAO Report. Downloadable from http://www.fao .org/righttofood/KC/downloads/vl/docs/AH264.pdf.

'Agricultural Policy Reform in Brazil'. OECD Policy Brief. October 2005.

'Agricultural Policy Reform in China'. OECD Policy Brief. October 2005.

Annual Report 2009–10. Ministry of Micro, Small and Medium Enterprises, Government of India.

Annual Report 2009–10. Ministry of Tourism, Government of India.

Annual Report 2008–09. Ministry of Home Affairs, Government of India.

Annual Report 2009–10. Ministry of Home Affairs, Government of India.

Ashley, Caroline, Peter Brine, Amy Lehr and Hannah Wilde. 'The Role of the Tourism Sector in Expanding Economic Opportunity'. Harvard University: John F. Kennedy School of Government, 2007.

ASSOCHAM Report on Rural Development 2010.

Barry, M. 'The Tail End of Guinea Worm—Global Eradication without a Drug or a Vaccine'. *The New England Journal of Medicine*. 21 June 2007.

Bajgain, Sundar, and Indira Shakya. Edited by Matthew Mendis. 'The Nepal Biogas Support Program: A Successful Model of Public Private Partnership for Rural Household Energy Supply'. World Bank. 2005. Available at http://siteresources.worldbank.org/INTENERGY/Publications/20918309/ NepalBiogasSupportProgram.pdf.

Barton, David N. 'Water Pricing as a Tool for Improving Water Use Efficiency'. Norwegian Institute of Nature Research.

Bornstein, David. *How to Change the World: Social Entrepreneurs and the Power of New Ideas.* New York: Oxford University Press, 2007.

Central Sector Scheme on Rural Business Hubs. Ministry of Panchayati Raj. 2009.

Chen, Fu (Prof.). 'Land Reform in rural China since the mid-1980s'. *Land Reform 1998/2.* 1999.

'China's village doctors take great strides'. World Health Organization Bulletin. 2008.

Cincotta, R.P., R. Engelman and D. Anastasion. *The Security Demographic: Population and Civil Conflict after the Cold War.* Washington DC: Population Action International, 2003.

Colombant, Nico. 'US Poverty Rates Grow'. *Voice of America.* 16 September 2010. http://www.voanews.com/english/news/usa/US-Poverty-Rate-Highest -in-15-Years-103060399.html

Compendium of Key Statistical Indicators by Country Groups. FAO.

'Consumption of Food (Rs per capita per month)'. National Sample Surveys.

'Cooperative Societies in India'. NCUI Publication. 2007.

'Current State of Organic Farming in India and Other Countries'. *Indian Journal of Fertilizers.* 2005.

Dabholkar, S.A. *Plenty for All.* Mehta Publishing House, 1998.

Datta, Samar K., Srijan Pal Singh, Milindo Chakrabarti, Subho Biswas and Sah Bittu. 'A Perspective on Fisheries Sector Interventions for Livelihood Promotion'. Ahmedabad: Research and Publications Department, Indian Institute of Management, 2010.

'Delivering on Commitments'. UNDP in Action. 2009–10.

Dholakia, Ravindra H. *Frontiers of Agricultural Development in Gujarat.* Ahmedabad: Centre for Management in Agriculture, Indian Institute of Management. 2007.

Dholakia, Ravindra H. and Samar K. Datta (eds). *High Growth Trajectory and Structural Changes in Gujarat Agriculture.* Ahmedabad: Centre for Management in Agriculture, Indian Institute of Management, 2010.

Dracunculiasis Treatment & Management. Emedicine. 2009. Available at http:// emedicine.medscape.com/article/997617-treatment.

Drop Out Rates in Class I–V and I–VIII and I–X. Abstract of Selected Educational Statistics. 2007–08.

Economic Survey of India 2009–10 and 2010–11.

'Ethical economics, endless enthusiasm'. A conversation with Rangasamy Elango. *India Together.* August 2002. Available at http://www.indiatogether.org/govt/ local/interviews/elango.htm.

Factsheet: Public Private Community Partnership. UNDP. Available at http://www.undp.org.in/content/factsheets/DG/PPCP.pdf.

'Farm Suicides: 12 year saga'. *The Hindu*. January 2010.

Gangopadhyay, S., and W. Wadhwa. NSS, 2004.

Gates, William H. (Sr). Presentation of the 2006 Gates Award for Global Health to the Carter Center.

General Report on the IAU Prague Conference. 'Education for a Sustainable Future'. Keynote address on 'Educating Earth-literate leaders' given by Stephen Martins (Open University, UK) and Rolf Jucker (University of Wales Swansea, UK). September 2003.

Global Health Indicators. World Health Organization. 2009.

Global Hunger Index 2009. The Challenge of Hunger: Focus on Financial Crisis and Gender Inequality.

Govinda, R., and K. Biswal. 'Mapping literacy in India: who are the illiterates and where do we find them?' Background paper for the Education for All Global Monitoring Report 2006, Literacy for Life, UNESCO. 2005.

'Grim Reapers'. Article in *The Economist*. July 2010.

Guidelines for the Nirmal Gram Puraskar. Ministry of Rural Development, Government of India.

Haig, Bryan. 'Review of *The World Economy: Historical Statistics* by Angus Maddison'. *Economic Record*. Vol. 81. 2005.

Haklev, Stian. 'Chinese barefoot doctors, a viable model today?' Paper written for IDSC11 class. 2005.

Handoo, Ashok. 'Naxalite Problem Needs a Holistic Approach'. Press Information Bureau. 22 July 2009.

Huang, Jikun, Yu Liu, Will Martin, Scott Rozelle. 'Agricultural Trade Reforms and Rural Prosperity: Lessons from China'. A Working Paper. The National Bureau of Economic Research. April 2008.

Human Development Report 1998: Consumption for Human Development. New York: UNDP.

'India finds cheap energy may be an easy nut to crack'. *Business Standard*. 13 March 2008.

Indiresan, P.V. *Vision 2020: What India Can Be and How to Make That Happen*. ICFAI Books, 2003.

IPCC Fourth Assessment Report: Climate Change 2007, Working Group I Report 'The Physical Science Basis'.

IPCC Fourth Assessment Report: Climate Change 2007, Working Group II Report 'Impacts, Adaptation and Vulnerability'.

IPCC Fourth Assessment Report: Climate Change 2007, Working Group III Report 'Mitigation of Climate Change'.

IPCC Fourth Assessment Report: Climate Change 2007, Working Group III Report 'The AR4 Synthesis Report'.

Jha, Brajesh. 'Employment, Wages and Productivity in Indian Agriculture'. Institute of Economic Growth (IEG) Working Papers Series No. E/266/2006. 2006.

Kalam, A.P.J. Abdul, and Y.S. Rajan. *Indian 2020: A Vision for the New Millennium.* New Delhi: Penguin Books India, 1998.

'Kalam's "PURA" vision set to be launched in Karnataka'. *Deccan Herald.* 14 September 2009.

'Karnataka to prepare report for implementing "Kalam PURA" project. *DNA (Daily News and Analysis).* Bangalore. 22 October 2009.

Kiehl, J.T., and Kevin E. Trenberth. 'Earth's Annual Global Mean Energy Budget'. National Center for Atmospheric Research. 1997.

Kotler, Philip, Kevin Lane Keller, Abraham Koshy and Mithileshwar Jha. *Marketing Management: A South Asian Perspective.* Prentice-Hall of India, 13th edition.

Kyoto Protocol Status of Ratification. UNFCCC. 2009. http://unfccc.int/files/ kyoto_protocol/status_of_ratification/application/pdf/kp_ratification.pdf

Lit by Bio Fuel. India Environment Portal. http://www.indiaenvironmentportal .org.in/node/266960?quicktabs_2=0

'Magarpatta: building a city with rural–urban partnership'. *The Indian Express.* 26 May 2010.

Material from Mali-Folkecenter website: http://www.malifolkecenter.org/.

'Meeting India's tree planting guru'. BBC News. 19 September 2009.

'Mumbai tops in accidental deaths'. *DNA.* February 2010.

Ostrom, Elinor. *Unlocking Public Entrepreneurship and Public Economies.* World Institute for Development Economic Research (UNU-WIDER), 2005.

Pakistan: where and who are the world's illiterates? UNESCO Report. http:// unesdoc.unesco.org/images/0014/001459/145959e.pdf.

Paroda, R.S. 'Meeting New Challenges in Food Production'. *Yojana.* 1998.

Patel, Raj. *Stuffed and Starved: What Lies Behind the World Food Crisis.* HaperCollins, 2008.

Percentage and Number of Poor. Planning Commission Estimates.

'Performance of States of India (Rural)—ACER 2009 (% of Children who can Read, Read English & Do Arithmetic)'. ACER 2009.

Pindyck, Robert, and D.L. Rubinfeld. *Microeconomics*. 6th Edition. Prentice-Hall, 2008.

Portal of NEGP, Government of India.

Prahlad, C.K. *The Fortune at the Bottom of the Pyramid: Eradicating Poverty through Profits*. Wharton School Publishing, 2006.

PURA Overview. Ministry of Rural Development, Government of India. Available at http://pura.org.in/content/pura-overview.

'REED Returns More Than Money'. REED Report. October 2005. Available at http://www.unep.fr/energy/finance/documents/pdf/REEDreport05.pdf.

Report on 'India: Food Processing Industry'. Compiled by Swiss Business Hub India. 2008.

Report on India Jatropha electrification initiative of Winrock International India (WII). Available at www.winrockindia.org.

Report on International Exhibition and B2B Meetings for Agriculture and Food Processing in South India. Agri and Food Processing Indian. 2009.

Report on Sarva Shiksha Abhiyaan. Available from education ministry website http://www.education.nic.in/ssa/ssa_1.asp.

Reports on algae oil. Available from Oilgae website http://www.oilgae.com/.

'Rural Business Hub idea gets good response in AP'. *Business Line*. 9 November 2006.

Rural Energy Enterprise Development (REED). UNEP. http://www.unep.fr/energy/activities/reed/

Rural Poverty Report 2001—The Challenge of Ending Rural Poverty. IFAD.

Rural Poverty Report 2011—New realities, new challenges: New opportunities for tomorrow's generation. IFAD.

Simmons, Craig. 'Can the Earth keep up with human consumption?' *The Guardian*. 22 February 2001. Accessed from http://www.guardian.co.uk/greenliving/story/0,,441590,00.html.

Somanathan, E. 'Biodiversity in India'. In *Oxford Companion to Economic in India*. 2007.

Space Technology Enabled Village Resource Center. http://www.isro.org/publications/pdf/VRCBrochure.pdf

'State of the World 2009: Into a warming planet'. The Worldwatch Institute.

Stewart, W.M. (Dr). 'Balanced Fertilization Increases Water Use Efficiency'. *News and Views*. 2001.

'Sustainable Bioenergy: A Framework for Decision Makers'. United Nations Report. 2007.

Swaminathan, M.S. *From Rio de Janeiro to Johannesburg*. Madras: East–West Books, 2002.

Swarnjayanti Gram Swarozgar Yojana (SGSY). Overview available from the Ministry of Rural Development, Government of India. http://www.rural .nic.in/anual0203/chap-5.pdf

'The Himalayas of Hiring', *The Economist*. 5 August 2010.

'The importance of Rangaswamy Elango'. GoodNewsIndia. 1 May 2003.

'The Irula tribal snake venom extraction cooperative'. UNDP Report. Available at http://ssc.undp.org/uploads/media/Snake_Venom.pdf.

The Millennium Development Goals Report. United Nations. 2009.

'The Naxalite Challenge'. *Frontline*. 8–21 October 2005.

The State of Food and Agriculture. FAO. 2009.

The State of the World's Children 2005: Children Under Threat. United Nations Children's Fund (UNICEF). 2005.

Thompson, David. 'Co-op Principles Then and Now'. *Cooperative Grocer*. No. 53. July–August 1994.

Tiwari, D.N. Sustainability Crisis 2009.

Tiwari, D.N. Sustainability Crisis 2010.

'Tourism set to boom in India: Deloitte'. *Livemint*. 25 March 2009.

Video on Ranidhera Project. Available at http://wn.com/jatropha_plant _winrock_succes_story_self_supporting_village_ranidhera_india_posted _by_gino_smit__youmanitas_energy_farms_foundation.

Web portal of Ministry of Rural Development, Government of India. www .rural.nic.in

Website of the Coca Cola Company.

'Why Algae?' Solix Biofuels. 2008.

Woodward, David, and Andrew Simms. 'Growth Isn't Working: The unbalanced distribution of benefits and costs from economic growth'. New Economics Foundation. London. 2006.

World Bank Database. Available at www.worldbank.org.

Yao, Shunli. 'Chinese Agricultural Reforms, WTO and FTA Negotiations'. Asia-Pacific Research and Training Network on Trade. 2003.

Yunus, Muhammad. *Banker to the Poor: Micro-Lending and the Battle Against World Poverty*. New York: Public Affairs, 2003.

Yunus, Muhammad. *Creating a World without Poverty*. New York: Public Affairs, 2009.

Zhang, Junhui. 'Tracking water use efficiency (WUE) of terrestrial ecosystems using MODIS-EVI images'. *Global Ecology and Biogeography*. 20 October 2009.